VATICAN II

VATICAN II

FIFTY PERSONAL STORIES

WILLIAM MADGES AND MICHAEL J. DALEY
Editors

ORBIS BOOKS

Maryknoll, New York 10545

Founded in 1970, Orbis Books endeavors to publish works that enlighten the mind, nourish the spirit, and challenge the conscience. The publishing arm of the Maryknoll Fathers and Brothers, Orbis seeks to explore the global dimensions of the Christian faith and mission, to invite dialogue with diverse cultures and religious traditions, and to serve the cause of reconciliation and peace. The books published reflect the views of their authors and do not represent the official position of the Maryknoll Society. To learn more about Maryknoll and Orbis Books, please visit our website at www .maryknollsociety.org.

Library of Congress Cataloging-in-Publication Data

Vatican II : fifty personal stories / William Madges and Michael J. Daley, editors. — [Rev. and expanded ed.].
  p. cm.
Includes bibliographical references (p.   ) and index.
ISBN 978-1-57075-993-2 (pbk.)
1. Vatican Council (2nd : 1962-1965). I. Madges, William, 1952-. II. Daley, Michael J., 1968-. III. Title: Vatican 2. IV. Title: Vatican Two.
BX8301962.V327 2012
262'.52—dc23

2012007212

To our families

June, Cara, Brendan, and Nora

Marsha, Katie, and Sarah

And to our former theology teachers at Xavier University

Contents

Acknowledgments

We would like to express our thanks to the contributors who agreed to share their personal reflections about the Second Vatican Council and its significance for their work and ministry. In addition, we would like to recognize publicly Robert Ellsberg for guiding this project and Maria Angelini for assisting in the preparation of the final manuscript. Finally, we wish to thank our spouses, June Pfaff Daley and Marsha Erickson, for their personal support and encouragement during this project.

Glossary

Aggiornamento—Italian for "bringing up to date"; speaks to church renewal and adaptation; as phrased by John XXIII, "opening up of windows."

Aula—Latin for "hall." The nave of St. Peter's Basilica served as the meeting place where the council's proceedings were held.

Constitutions—Vatican II issued four of these documents: two dogmatic constitutions (Church and Revelation), one constitution (Liturgy), and one pastoral constitution (Church in the Modern World). Among the most formal expressions of an ecumenical council, they usually describe or define doctrinal matters, but as the term "pastoral" suggests in the "Pastoral Constitution on the Church" (*Gaudium et spes*) they can also speak of the application of doctrinal beliefs and moral principles to specific situations.

Declarations—Vatican II issued three of these documents (Education, Religious Freedom, and Non-Christian Religions). They summarize and articulate the church's current teaching on the subject at hand (often showing significant development).

Decrees—Vatican II issued nine of these documents (Eastern Catholic Churches, Ecumenism, Priestly Formation, Laity, Religious Life, Office of Bishops, Missionary Activity, Social Communications, and Priesthood). Like constitutions, these documents can contain doctrinal matter. Similar to declarations, they contain more specific recommendations and suggestions of reform pertaining to the topics under discussion.

Encyclical—Latin for "circular letter." Formal letter, written by the pope, which addresses doctrinal, moral, and/or disciplinary matters.

Osservatore Romano—first published on July 1, 1861, it serves as the semi-official newspaper of the Vatican.

Papabili—used as a reference to those who are considered papal front-runners before and/or during a papal election.

Pensioni—lodgings, dwellings, hotels.

Peritus, periti—Latin for "expert" or "advisor," theological advisors. Bishops were able to appoint their own theological advisors and to bring them to the council.

Secretariats—some originated as preparatory bodies (Promoting Christian Unity and Social Communications); others (Dialogue with Non-Christians, Dialogue with Non-Believers) came about as fruits of the council. Served to promote conversation and be a resource concerning their respective topic. Their work found its way into some council documents. After the council some became offices of the Roman curia.

Secretary General—did preliminary and organizational work for the council. Kept the council's proceedings orderly and timely. Appointed by John XXIII, Archbishop Pericle Felici served in this role.

Theological Commission—one of the council's ten preparatory commissions. Headed by Cardinal Alfredo Ottaviani and closely connected with the Holy Office, it saw itself as the guardian of orthodoxy throughout the council as all doctrinal matters passed through it.

FOREWORD

An Interpretive Introduction to Vatican II*

DENNIS M. DOYLE

IN MANY WAYS THE PUBLICATION of *Vatican II: Fifty Personal Stories* is more significant and vital today than when the first edition appeared ten years ago. The focus of present-day debate over the meaning of the council and its documents revolves around matters that are centrally related to the contributions of this book.

Sharp differences among Catholics concerning the interpretation of Vatican II surfaced soon after the council's end.[1] Those differences, however, reflected not only differences already present at the council but could also be connected with differences that had been in place for many years prior to the council's inception.[2] There was a confrontation that took place on the floor of the council between traditionalists and progressives. The progressives got much more of what they wanted than did the traditionalists. For many who lived through this confrontation process the outcome was revolutionary.

Differing interpretations of the council, and of the tremendous changes in the church that it inaugurated, are reflected in the mission statements of two international Catholic journals. *Concilium*, a journal founded in 1965, articulates its purpose: "Our international journal walks in the footsteps of those who shaped the vision arising from the Second Vatican Council. During the Council (1962-1965) the Roman Catholic Bishops decided to open the Church to a changing world and read the signs of the times in the light of the Gospel. This has been a modern starting point

---

* DENNIS M. DOYLE received his doctorate in religious studies from the Catholic University of America. He has taught at the University of Dayton for twenty-eight years. He is the author of numerous articles and two books, *The Church Emerging from Vatican II: A Popular Approach to Contemporary Catholicism* (Bayard, updated 2002) and *Communion Ecclesiology: Vision and Versions* (Orbis Books, 2000).

for church renewal and for theological re-foundation."[3] The stress on
aggiornamento, bringing the church up to date, is notable.

Within the first few years, however, a group of scholars moved away
from *Concilium* in search of a different balance between the new and
the old. By 1972 they had founded their own international journal, *Com-munio*, which now expresses its mission in a way that includes the vision
of John Paul II: "John Paul II unarguably set the Church on the path
to the genuine renewal called for by the Second Vatican Council—a
renewal that eschews both accommodation to the zeitgeist and sectarian
bitterness in order to let the light of the Gospel shine on the questions,
problems, and anxieties of the age. Ever since its inception, *Commu-nio* has been committed to this program of renewal through return to
the sources of the authentic Tradition."[4] *Aggiornamento* is by no means
rejected, but the stress is placed on the need to avoid mere accommoda-tion by contextualizing any updating within a yet deeper stress on *res-sourcement*, a return to the sources.

Tracing out the existence of two schools of thought is fraught with
difficulties. Many scholars do not fit neatly into either camp, and those
who do still manifest a variety of opinions among themselves. Both
schools of thought find a way to emphasize both *aggiornamento* and
ressourcement, but they differ in their definition and application of the
terms as well as in their understanding of what constitutes the proper
balance. Some members of each group have some basic appreciation
for the other, yet there are varying degrees of partisanship evident in
loud voices demonizing and distorting their opponents' positions. Both
camps have a long history of their own positions being shaped by reac-tion against their critics.

I do not wish to suggest that we have two virtually equal but contrast-ing opinions here, though one might intelligently argue for such a posi-tion. I consider it quite evident, though, that in either camp are scholars
of great stature who are also recognizably holy people. When the late
Cardinal Avery Dulles, whom I loved and esteemed, came to the Uni-versity of Dayton to receive the Marianist Award in 2004, I asked him
in a public forum if it were not the case that a great task in the present
lies in finding the proper balance between the *Concilium* people and the
Communio people. He began his response by saying that he thought that
Communio itself was already the balance. I would have answered my
own question with a resounding YES! though, again, without wanting
to imply necessarily that both sides are equally wrong and equally right.
And I am good friends with some scholars of significant note whose
answers would sound almost exactly like that of Cardinal Dulles with

the exception that they would substitute the word *Concilium* for that of *Communio*. Differences of this nature run deep, and we need to be careful about attributing shallow motives to those who swim in a different direction.

The latest round of tense exchanges began with charges made by Archbishop Agostino Marchetto in a 2005 collection of highly critical and mostly negative reviews that he had written of books that address the history of ecumenical councils and particularly Vatican II.[5] The main target of his criticism is the five-volume *History of Vatican II* edited by Giuseppe Alberigo and Joseph A. Komonchak. Although Marchetto regularly criticizes Komonchak for what he takes to be his negative attitude toward the curia, he is generally respectful and at times positively appreciative of Komonchak's contributions. When it comes to Alberigo, however, Marchetto consistently portrays him as one who regularly substitutes his own opinions about what he wished Vatican II had said for what the council truly taught. He judges that Alberigo minimizes the importance of the documents themselves in favor of a vague category that can be called the "spirit" of the council. He finds the main bias of Alberigo to lie in stressing the discontinuity of Vatican II with anything previous in Catholic tradition and thereby interpreting the council as a "rupture" that has produced a new church for a new age. Marchetto thinks that Alberigo, rather than explaining how the council struggled to reach a true consensus between what is often labeled the majority view and the minority view, instead pushes a misleading interpretation that selectively highlights and exacerbates continuing divisions. When Marchetto's book was first released, Cardinal Camillo Ruini gave a speech in which he provocatively affirmed the most sensational of Marchetto's denunciations.[6]

On December 22, 2005, Pope Benedict XVI gave a speech to the curia in which he advocated that Vatican II be approached with a "hermeneutics of reform" that would account for significant elements of both discontinuity and continuity.[7] There appeared to be enough presents in this Christmas speech to make both the Marchettos and the Alberigos of the world very happy. Supporters of Marchetto read the work as completely on their side; Alberigo, Komonchak, and others have since interpreted the pope as including support for their own approaches.[8] On the one hand, Benedict did reject a "hermeneutics of discontinuity and rupture." On the other hand, however, he did not simply replace it with a "hermeneutics of continuity," but rather went to great lengths to account for elements of discontinuity in his "hermeneutics of reform." Moreover, he associates the rejected approach not directly with Alberigo but with radical views that emerged soon after the council.

One of the things that makes the appearance of this new edition of *Vatican II: Fifty Personal Stories* so timely is the way in which these recent debates have focused on the importance of historical context. Komonchak has argued for the need to understand Vatican II as an "event." One cannot adequately interpret the documents apart from an understanding of the history of the council.[9] The history of the council includes not only what led up to it and what happened in the proceedings and the discussions and in the drama of events, but also what has been happening since the council in terms of how it has been received and lived out. From an historically conscious viewpoint, the meaning of Vatican II is still being worked out in the life of the church.

This position is not advocating a simplistic substitution of the "spirit" of the council for the actual documents. Rather, it is making a case that studying the documents themselves without treating their historical context and continuing reception as integral to their meaning is both insufficient and potentially distorting. Seen in this light, William Madges and Michael Daley are not only offering useful background for understanding the sixteen documents, but beyond that are providing a type of material that is integral for coming to grips with the meaning of Vatican II understood as an event.

Vatican II: Fifty Personal Stories provides three layers of contextualization of the council.[10] The stories themselves, written by a Who's Who of postconciliar Catholicism, supply the first layer. These stories provide behind-the-scenes details of what went on at the council as well as what went on in the lives of those it affected. Many of the anecdotes are touching, revealing, or funny; and they offer insightful points about the development of the documents and about the underlying theological debates. The common buzz-phrases about *aggiornamento* and human dignity and collegiality and inculturation take on form and texture as they are discussed by prominent Catholics who have a deeply internalized understanding of such concepts. The reader comes away with a grasp of what the actual teachings were in liturgy and revelation and church and ecumenism.

A second level of contextualization can be found in the brief, yet not too-brief, biographical statements that introduce each of the stories. Although their primary function is to provide background for the personal stories, a secondary yet perhaps even more important function is to give readers information about fifty people, some of whom helped to shape and all of whom were shaped by the council. In other words, as these bios directly provide context for each personal story, in their own way they also provide context for the council itself and for its implementation over the past fifty years.

The third level of contextualization consists in the six introductory essays that mark the beginning of each major section, devoted to history, liturgy, church, revelation, dialogue, and social justice. Madges and Daley provide historical and theological sketches that are critical for understanding the personal stories and the council documents.

The progressive voices in this volume clearly outnumber the conservative and the traditional, though all of these are outnumbered by voices hard to label. This is a complex text about a complex council, yet written in a way to give a wide readership the ability to grapple with both the sixteen documents themselves as well as with the meaning of Vatican II understood as an event.

All Is Story

LIFE IS ALL ABOUT THE story we tell ourselves and others. If we want to make a point with our children (young or old), we can repeat a rule or we can tell a story. The story is often more effective. If we want our students to remember an event, we can give the date and relate the facts about the event. Or we can tell a story that captures something of the essence of the event. The effect of telling the story is usually lasting and substantial.

Yet, in the context in which we find ourselves today, the story and its telling are in crisis. Which leads us to a story. In his book *Leadership Is an Art*, Max DePree tells of the struggle between the campfire and the light bulb.[1] A friend of his had been doing some work in Nigeria in the sixties. Electricity was working its way into the villages. In the hut of each family was a single outlet. As evening came, after all the work was done, families would gather in their huts and look up at their light bulb. They were proud and excited to have such a tangible symbol of technology in their very own homes.

In the middle of the village, where the tribal fire burned, the chief and tribal elders gathered. Except no one came. It appeared that the allure of the light bulb was keeping the villagers in their huts. There, with nothing to read, families sat mesmerized by the light. "Progress," they said. All the while the village storytellers waited by the fire to pass on the tribe's history and traditions. Unfortunately, a few light bulbs were beating hundreds of years of community.

So it is with us as Catholics. We are our stories. Catholics have never been "Dragnet" Christians. We are not like Detective Joe Friday, people who want "just the facts." Christian faith began with the telling of a story: the life, death, and resurrection of Jesus of Nazareth, and ever since Catholics have done their utmost to embellish and add to this foundational story. A story is not a story, though, unless it is told. Yet the story must also be told well. Stories about "bad" things—excessive power, political intrigue, or outright deception—can become "good" stories, if they are told well. Likewise, we have heard good stories told so poorly that their potential is lost. So the challenge becomes one of telling our good stories well. That is when the "Wow!" happens, when the possibility of transformation appears. The question we ask then is, "What stories are we telling?"

Now more than ever, one chapter in the church's story that must be told involves an event that took place five decades ago: the Second Vatican Council (1962-1965). Along with its sixteen documents, the council produced some wonderful stories—stories that, if we are not vigilant in preserving and telling them, will be lost. With this in mind, what we seek to do in this book is to introduce the reader to some of the council's stories and their various characters (and there *were* some characters).

Thus, we have adopted a narrative, or storytelling, approach to the Second Vatican Council. Due to the good will of numerous individuals (some of whom were participants at the council itself; all of whom live in its shadow), we have collected fifty stories that describe how Catholics and others responded to the council and its teachings. The significance of this collection becomes all the more clear when one recognizes that most of those who experienced the council firsthand are moving into their senior years—if they have not already left the stage. These stories must be told!

Related to this invitation to storytelling, we believe this book can meet the needs of a variety of different audiences. For general readers, the book can serve as an introduction to the state of the church today as reflected through the teachings of Vatican II. For college students, the book can be used in connection with another text about Catholicism or the council to give students a variety of perspectives on Vatican II's meaning and its effects. For adult education classes and faith-sharing groups, the book can provide stories that connect with their own lives and encourage them to tell their own stories about what it means to be church.

In general, we think the book will appeal to people who seek to have their perspectives broadened or their spirits affirmed by opening themselves to these stories of Vatican II.

INTRODUCTION

*The Contexts of the Council**

JOHN W. O'MALLEY, S.J.

WHEN THE COUNCIL OPENED ON October 11, 1962, no one knew what to expect. Reliable indicators, such as the Roman Synod of 1960 and the draft documents drawn up by the Preparatory Commissions, pointed to a modest or even regressive outcome. While some quarters entertained hope that the council would validate the findings of recent biblical, patristic, and liturgical research and take account of significant philosophical shifts, they also feared that it might, instead, reaffirm positions codified in seminary textbooks that by and large ignored such scholarship. There were, of course, contrary indicators, not the least being Pope John's invitation to "the separated brethren" to attend the council.

As young men, the bishops coming to the council had been indoctrinated by the textbooks. Why, then, would they not go along with what was presented to them by the commissions, which enjoyed the added authority of being headed by cardinals of the Roman Congregations? Nobody expected that almost as soon as the council opened two groups of leaders, both relatively small, would emerge from among those thousands of bishops, and that the rest of the bishops would have to judge between the two sides not only on a number of specific issues but also on a general orientation of the council. The conflict between the two parties that soon broke out constituted the drama of the council. Had the conflict been foretold, few would have wagered that an overwhelming majority of bishops, hovering between 85 and 90 percent, would so early on, so consistently, and so insistently side with "the Transalpines." . . .

---

* Reprinted by permission of the publisher from O'Malley, *What Happened at Vatican II?* (Cambridge, MA, and London: Belknap Press of Harvard University), pp. 290-94, 298-99, 302-3, 305-8 (Copyright © 2008 by the President and Fellows of Harvard College).

The conflicts in the council, so bitterly and doggedly fought, unmistakably show that some basic values were at stake. Since the leading protagonists on both sides of the debate were for the most part the same no matter what the issue under discussion, there had to be fundamental, across-the-board issues in play to account for the polarity. As the bishops debated a specific issue, whether they were aware of it or not, they wrestled with the issue's more profound implications.

Commentaries on the council have obscured rather than clarified the difference between the two parties by describing the contest as pitting liberals or progressives on the one side against conservatives or reactionaries on the other. I have preferred the terms "majority" and "minority" because they are less prejudicial and are directly verifiable. Nonetheless, the bishops of the minority emerged as conservative in the conventional sense of defending positions current at the time. . . .

Were the bishops who were leading the majority progressive? They were certainly more in touch with current philosophical and theological developments than were their counterparts in the minority, and they made use of theologians who were partly responsible for those developments. On that level, therefore, this partisanship of theirs was an aspect of *aggiornamento* and was progressive in that sense. These bishops were in general more open to updating and willing to apply it more broadly than those of the minority. In that regard, too, they could be called progressive.

For the most part, however, they argued that their positions were more conservative than those of the conservatives because they were retrievals of traditions fundamental and ancient. . . . But the Western bishops leading the majority also came to the council with a sense of breadth and malleability. They had imbibed it from theologians aware of the limitations of the textbooks and engaged in a battle to correct them. That was the strength of such bishops and theologians. To some extent it was also their weakness. They assumed an easier translation of ideas from the scholars' study to the social reality of the church than proved to be the case. They were, moreover, not untouched by elitism and sometimes played fast with the historical record. . . .

The leaders of the minority worked within a narrower theological and cultural horizon. For their contemporaries they fit the stereotype of the proponents of "Roman theology," a theology heavily conditioned by canon law, indifferent to the problems raised by historical methods, and often hermeneutically naïve. They had been schooled to disdain modern approaches to theology as passing novelties or, still influenced by *Pascendi* and *Lamentabili,* to attack them as dangerously subversive. Of them the majority asked a great deal. By trying to convince them to go along with this or that position, the majority essentially asked them to adopt a new mindset and a new value system and to affirm assumptions they feared or abhorred.

The leaders of the minority conveyed in word and deed an entitlement that irked and sometimes enraged the majority. It fueled the antagonism that the assembly sometimes directed toward them, as when the bishops applauded or withheld applause at the wrong times. Insofar as they were part of the curia, they made use of organizational machinery and a network of communication to advance or defend their causes, which further fueled resentment and suspicions of conspiracy. They were, however, more keenly aware than their opponents of possible negative consequences of decisions the council might make, almost to the point of wanting no changes except a further tightening of the screws.

Mediating between the two parties were the two popes. John by temperament, choice, and even spiritual conviction was a noninterventionist. . . . His successor was of a different, more worrisome temperament. Paul VI came into office with a council already steaming ahead—or, in the eyes of the minority, careening out of control in the wrong direction. . . . As a young man he had a virtually private theological education, improved upon when he moved to Rome as a young priest, but it was essentially parochial. He spent his middle years in the curia.

He was well read in contemporary theology and a personal friend of the philosopher Jacques Maritain and the lay theologian Jean Guitton. He was sympathetic to French thought and culture, secular and sacred. . . . He pored over council documents with a meticulous "red pencil" in hand, and he edited them as they were in the making, a papal action unprecedented in the annals of ecumenical councils. He firmly kept four issues off the agenda—priestly celibacy, birth control, reform of the curia, and the mechanism to implement collegiality at the center.

He had a complex relationship to the assembly in St. Peter's. He sometimes acted as a council father like any other, sometimes as a promoter of the council's direction, sometimes as a brake to it, sometimes as an agent to promote consensus, sometimes as the arbiter of procedural conflicts for which he was occasionally responsible, sometimes as interpreter to the council of its meaning, sometimes as monitor of its orthodoxy, and sometimes as rival to its authority. . . .

Thus we come back to the three across-the-board issues. At the council the leading protagonists on both sides came to Vatican II with different theological and cultural sensitivities and with different expectations or hopes for the outcome. They clashed over specific issues, underneath which lay the three more general and fundamental ones. The first was how the church would deal with change. By its own definition the Christian church is a conservative society whose essential mission is to pass on by word and deed a message received long ago. If it adulterates the message or loses sight of it, it has lost its soul, its reason for existence. Yet the church has in one form or another recognized that the message is not an abstraction above and beyond the human beings who first received it or the human beings who have interpreted and passed it on through the centuries. Thus the message entered the historical process, and thus it to some extent became subject to change. . . .

Collegiality brings us to the heart of the second issue-under-the-issues, the relationship between center and periphery. . . . The minority bishops opposed collegiality (as they understood the majority to describe it) most pointedly, however, because it was incompatible with papal primacy. Since they often seemed to understand primacy in Bismarck's terms as an absolute monarchy possessing all authority in the church, which it doled out or recalled at will, primacy and collegiality were by definition irreconcilable. The minority opposed collegiality, therefore, on sincerely held theological and logical grounds, yet it is no accident that some leaders among them were from the curia or associated with it. They worked in and for the center.

The majority at the council certainly did not press for a statement on collegiality merely to make a theological point. They brought it to the fore, like other *ressourcements*, because it had practical ramifications. The bishops who promoted the doctrine and fought for it so passionately wanted to redress what they saw as the imbalance between the authority exercised especially by the Roman Congregations and their own authority as heads of "local churches." Collegiality was the supreme instance in the council of the effort to moderate the centralizing tendencies of the ecclesiastical institution, of the effort to give those from the periphery a more authoritative voice not only back home but also in the center. . . .

The center-periphery issue thus blends into the style issue (the third across-the-board issue), though the latter is much broader. With what style does the church communicate and operate? How does it present itself, and how does it "do business"? What is its personality? The style of the documents of Vatican II is what at first glance as well as most profoundly sets it apart from all other councils. During the council bishops, following the orientation from John XXIII, consistently and repeatedly described the council as pastoral in nature, and they sought a style for the documents to conform to it. The leaders of the majority came to the council with a clear idea that the style was to be biblical and patristic, and by the second period they had won their point. . . .

A style choice is an identity choice, a personality choice, a choice in this instance about the kind of institution the council wanted the church to be. The fathers chose to praise the positive aspects of Catholicism and establish the church's identity on that basis rather than by making Catholicism look good by making others look bad. In this way and in others the style shift expressed and promoted a shift in values and priorities. . . .

The first element in the style shift was the substitution of a rhetorical form for the judicial and legislative forms that had characterized previous councils. In this new style canons, anathemas, and verdicts of guilty-as-charged found no place. The Roman Synod of 1960, the "dress rehearsal" for Vatican II, issued 755 canons. The council, which ended just five years later, issued not a single one. . . .

Despite the way leaders at the council sometimes expressed themselves, they fully realized that Vatican II as a self-proclaimed pastoral council was for that reason also a teaching council. Vatican II taught many things, but few more important than the style of relationships that was to prevail in the church. Its style of discourse was the medium that conveyed the message. It did not, therefore, "define" the teaching but taught it on almost every page through the form and vocabulary it adopted. In so doing it issued an implicit call for a change in style—a style less autocratic and more collaborative, a style willing to seek out and listen to different viewpoints and to take them into account, a style eager to find common ground with "the other," a style open and above board, a style less unilateral in its decision-making, a style committed to fair play and to working with persons and institutions outside the Catholic community, a style that assumes innocence until guilt is proven, a style that eschews secret oaths, anonymous denunciations, and inquisitorial tactics. The majority believed that Pope John XXIII pointed to something along that line when in his opening allocution to the council on October 11, 1962, he said that the church should act by "making use of the medicine of mercy rather than severity . . . and by showing herself to be the loving mother of all, benign, patient, full of mercy and goodness."

PART ONE

THE COUNCIL IN CONTEXT

*What Story Will We Tell?**

MICHAEL J. DALEY

WHENEVER I THINK OF VATICAN II, of all the possible images that come to mind, a small, thick, paperback book enters my head. On the cover of it, in front of a red background, is a gold medal engraved with the faces of Popes John XXIII and Paul VI, the fathers of the council.[1] The title of that now classic book is *The Documents of Vatican II*. As the title suggests, it contains the sixteen documents of the Second Vatican Council—from church to liturgy, revelation to ecumenism, laity to missions.

As we continue to move further and further away from the actual, historical event itself, which consisted of four sessions beginning on October 11, 1962, and ending on December 8, 1965, a new understanding and image of the council is emerging. It is one that speaks to the process of Vatican II—the story, if you will, not only then but now—rather than the product. Cardinal Lawrence Shehan, archbishop of Baltimore during the council, captured it well when, writing in the introduction to the above-mentioned text, he said, "The Council has ended; the Council has just begun."

The Process Begins

If asked for one of the more important dates in the history of the church I would be willing to bet that few, if any, persons would offer January

---

* Material used in this introductory chapter was previously published in *St. Anthony Messenger*, 104 (December 1996): 50-51; 106 (April 1999): 50-51; 109 (August 2001): 50-51. I am indebted to the editors and authors of the first three volumes of *History of Vatican II*, ed. Giuseppe Alberigo; English version ed. Joseph A. Komonchak (Maryknoll, NY: Orbis Books, 1995-2000).

25, 1959. And yet it was on that day that John XXIII, having been pope for only ninety days, announced his decision to convoke a new council. This announcement, as indicated by Etienne Fouilloux in *History of Vatican II*, occasioned on the part of many a two-fold surprise: (1) that a reigning pope would admit the need to update the church; and (2) that he would choose a council as the way to do so rather than papal fiat.[2] So began the surprising and irreversible undertaking that his predecessors had resisted.

Although it was called "A Gesture of Serene Boldness" by the French newspaper *La Croix*, historian Giuseppe Alberigo relates that Pope John XXIII's announcement of a council before a small gathering of cardinals was met with "impressive, devout silence."[3] While the response of the public to the prospect of a new council was one of open-mindedness and expectation,[4] the response of the college of cardinals was one of "bewilderment and worry."[5]

This sentiment is best conveyed through one of the council's many anecdotes. Trying his best to explain what *aggiornamento* meant to a group of bishops, Pope John XXIII sensed his words about church renewal and responding to the "signs of the times" were falling on deaf ears. To better illustrate what "bringing up to date" entailed, John XXIII went to the nearest window, opened it, and said, "The church needs to let in some fresh air." Referring both to personal, interior renewal of self and adaptation of the church's teachings and structures to modern times, *aggiornamento* quickly became part of the Catholic vocabulary. Its familiarity to all was secured due to its frequent usage by Pope John XXIII and eventual acceptance by the majority of the close to 2,500 bishops at Vatican II.

Adding to the mood of reservation and resistance from some, and hope and confidence from others, was the ambiguity surrounding the character of the council. In his book *Pope John XXIII: Shepherd of the Modern World*, Peter Hebblethwaite conveys this sense in a conversation at the last and decisive meeting of the Central Commission, whose task it was to prepare the documents for the council's discussion. Some time prior to the meeting, John XXIII had taken out a ruler and measured a page from a preliminary draft and said, "Seven inches of condemnations and one of praise: is that the way to talk to the modern world?" (These words would soon be echoed by him again in his opening address to the council when he said, "Nowadays, however, the Spouse of Christ prefers to make use of the medicine of mercy rather than that of severity. She considers that she meets the needs of the present day by demonstrating the validity of her teaching rather than by condemnation."[6])

Cardinal Giovanni Battista Montini, the then archbishop of Milan and future Pope Paul VI, went to that final meeting of the Central Commission and said that mercy, charity, and Christian witness—not anathemas and condemnations—were the way to reach the modern world. Realizing that Cardinal Montini spoke with the authority of the pope, Cardinal Alfredo Ottaviani, one of the council's more conservative voices and secretary of the Sacred Congregation of the Holy Office (today called the Congregation for the Doctrine of the Faith), was heard to murmur: "I pray to God that I may die before the end of the Council—in that way I can die a Catholic."[7] As evidenced in Cardinal Ottaviani's words, "conservatives" at the council thought that to approach the modern world without condemnation meant to abandon traditional Catholic beliefs and practices.

Initially many people sought to understand the reason for the calling of the council by referring to previous ones, specifically the Council of Trent (1545-1563) and Vatican I (1869-1870). Yet, as Alberigo makes clear, there was neither a similar historical situation nor any of the traditional reasons—"doctrinal errors or disciplinary divisions"—for calling a council.[8] Still, many thought Vatican II would be a completion of Vatican I, which began on December 8, 1869, and was suspended on October 20, 1870. This council, in its constitution *Pastor aeternus*, declared the dogma of papal infallibility. In response to these tendencies, John stressed that the orientation of the upcoming council would be pastoral rather than doctrinal. He also emphasized its ecumenical character, foreseeing it as a "new Pentecost."

The next major step toward Vatican II began on Pentecost Day, May 17, 1959, with the establishment of the Antepreparatory Commission.[9] The main tasks of this commission would center around a universal consultation of the episcopate, creation of an outline of subjects to be discussed at the council, and suggestions regarding the membership of the preparatory groups. This herculean task was entrusted to Cardinal Domenico Tardini, Pope John's secretary of state.

Unfortunately, he did not live to see the fruits of his labors; he died on July 30, 1961.

Father Francis X. Murphy, C.Ss.R., the long-suspected but now-revealed "Xavier Rynne" of conciliar fame (see page 6), says that "in organizing the council, Tardini followed the pattern of curial congregations or offices, gradually employing their prelates and advisors—conservatives to a man—in proposing some seventy schemata for debate and excluding forward-looking cardinals and theologians. Thus the preparatory stages revealed a fundamental split in the church's thinking between the static, juridical theology of the curia and the mindset of prelates who accepted Pope John's challenge to consider the church as the People of God rather than the political entity suggested by the traditional phrase of a 'perfect society.'"[10]

According to Fouilloux, the episcopal responses, or *votas*, to this invitation of the Antepreparatory Commission followed three major lines of thought.[11] The first group expressed "intransigence." Here definitions and condemnations prevailed, and Mariological declarations were championed at the expense of ecumenism. The second group of responses favored adaptation in diverse areas. This response presaged the final concerns of Vatican II: episcopal collegiality, liturgical renewal, and greater lay participation. Alongside these two lines of thought was the Roman viewpoint on the upcoming council, which was gradually shifting from an initial "contempt" or "indifference" to a more measured response of "distrustful cooptation."

The Speech Heard Round the World

In his opening speech, on October 11, 1962, Pope John XXIII gave the council fathers a personal and collective spiritual challenge to engage in the process of *aggiornamento* rather than take refuge in negative readings of the state of the church and the world. In these now-memorable words, Pope John said:

> In the daily exercise of our pastoral office, we sometimes have to listen, much to our regret, to voices of persons who, though burning with zeal, are not endowed with too much sense of discretion or measure. In these modern times they can see nothing but prevarication and ruin. They say that our era, in comparison with past eras, is getting worse, and they behave as though they have learned nothing from history, which is, none the less, the teacher of life. They behave as though at the time of former Councils everything was a full triumph for the Christian idea and life and for proper Christian liberty.
>
> We feel we must disagree with these prophets of gloom, who are always forecasting disaster, as though the end of the world were at hand.
>
> In the present order of things, Divine Providence is leading us to a new order of human relations which, by men's own efforts and even beyond their very expectations, are directed toward the fulfillment of God's superior and inscrutable designs. And

everything, even human differences, leads to the greater good of the Church.[12]

For Pope John, then, the council's agenda wasn't to be focused on retrieving or restoring some golden age of the church, as if there ever was one, but instead on bringing about a renewal in dialogue with the modern world.[13] As John was very apt to say, "The substance of the ancient doctrine of the deposit of faith is one thing, and the way in which it is presented is another."

The question still remained as to how to use the prepared schemas, written by the largely Roman and curial-controlled preparatory commissions. That question was answered in large measure on October 13, the first working session of the council. Supported by Cardinal Frings of Germany, Cardinal Liénart of France asked for and was granted a postponement of several days for the bishops to consult with members of their national or regional conferences as to whom to elect to the council's commissions. This was in response to the basically predetermined curia-approved members of the various commissions, which likely would have led to the adoption of the schemas already prepared. Without this intervention, many argue that Vatican II would have become a charade rather than a council.[14]

As evidenced in the preparation for the council and its subsequent unfolding, there could be said to have been two different and, at times, competing understandings about the purpose and goal of the council. This is seen in two of the council's more dramatic personages. Pope John's vision was open, conciliatory, pastoral, and oriented toward the future. Cardinal Ottaviani's vision was more defensive, doctrinal, and oriented toward the past. The motto on his episcopal coat of arms was, after all, *Semper idem*, "Always the same."[15]

Which understanding of Vatican II carries us into the future will be determined by what stories we tell. Have you heard the one about . . . ?

FRANCIS XAVIER MURPHY, C.SS.R.
(AKA XAVIER RYNNE)

Reporting the Secrets of the Council*

Francis Xavier Murphy was born in the Bronx, New York, on June 26, 1914. He progressed through the usual stages of education and was ordained a Redemptorist priest on June 23, 1940. Over the next sixty years he marked out a distinguished career as theologian, professor, and journalist. Father Murphy served as chaplain to the Catholic midshipmen of the U.S. Naval Academy, and he worked with Catholic War Relief Services in Italy and Germany. He joined the U.S. Army and served in Korea, Germany, and France from 1951 to 1958. After completing military service, Father Murphy accepted a university position at the Accademia Alphonsiana in Rome, where he taught patristic and moral theology from 1959 to 1975. Among some of the many books he published during this time were A Monument to St. Jerome *(1953),* Peter Speaks through Leo *(1954), and* Pope John XXIII *(1958).*

During the Second Vatican Council, Father Murphy gathered information about, as well as reported his personal observations concerning, the course of the debates about the subject matter of the various conciliar documents. In addition, he documented the church politics engaged in both behind the scenes and during the debates on the floor of the council. His detailed reports first appeared pseudonymously in The New Yorker *magazine. These reports, augmented with additional material, were eventually published in four book-length volumes, each devoted to one of the four sessions of the council.*[16]

For his scholarly and other accomplishments, he was recognized with honors from the Aspen Institute, the Folger Shakespeare Library, and the Woodrow Wilson International Center for Scholars.

Father Murphy died on April 11, 2002.

---

* This excerpt is taken in modified form from Xavier Rynne, *Vatican Council II* (Maryknoll, NY: Orbis Books, 1999).

I WAS TEACHING AT THE Redemptorist Accademia Alfonsiana, on the Faculty of Moral Theology, during the preparations for Vatican II as well as throughout the council. Never one to shrink from politics at any level, I began compiling notes about the intrigues and secretive manipulations by a number of prominent prelates as the agenda for the council was being formulated. I pulled these notes together into an article and submitted them to John Chapin, a literary agent. He in turn put me in touch with Robert Giroux, vice president and senior editor of Farrar, Straus & Cudahy. He liked my piece and thought it worthy of publication. When he asked me where I'd like to have it placed, I replied, without the slightest hesitation, "In *The New Yorker*." Somewhat taken aback, Bob said, "Oh Father, I think there's too much religion for *The New Yorker*." I stuck to my guns, and after some discussion Bob agreed to send it to Bill Shawn, the editor of *The New Yorker*.

Two days later Bob called me with the good news that my piece had been accepted. Going over the manuscript in preparation for its final submission, Bob suddenly said, "And what name are you going to use for the author? Since you are involved with the papal curia, it might be dangerous." Although the article contained nothing heretical or unorthodox, its revelations of the gossip and activities of the curia might infuriate members of that group. "They might report you to the Holy Office and have you relieved of your professorship," he said. All of a sudden the name Xavier Rynne (my middle name and my mother's maiden name) popped into my mind. "Excellent," Bob said. And that was the name I used.

The article, "Letter from Vatican City," was published in *The New Yorker* at the very start of the first session of the council. A long and apparently authentic account of names and activities, guesswork and facts about the preparations for the council, it sent shock waves through the assemblage of cardinals, bishops, and priests. Many were outraged, and some frankly appalled. A surprising number became hell-bent on pursuing the whereabouts of Xavier Rynne, an effort that, fortunately, except for a few close calls, was unsuccessful for the duration of the council. "Who the hell is Xavier Rynne?" became a persistent question throughout the council and for many years after the deliberations ended.

Although the conciliar debate resulting in the church's historic self-critique was supposed to be conducted under the rule of secrecy, the fanfare with which the council opened and the gravity of the matters under consideration proved too great a burden for the traditional Vatican organs of information.

Meanwhile, thanks to Xavier Rynne, a rare spotlight had been focused on the Vatican's entrenched inner circle. The prelates and clerics of the Roman curia, who determine church policies from the top, were thus exposed to conciliar criticism, much to the chagrin of their supposititious leader, Cardinal Alfredo Ottaviani of the *ancien* Holy Office (formerly known as the Inquisition), who considered himself the paragon of orthodoxy.

From its inauguration, the council had proven a startling event, providing journalists and TV and radio commentators by the hundreds with hard news: Pope John referring to some of his counselors as "prophets of doom"; Cardinal Liénart and Cardinal Frings upsetting the first meeting by demanding a free election of the commissions that would produce the council's documents; the frequent skirmishes between curial cardinals and their opponents; the gracious confrontations of adversary prelates and *periti* in the *Bar Jonah* and the *Bar Rabbas*. (These were the coffee, snack, and toilet facilities provided by Pope John in the sacristy and interior vestibule. "If we do not let them smoke somewhere," he is reported to have advised, "they'll be hiding their cigarettes under their miters.")

Over the course of the next three years, the council's annual two-month sessions were reported in extraordinary detail through twelve subsequent *New Yorker* articles by the stealthy Xavier Rynne. Each article created a firestorm of controversy within the assemblage. But, for all the hue and cry, the speculations and interrogations, no one seemed capable of identifying the author of the missives.

It was only at a clerical gathering in Baltimore some twenty years later that I admitted authorship to the departing Apostolic Nuncio, Pio Laghi. Asked why, after all these years of pseudonymity, I was coming up out of the catacombs, I replied, "If I died tomorrow the Jesuits would claim him [Rynne] and the Redemptorists would be delighted to be rid of him." Nonetheless, as I had been writing articles for *America*, *Catholic World*, the *New York Times*, *Boston Globe*, *Los Angeles Times*, *Baltimore Sun*, and other journals, suspicion soon fell on me. In particular, the professors at the Jesuit-run Biblicum questioned me strenuously and often. However, by the assiduous use of casuistry, I managed to preserve my anonymity, although some of my closer friends and an occasional sharp critic were certain that I was their man.

I had been appointed a *peritus* through the good graces of the Redemptorist bishop of Monterey-Fresno, Aloysius Willinger, a close friend of Cardinal Cicognani, the Vatican secretary of state. Shortly after the arrival of the first *New Yorker* article in Rome, he questioned me as to the authorship, concluding with the observation that there were many expressions that sounded like mine. That evening he had Archbishop Egidio Vagnozzi and a few younger bishops to dinner and, finding them ignorant of the Rynne article, took great glee in disabusing them of their ignorance.

About a month later I learned that I was going to be called to the Holy Office to be put under an extremely rare oath of secrecy, under pain of excommunication. When I inquired as to the subject matter for the oath, I was told I would be informed after I arrived at the Holy Office. I replied that I simply refused to take a blind oath. The next morning I sought out both Cardinal Spellman and the English Cardinal John Heenan, suggesting that if I were not back in the conciliar hall by noon, they should send somebody after me.

I arrived at the Holy Office and awaited the arrival of Archbishop Pietro Parente, Assessor of the Congregation, who entered promptly at ten o'clock. He was accompanied by two monsignori, one of whom was Henry Cosgrove, an acquaintance of mine from Brooklyn.

"Kneel down," said the archbishop in Italian, "and we will take the oath of secrecy."

"Not until I know why," was my caustic response.

"I will tell you after the oath."

"No, Monsignor. I am not taking an oath about something of which I do not know the substance."

"You will be told . . ."

"No, Monsignor," I interrupted. "And what are these two gentlemen doing here?"

"One is my secretary, the other a translator."

"It is obvious that I need no translator. Henry," I said, turning to the American monsignor, "you can be my secretary."

With the archbishop's temper rapidly rising, I asked if he wanted to interrogate me regarding the magazine with little pieces of paper he had tucked under his arm. On his acquiescence, I took an oath about what I might know regarding that particular magazine. He began reading me a series of quotations, and for each I agreed that they were written by one Xavier Rynne, but carefully added that I was Father Francis Murphy. Then he came to a defamatory passage about himself, describing his expulsion from Rome some twenty years earlier by Pope Pius XI. "*Listen,*" he said, "*you understand that Pius XI was a little sick in the head.*"

"Henry," I shouted to my newly acquired secretary, "write that down!"

Suddenly realizing the significance of what he had just said, the archbishop bolted out of the room. The three of us stood silently, not knowing exactly what to do. Finally, I whispered the closing prayer of the oath, dismissed the monsignori, and walked quietly back to my quarters. I never heard from the archbishop again.

JOHN W. O'MALLEY, S.J.

Vatican II and My Many Contexts

John W. O'Malley, S.J., is University Professor at Georgetown University, Washington, DC. A specialist in the religious culture of early modern Europe, he received his doctorate in history in 1966 from Harvard University. His monographs have received best-book awards from the American Historical Association, the American Philosophical Society, the American Society for Church History, and the Sixteenth Century Studies Conference. His best-known book, The First Jesuits *(Cambridge, MA: Harvard University Press, 1993), has been translated into ten languages. In 2008 he published with Harvard* What Happened at Vatican II, *translated into French, Italian, and Polish. The same press will in 2012 publish* What Happened at Trent: A History of the Council. *A full list of his publications up to 2001 can be found in* Early Modern Catholicism: Essays in Honor of John W. O'Malley, S.J. *(Toronto: University of Toronto Press, 2001).*

John O'Malley has lectured widely in North America and Europe on both popular and professional topics. He has held fellowships from the Guggenheim Foundation, the National Endowment for the Humanities, the American Council of Learned Societies, the American Philosophical Society, the American Academy in Rome (Prix de Rome), and Villa I Tatti, the Harvard University Center for Italian Renaissance Studies, Florence. He is a past president of the American Catholic Historical Association and of the Renaissance Society of America. In 1995 he was elected to the American Academy of Arts and Sciences, in 2001 to the Accademia di san Carlo (Ambrosian Library), Milan, and in 1997 to the American Philosophical Society, of which he is currently vice-president. Besides holding a number of honorary degrees, he in 2002 received the lifetime achievement award from the Society for Italian Historical Studies and in 2005 the corresponding award from the Renaissance Society of America.

VATICAN II DID NOT TAKE place in one context. Because of the worldwide span of the Catholic Church and the socio-economic range of its members (from royal pretenders to the humblest peasants), the council took place in many contexts. I had direct experience of one as I grew up in a small town in Ohio, where 45 percent of the population was Methodist, 45 percent Catholic, and 10 percent nondescript. My parents were practicing Catholics, but they considered themselves liberal in their views about the church. (Yes! Even in those pre-Vatican II days such creatures existed!) Their waywardness was probably due in part to the fact they had so many Protestant relatives and friends.

The town had no Catholic school. Two or three nuns from a slightly larger neighboring town came to ours every Sunday morning to teach a half-hour of catechism between the two Masses. This was done in the pews of the church. If the numbers warranted it, some lay women also taught along with the nuns. Of my two best friends as I was growing up, one was a non-practicing Methodist and the other, as best I could tell, a casual agnostic. I did not have, therefore, a "typical Catholic boyhood." The fact that I was an only child was also not typically Catholic.

Nonetheless, Saint Joseph's church played a central role in our lives. My parents would not think of missing Mass on Sunday, and at a certain point my mother became director of the choir. We faithfully attended May devotions in honor of the Virgin Mary and, during Lent, the Stations of the Cross. Although my parents abstained, I never missed a Bingo Night or Card Party Night at the church. My parents, like virtually everybody in their generation, also abstained from receiving Communion except once a year "during the Easter season." At Mass they recited the rosary.

The nuns convinced some of us kids that receiving Communion more often was a good idea, and about my sophomore year in high school I began to do so every Sunday and then, as an altar boy, even during the week. The nuns also introduced us to the little paperback (price 25 cents), My Sunday Missal, with which we could follow what the priest was reading. "Pray the Mass" was the mantra.

That was my first context. The second was Jesuit training in the late 1940s and 1950s. Our novitiate was very strict, but, even so, one day we had a formal debate about the possibility of a vernacular liturgy. Although I was inclined to the negative, I was chosen to speak in favor of the vernacular. The arguments stuck with me. The very fact that in such a situation a debate like that could be officially sponsored says a lot about what some educated Catholics were thinking. Other than that debate, Catholic life in the Jesuits was standard for the era until I began my theological studies.

The Jesuit house of study was in southern Indiana, Bible-belt country, hardly where you would expect "progressive thinking." Our faculty, however, was very much aware of what was going on in the wider world and introduced us to it. We read Bernard Lonergan, and, even more daring, Karl Rahner, Josef Andreas Jungmann, Jean Daniélou, and Henri de Lubac. In a vague way we students were aware that at least some of these authors were under suspicion, but we did not realize what a break they represented with how theology was presented in standard textbooks.

At the same time John Courtney Murray rose to prominence in the church-state question, and he became a hero for us because he seemed to be opening the possibility that a Catholic could be president of the United States. In retrospect I see how prepared I was in comparison with most American Catholics at the time for what transpired at the council.

In 1963, while I was writing my dissertation in history for Harvard University, I was awarded a fellowship to the American Academy in Rome. My two years at the Academy were transforming for me in many ways, one of which was through the excitement of being in Rome while the council was going on. My third context! Through the Academy I had tickets to several of the public sessions of the council, and many times snuck into the press briefings that took place every afternoon. Because of the kind of theological training I had received, I easily absorbed the council's decisions as they document-by-document appeared.

Engaged though I was in what was happening at the council, I never dreamed that I would one day write about it on a professional basis. My specialty, after all, was the sixteenth century, not the twentieth. I wrote my dissertation, however, on a church reformer, Giles of Viterbo, and I began to see connections between "reform" in the sixteenth century and the council's *aggiornamento*. I also began to believe that my training in history provided me with a rather unusual frame of reference with which to understand the council.

I finished my dissertation, returned to the States, and was assigned to teach at the University of Detroit (today, Detroit-Mercy). One evening during a casual conversation in the Jesuit recreation room several years after the council ended, I was asked a question about the council. That did it! I said to myself, "You need to write an article about that." I did. It was published in 1971 in *Theological Studies*.

I thought that was the end of the matter for me, but it certainly was not. It fell to my generation to "implement the council" and to try to explain it to people. This was the fourth context. These were not tasks we asked for, nor were they always easy. They have, in any case, engaged me for most of my adult life. I have kept my grounding in the sixteenth century, but I don't live there. I live in the present, the twentieth and now twenty-first century. In that present there is for us Catholics no way not to be affected by Vatican Council II. That's why I keep thinking and writing about it. It is an important part of my identity . . . and yours too!

MONIKA K. HELLWIG

Vatican II: The Glorious Years

Monika K. Hellwig was born in Breslau, Germany, on December 10, 1929. After earning degrees at the University of Liverpool (England), she came to the United States, where she completed the M.A. in 1956 and the Ph.D. in 1968, both at the Catholic University of America. In addition to visiting professorships at a number of colleges and universities, Hellwig taught at Georgetown University for about thirty years, completing her tenure there as the Landegger Professor of Theology (1990-1996). From 1996-2005 she was the Executive Director of the Association of Catholic Colleges and Universities of the United States. She died September 30, 2005.

Dr. Hellwig served on the editorial board of prominent theological journals, such as Theological Studies *and the* Journal of Ecumenical Studies. *In addition, she was a member of national committees established by the U.S. Catholic Conference and held the office of president of the Catholic Theological Society of America (1986-1987). She published more than one hundred articles and more than twenty books. Some of her more important publications include* Understanding Catholicism *(1981),* Jesus, the Compassion of God *(1983), and* The Modern Catholic Encyclopedia *(1994), which she co-edited with Michael Glazier. In recognition of her outstanding contributions to Catholic theology, Hellwig was awarded more than twenty honorary doctorates.*

During the Second Vatican Council she was in Rome, first to ghostwrite a book for a Vatican official, then as part of a retreat team for Movemento Mondo Migliore, and finally as a broadcaster for the English-language program of Vatican Radio while making abstracts of the council documents.

THOSE OF US WHO HAD the privilege of being in Rome during the Second Vatican Council are not likely ever to forget the intellectual excitement of those times. Every autumn of those four years the streets in the neighborhood of St. Peter's and around the pontifical universities bustled.

There was talk about what was happening in the *aula* and about what was happening behind the scenes. The debates spilled into restaurants and bars. There was speculation about the strategy sessions going on behind doors in *pensioni* and religious houses. Sometimes the debates spilled into the streets with bishops and long-robed cardinals striding along engaged in discussion with their own *periti* or trying to shake off importunate journalists or petitioners.

The four sessions took place always and only in the autumn, when the weather in Rome was gracious and it was good to be out of doors. Even before the bishops arrived from all over the world, lectures and press conferences by the *periti* would be announced. This would be a little before the beginning of the academic year at the Roman universities, and some world-renowned speakers would be billed. Much as the organizers would try to limit attendance to those with press credentials, those of us who were in Rome on other pursuits would crowd the halls, thirsty for the kind of theology and scripture scholarship to be had so freely at that time.

Once the sessions began, the *Osservatore Romano* would report daily. Of course the editors observed scrupulously the rule that the actual speeches should not be reported because it was not to be known which participant bishops were taking which positions in the discussions. No documents were actually published until the end of the second session. Until they were passed, the matter of the discussions was to be kept *segreto* (secret). *Osservatore Romano*, therefore, gave on the front page only the list of speakers in the order in which they had spoken on the previous day. From the second session onward, however, one could read the entire texts of the speeches without attribution toward the back of the paper. The speeches were printed in the same order as the list of speakers on the front page. This material, after all, was *segreto*, or at most *segretissimo*, by no means classified as *segretissimo segretissimo* (!) And so we who read Italian were getting day by day the most wonderful theological education. The speeches, but for rare exceptions, were assuredly written not by the bishops but by their *periti*, and many bishops had picked their *periti* from among top-rank scholars.

Between the first and second sessions of the council, Pope John XXIII died, a truly saintly and pastoral pope. A man of great common sense and shrewdness, he was the visionary, prophetic leader who had launched the council with such great expressed hopes for a new Pentecost of the Holy Spirit. He died saying that he offered his life for the continuation of the council. We all held our breath over the coming election of the next pope as the rumors flew around Rome. There had been much calculation as to who were the *papabili* and which among them was the front-runner. Everyone had both hopes and fears concerning the impact that a change in the papacy would have on the council and its outcome. It was very well known that there were curial cardinals who, along with their permanent staffs, had been and remained utterly opposed to the very idea of the council. They were convinced that they were running the church very efficiently so that no changes were needed. Moreover, they knew that the German bishops and those of Asia and Africa were a great threat to this excellent established order of the church, properly governed out of Rome to preserve changeless uniformity even in small matters. Already they were saying, "I told you so," and "Look at the disturbance they have caused." A refrain one could pick up sometimes in the street was, "Fifty years, fifty years, it will take us fifty years to get the church back in order after this council." Looking back now, after forty [*sic*] years since the opening, the refrain sounds more ominous in light of recent developments than it did then when we laughed at it as a huge joke.

In the event, it was Montini of Milan who was elected, and it was assumed that he would move in the same direction as Pope John XXIII. Indeed it was Montini who had made a very strong speech on collegiality in the church during the first session. On the day after his election he announced publicly that the main business of his pontificate would be the continuation of the council. Moreover, his inaugural encyclical opened some of those windows of which John XXIII had spoken in initiating preparations for the council: "I want to open the windows of the church and let some fresh air in." It was rumored in Rome that Pope Paul VI, having had experience of the kinds of tricks played on popes by some gentlemen of the curia, and having been a papal speech writer himself under Pope Pius XII, was taking no chances with his inaugural encyclical. He wrote it word for word himself and, so I was assured by one in a position to know, stood at the presses all night to make sure that what was printed was what he had actually written and not someone else's "correction" of his text.

Unfortunately in the general excitement of the council, this encyclical, *Ecclesiam suam*, did not attract, then or since then, the attention it should have received. Presenting the church as essentially a process of dialogue, the encyclical opened possibilities for great progress in ecumenism (which some in the curia have diligently tried to close since then). Pope Paul VI certainly began his pontificate with a very dynamic, forward-looking concept of the church, with imagery that effectively complements the imagery used in *Lumen gentium*, the "Dogmatic Constitution on the Church," already then under discussion, though not promulgated until the end of the third session.

Meanwhile, the council went on. In the second session *Sacrosanctum concilium*, the "Constitution on the Sacred Liturgy," was promulgated along with two lesser documents. There had, of course, been a ferment of liturgical scholarship both in Europe and in America. In the fifties, some of us in the United States who were fortunate had been attending summer sessions at the Catholic University of America and at the University of Notre Dame. Many of the great European scholars in scripture, patristics, and liturgy were lecturing there, along with towering American scholars such as Godfrey Diekmann. The passing and promulgation of *Sacrosanctum concilium* seemed like a vindication of our professors, almost all of whom had at some time suffered from curial disapproval and sanctions. The passing of this document initiated years of wonderfully happy rediscovery and retrieval of the spirit of the liturgy, all now firmly legitimated. However, it was not in Rome, but later upon return to the United States and to the graduate programs in theology at the Catholic University of America that I actually experienced this excitement of rediscovery with like-minded congregations of worshipers.

One by one the great Vatican II documents opened vistas of possibilities for Catholics around the world. There was the battle led by Cardinal Suenens over the placement of chapters in *Lumen gentium*. Symbolically this was an important issue: was the church to be described primarily as the People of God, or primarily as a hierarchic structure? Clearly the stance of a powerful group of curial cardinals and bishops was that this was not even a question. In their view the church was essentially a hierarchic structure, to be maintained with an unswerving fidelity that was equated with unqualified changelessness. Therefore there was no question that after an introductory chapter, more homiletic than consequential, the next step was to set out the centralized hierarchic structure of the church.

Against this Suenens pressed for a second chapter on the People of God as describing the true nature of the church. This in turn had consequences for the large document on the church in the modern world, *Gaudium et spes*, and for the documents on the role of the laity, on revelation, on ecumenism, and more.

Because of the press conferences and public lectures of the *periti*, these discussions conveyed to us who were living in Rome at the time a real ferment of hope for a renewed church. We began to share the vision of a church immediately relevant to the real problems and challenges of the world of the twentieth century. We began to see the integration of what we had studied with what was actually happening. We began to have hope of wide-awake Catholic communities in lively participatory liturgies. And we began to realize in a whole new way that not only the hierarchy and clergy, but we ourselves, the laity, were this church that was being talked about. Already at this time in the sixties, this was perceived as especially good news for women, though in the council itself the women were totally excluded, even such as economist Barbara Ward, who had contributed massively to the preparatory work for *Gaudium et spes*.

When the council ended, it was on a great surge of hope and new energy. The liturgy was to be thoroughly renewed for intelligibility, more biblical content, and more active participation by the congregation. There was to be a substantial reform of the curia. There were to be regular means for the exercise of episcopal collegiality to express the voices of the local churches. There was to be a whole new approach to and emphasis on ecumenism. The church was to engage the reality of the modern world on a note of hope and collaboration, not with a predetermined stance of rejection and condemnation. And this engagement was largely to be in fields where the combined expertise of the laity was to play the key role, with room for multiple initiatives. Postconciliar commissions were to be put in place to make sure it all happened. What was perhaps not-well-enough thought out was the extent to which the huge, complex, change-resistant Roman curia was in the strategic position to control whether or not it all happened.

Soon after the council, I traveled in Switzerland, Germany, and Britain, and then returned to the United States to complete doctoral studies at the Catholic University of America. Implementation of the liturgical changes was, of course, piecemeal as directives came out from the postconciliar committee, and patchy as parish clergy responded with varying degrees of enthusiasm or lack of it. Slowly parish councils came into being, implementing at the grassroots level the principle of collegiality introduced by the council with references to the bishops of the local churches. In fact, as the years wore on, it could be observed that the principle of collegiality was implemented rather better within the local churches than at the global level, where the curia remained implacably opposed to it.

Within the Graduate Department of Religion and Religious Education (then part of the Graduate School of Arts and Sciences), scripture, theology, and liturgy had truly come alive. Immense enthusiasm and creativity were expended on the preparation and celebration of the regular eucharistic liturgies, as well as on paraliturgical occasions, and eventually community penance celebrations. It constituted a training ground for many who would later be lay ministers in the parishes, and gave them an experience of Christian community that carried over into religious education, musical and liturgical ministries, publishing, and other fields. In those days everything was still possible, and, at least on the university campus, enthusiasm was not spontaneously met with suspicion.

It was not only in liturgical celebration but also in the classroom that profound change and renewal were taking place. In the fifties at the Catholic University of America (as was probably the case elsewhere on Catholic campuses) the Index of Forbidden Books loomed so large that a considerable collection of modern philosophy and theology was literally padlocked in cages in the library. The zeal of the librarians was such that even Romano Guardini's *The Lord* (in its English translation) was locked away because scripture quotations had been taken from a better translation, which was therefore closer to the German but which had not been officially approved for use by American Catholics. After the Second Vatican Council many of the books in the cages had been liberated and had migrated onto the graduate reading lists, where they were absorbed with recognition and appreciation. We were making a transition from dogmatic theology to systematic theology, from explanation of established positions assumed to be formulated in unchangeable ways to a mode of inquiry that began with existential questions and explored the tradition for resources to answer those questions. We were reading and discussing across Christian denominational boundaries, and going further afield to learn from Jewish authors, eventually moving into the whole sweep of human religious traditions.

Lay students in those days were flocking to the graduate religious studies and theological programs both during the academic year and during the summers, when many of them were using their vacation time from full-time jobs to pursue these studies with a passion. Some certainly hoped to be active in various church ministries, but many were simply in pursuit of knowledge and understanding of this remarkable rebirth of the church that had happened with Vatican II. Most significant was the number of women, both religious and lay, with this thirst for a deeper understanding of theology and of the Catholic tradition. Combined with the Sister Formation movement that had been so widespread in the fifties, boosted by the personal urging of Pope Pius XII, this new enthusiasm on the part of women for biblical, theological, and liturgical studies contributed to a certain gap between an increasingly educated body of Catholic women and a commonly much-less-educated parish clergy. Typically at public theological lectures and at seminars and institutes on theological and church topics, the clergy were absent and the women turned out in force.

Of course, it was not long before the reaction set in. The changes were so swift and so central that many in the church, both lay and clerical, feared that everything was falling apart. It must indeed be acknowledged that with less-rigid catechetical instruction, younger Catholics seemed to know less about the traditional teachings. With a more personal approach to morality and church law, many followed their own conscience on matters such as birth control, and took ritual laws like Sunday eucharistic attendance much more lightly. With a new understanding of sacramentality, few could make sense of the sacrament of penance in the way we had been practicing it. On the other hand, those who longed for a more meaningful celebration within a context of spiritual direction were hard put to find such a confessor among the parish clergy. Many simply drifted away. Meanwhile, slowly, we rediscovered the Rite of Christian Initiation of Adults, which put new demands both on the clergy and on the parish communities—demands for which not all of them were ready either intellectually or in terms of lived Christian community.

It cannot be denied that the aftermath of Vatican II left us with great inspiration and hope, but also with great confusion and tension that constantly has threatened to polarize the community. In the midst of that confusion the social justice concerns of *Gaudium et spes* came to the forefront among some clergy and theologians in Latin America and elsewhere, and in a whole new way in the U.S. Catholic Bishops' Conference. The Catholic Church has become a political force on behalf of the poor and excluded, and it is increasingly a force to be reckoned with. But precisely where the bishops' conference has become very forward-looking, pro-active, and ready to undertake radical social justice initiatives, the Catholic community in the pews has largely been unwilling to follow, holding instead the values and opinions of the general American population.

Have we realized the potential created by the Second Vatican Council? Yes, in some aspects and to some degree. We shall not be able to reenact that council and try over again. But how about Vatican III soon?

GREGORY BAUM

A Changing Church

Gregory Baum was born in Berlin, Germany, in 1923. He came to Canada from England in 1942. There he received a B.A. in mathematics (McMaster University, 1946); an M.A. in mathematics (Ohio State University, 1957), and a Th.D. (Fribourg University, Switzerland, 1956). He later studied sociology at the New School of Social Research (New York City, 1969-1971).

Both in its preparatory stages and during the council itself, Baum was a peritus, or theological advisor, at the Vatican Secretariat for Promoting Christian Unity (1960-1965).

Over his distinguished career, Baum has been a professor of theology at St. Michael's College in the University of Toronto (1959-1986); professor of social ethics, Faculty of Religious Studies, McGill University, Montreal (1986-1998); and, presently, is an associate at the Jesuit Centre justice et foi in Montreal.

Baum has been a frequent contributor to the international Catholic review Concilium, *and served on its board of directors from 1970 to 1990. He is also the founder and editor of* The Ecumenist, *1962-2003.*

The books Baum has published since 2000 include the following: Nationalism, Religion and Ethics *(2001);* Amazing Church *(2005);* Signs of the Times: Religious Pluralism and Economic Injustice *(2007); and* The Theology of Tariq Ramadan: A Catholic Perspective *(2009). In 2006 Novalis and Orbis Books republished his highly praised book* Religion and Alienation.

MY DOCTORATE AT THE UNIVERSITY of Fribourg in Switzerland dealt with the church's understanding of Christian unity. Published as a book, it attracted the attention of ecumenically minded Catholics. In 1959 when Pope John XXIII convoked Vatican Council II and created the Secretariat for Promoting Christian Unity, its prefect, Cardinal Bea, appointed a number of bishops and priests to work with him. I had the good fortune of being named *peritus* at the Secretariat, a task that brought me to Rome several times a year between 1960 and 1965. The work of the Secretariat included the preparation of three draft documents: on the ecumenical movement, on religious liberty, and on the church's relation to the Jews and the world religions, all controversial topics in the church at that time.

I was greatly impressed by the willingness of the bishops to change the church's official teaching. I remembered the strictures imposed upon theologians in 1950 when I began my study of theology. Pius XII had just published his encyclical *Humani generis*, in which he defended neo-Thomism as the church's official theology and philosophy and repudiated the efforts of Catholic thinkers to enlarge their perspective and promote theological and philosophical pluralism in the church. In the 1950s, biblical scholars who applied the historical-critical method in their research were under great pressure from the Roman magisterium. My association with Catholic theologians who engaged in dialogue with Protestant thinkers made me keenly aware of Rome's disapproval of the ecumenical movement, especially its formal condemnation in Pius XI's encyclical *Mortalium animos* (1928) and the subsequent Vatican decrees prohibiting Catholics from participating in ecumenical meetings. Among ourselves we whispered that the Roman resistance to ecumenism was needlessly narrow and based on an inadequate understanding of its nature and potentiality.

Yet I remember how shocked I was during a conversation with a dedicated young Catholic woman who worked in Fribourg at the head office of Pax Romana, an international association of Catholic intellectuals. Pax Romana provided an opportunity for progressive Catholic lay people to discuss among themselves the ethical imperatives of the Catholic faith in contemporary society. What shocked me was the firm declaration of this young woman that in condemning the principle of religious liberty, the popes were mistaken. She grieved over the restrictions imposed upon Protestants in some Catholic countries and was unimpressed by the reply that Protestant countries themselves fostered anti-Catholic bigotry. She argued that the human conscience wrestling with sacred texts and seeking obedience to the divine voice deserves the respect of society and the church. Yet I was disturbed by her insistence that the magisterium was wrong.

Later, at the council, I was grateful for the evolution of the church's teaching. The magisterium has come to respect dissident Christians and their churches, to see them as members of Christ's body in an as-yet imperfect communion with us, and to look upon ecumenism as a movement initiated by the Holy Spirit. The magisterium has come to acknowledge the ongoing validity of God's ancient covenant with the Jewish people and to recognize in the world religions truths and values shared by the church, an echo of the Word of God, incarnate in the man Jesus Christ. The magisterium has come to uphold religious liberty and human rights, despite the papal condemnations of these liberal institutions in the nineteenth century. In the first sentence of *Gaudium et spes*, the church declares herself in solidarity with the entire human family, beginning with the poor, the afflicted, and the weak. The magisterium has come to hold that God's grace, announced and celebrated in the church, is actually at work in the whole of human history (*ecclesia ab Abel*) and offers every human being, in a manner known only to God, the chance to share in Christ's work of redemption.

The ecumenical Council of Florence in the fifteenth century had said the opposite, insisting that pagans, Jews, heretics, and schismatics will be sent to the torments of hell when they die. Even great charity won't help heretics and schismatics; even if they shed their blood giving witness to the Christian faith, the council said, they will go to hell (Denzinger 1351). We are by this and other examples made aware that the church can change its mind. We now recognize that the ecclesiastical magisterium is exercised in history and, guided by the Spirit, evolves in history.

How can one explain the doctrinal evolution that took place at Vatican Council II? I propose two factors.

First, there existed in the churches specialized movements in which Catholics explored the meaning and power of the gospel in modern society: theological movements, open to pluralism, and inspired by biblical and patristic scholarship, the lay movement, the biblical movement, the liturgical movement, the ecumenical movement, the peace movement, and the social justice movement. Some of these movements were frowned on by the ecclesiastical hierarchy. But thanks to Pope John XXIII and the council, the ideas promoted by these movements were able to influence the thinking of the bishops.

Second, the council made possible the free conversation among bishops, an open dialogue that stimulated their thinking, an unusual opportunity in the church where conversations among bishops tend to deal with what has been settled in the past. The open dialogue at Vatican II was creative, making possible the emergence of new ideas replacing the old ones.

Thinking about the council today saddens me because the promises it made were not kept. The council tried to transform the monarchial papacy into a collegial one, one that would include the bishops in the decision making at the top and respect the authority of the local church to make the gospel relevant in the local culture. Yet the papal monarchy returned soon after the council: the bishops' conferences were deprived of their authority, and the church's central administration controlled the liturgy, the catechism, and the theology without respect for the creativity of the regional churches.

The council recognized the prophetic and priestly vocation of the baptized, honoring the contribution of lay Catholics to the church's teaching and their active part in the church's liturgy, a conciliar teaching that quickly was forgotten by pushing lay people back into the margin.

The council encouraged Catholic theologians to be creative, to wrestle with the issues raised in contemporary society, and to remember that, while the gospel is unchanging, its formulation must change so as to make it more understandable to people in their situation. Today theologians who do this are told by the authorities to stick to the old formulation.

The council emphasized what the church had in common with other Christians, with the followers of other religions, and with secular people in order to foster cooperation in promoting the common good. Only after recognizing what we share in common does the council specify the difference between us and them. With the instruction *Dominus Jesus* of the year 2000, the ecclesiastical magisterium puts the emphasis on the difference between us and others, and only afterward recalls that we share something in common with them. This approach has made cooperation with others more difficult. Its spiritual consequences are that Catholics no longer feel they share with Protestants a common faith in Jesus Christ, nor share with other religious people a common yearning to be led by God into the truth, nor share with secular humanity the desire for peace and justice. If this current continues, the church will become a giant sect, a walled garden, unable to recognize truth and goodness outside of its boundaries.

The great disappointment that the promises of Vatican II have not been kept drives some Catholics out of the church, while others assign increased importance to deepening their spiritual life and being comforted by God's presence in the heart.

LISA SOWLE CAHILL

The Council as Seen from a Catholic Girls' School

Lisa Sowle was born in Philadelphia in 1948. After attending elementary and secondary schools in Virginia and Washington, DC, she studied at the University of Portland and Santa Clara University, where she received her undergraduate degree in 1970. She earned the M.A. and Ph.D. degrees from the Divinity School of the University of Chicago in 1973 and 1976.

Ms. Sowle married Larry Cahill, an attorney, in 1972, and they became the parents of five children, three of whom are adopted from Thailand. Currently Dr. Cahill is the J. Donald Monan Professor of Theology at Boston College, where she has taught since 1976. She has been a visiting professor at Georgetown University and Yale University. In addition, she has received ten honorary degrees. Dr. Cahill has held leadership positions in important professional organizations, such as president of the Catholic Theological Society of America and president of the Society of Christian Ethics. In 1996 she was elected as a fellow of the American Academy of Arts and Sciences. She has published widely on bioethics, reproductive issues, war and peace, and social ethics. Among her books are Love Your Enemies: Discipleship, Pacifism, and Just War Theory *(1994);* Sex, Gender, and Christian Ethics *(1996);* Family: A Christian Social Perspective *(2000);* Bioethics and the Common Good *(2004); and* Theological Bioethics: Participation, Justice, and Change *(2005).*

Dr. Cahill has frequently been called upon as a theological consultant. For example, she was a consultant to the U.S. Catholic bishops in preparation for the 1987 Synod on the Laity as well as a consultant subsequently on a variety of marriage and family-life issues. She has been a member of the Catholic Health Association Theology and Ethics Advisory Committee, the National Advisory Board for Ethics in Reproduction, and the March of Dimes National Bioethics Committee. Dr. Cahill is a theological consultant to the Catholic Peacebuilding Network, and serves on the steering committee of the Catholic Common

Ground Initiative. She continues to serve on the Advisory Board of the Cardinal Bernardin Center at the Catholic Theological Union in Chicago.

I ATTENDED THE SISTERS OF Mercy Holy Trinity High School in Washington, DC, from 1962 to 1966, years roughly coinciding with the Second Vatican Council. One of my most vivid memories is listening with rapt attention as my senior-year theology teacher conveyed to us the contents and significance of the almost-daily bulletins from Rome, extensively covered by both religious and secular news media. Granting that my memory more than forty years later is highly selective and occasionally inventive, and that many events and details are recollected as having a significance that they could only have acquired later, I still look back on those years as emblematic of the situation of Catholic women "then" and "now," and the changes that both connect and disconnect the past and the present.

My childhood in the 1950s and early '60s is suffused with memories of Catholic piety and practices that were at once parochial, romantic, prayerful, stifling, uplifting, fear-inducing, identity-forming, spiritual, hopeful, and sexist. I can remember my dad's love for the sisters who taught him in grade school in Michigan and, by his account, consistently outsmarted his shenanigans. I can remember my dad taking us into church on All Souls' Day, so that we might offer magical prayers that would suddenly (and on that day only) release my grandparents from the torments of purgatory. I can remember having holy water fonts full of (diluted) Lourdes water in our bedrooms. I remember being in Rome, about nine years old, pressed in throngs of people in St. Peter's, who craned for a glimpse of Pius XII being carried about on a gilt chair. I can remember Mass in Latin and CYO dances. I can remember parading with the other eighth-grade girls, dressed in white, to crown the Virgin Mary.

I can remember the class being called up to sister's desk one by one after we had taken a career aptitude test, and her strained smile as she read off the testing service's first career choice for me ("priest or minister"), and quickly moved on to the second ("volunteer or social worker"). I can remember my convert mother's stiffness in and around Catholic religious services, the baby brother who lived a few hours (my parents had been advised by doctors to use birth control), and my mother's increasing hostility toward Catholic moral teachings and trappings of just about any sort. But I also remember that she kept in her room a crucifix and a small bust of Mary handed down from her own "fallen away" mother.

All this is background to my personal experience of the Second Vatican Council, refracted through my Catholic girls' school experience. It is often said that single-sex education is a good seedbed for the self-confidence of young women, and I believe that was generally true in the case of myself and most of my schoolmates at Holy Trinity. It was a small school; most members of our graduating class of about twenty-five are still in touch. My teachers reflected in microcosm many blessings, tensions, and revolutions in Catholic women's experience of the time. Sisters Perpetua and Joseph taught us math and science, respectively; some of us may have had difficulties with the subject matter, but we never believed it due to a design flaw in the female brain. Sister Mary Nivard took an interest in me when I was a shy freshman, and left a pastel statue of the Virgin Mary in my locker. In recent years she has worked in AIDS ministry. Sister Mary Frederick, our lively English and drama teacher, later married a young priest assigned to the adjoining parish. They are both active in CORPUS, an association of former priests and activists for change in church rules mandating clerical celibacy. A few years ago, after I had given a lecture on feminist theology in a series sponsored by the Mercy Sisters and Jesuit Spring Hill College in Mobile, Sister Rosalie, who taught Spanish and was from Alabama, wrote to me to tell me she is proud of my work. Her vocation later in life has been ministry to the sick and dying.

Our theology instructor in senior year was Lucy Denise, a young lay woman studying for a master's degree in theology from a Catholic women's college, Dumbarton Oaks. Although I think few of us were even aware of the term "feminism," Miss Denise provided an alternative to the reigning expectations for girls like us. Engaged to be married and a paragon of style in the eyes of her fascinated charges, she sought an advanced degree in an area of study considered almost exclusively a male preserve. Her enthusiasm for the council and a message of lay empowerment fairly flowed from her coverage of the "Pastoral Constitution on the Church in the Modern World" (*Gaudium et spes*). Miss Denise's very presence signified the seismic shifts that were taking place not far below the surface of the Catholic culture of the day.

I appreciate the paradoxical complexity that probably accompanies every paradigm shift when I recall that in my senior year I lived in an Opus Dei residence for women, recommended by my high school principal to my parents, whom an employment change took out of state. In

1965, Opus Dei piety did not seem closed, elitist, or bizarre; a lot of Catholics acted as if they belonged to a secret society.

The experience of Vatican II was definitive for my self-consciousness as a Catholic and especially as a Catholic woman. The Catholicism of the '50s could be narrow and superstitious, but it imbued me with a sense of the transcendent and of the presence of God in everyday life that carried many of my generation through the turmoil of change and its aftermath, steeped in a tradition that has always remained a home, even if not always a peaceful or comfortable one. As a woman who grew up largely before the council, I remain indelibly marked by the role expectations that went with the territory (wife and mother, and in a pre-scribed mode). Yet I have benefited from and thrived in the liberation of Catholic women now praised, if within limits, by the pope himself. My vocations as wife, mother, theologian, and professor are combined and intertwined in ways that were barely even conceivable before 1962. The reconstitution of women's place in Catholic life, theology, and liturgy is unfolding, increasingly carried forward by the experience, practices, and voices of women themselves.

In the twenty-first century, women's contributions to theology, to church life, and to society have assumed a more prominent global dimension. New communication technologies afford U.S. women much greater opportunities to learn from and cooperate with our sisters world-wide. Taking up the call of post-Vatican II popes for solidarity with and empowerment of "the poor," women from many contexts and continents join forces not only to improve their own lives, but to enhance the conditions of dignified life for all the world's inhabitants.

JOAN CHITTISTER, O.S.B.

The Struggle between Confusion and Expectation: The Legacy of Vatican II

Joan Chittister, O.S.B., is one of the most articulate social analysts and influential religious leaders of our age. For over thirty years she has put her energy into advocating for the critical questions impacting the global community. Courageous, passionate, and charged with energy, she is a much-sought-after speaker, counselor, and clear voice across all religions. A Benedictine Sister of Erie, Pennsylvania, Chittister is the author of more than forty books.

Currently she serves as co-chair of the Global Peace Initiative of Women, a partner organization of the United Nations, facilitating a worldwide network of women peace builders.

Chittister also writes a regular column, "From Where I Stand," for the National Catholic Reporter *and* Huffington Post *and has received numerous awards and recognition for her work for justice, peace, and equality, especially for women in the church and in society.*

Chittister has held positions of religious leadership among women in the Catholic Church for over thirty years, including that of prioress of her Benedictine community. She holds a master's degree from the University of Notre Dame, a doctorate from Penn State University in speech communications theory, was an elected-fellow of St. Edmund's College, Cambridge University, and is the founder and director of Benetvision: a resource and research center for contemporary spirituality located in Erie.

Her recent books include The Rule of Benedict: A Spirituality for the 21st Century *(2010);* The Gift of Years *(2008); and* Welcome to the Wisdom of the World: And Its Meaning for You *(2007).*

As VATICAN II ENDED, I was just about to begin doctoral studies in communication theory and social psychology. I didn't know a lot about either subject at the time, but, with one foot in a religious life spawned by the Council of Trent and the other in a religious life awash in Vatican II, I knew that anthropologists and social psychologists were missing the academic news of the century. Right in front of their eyes, a subculture was about to unleash its own cultural transformation—by design, with impunity, and *in toto*. It was a human undertaking of massive proportions. It added a great deal to religious life, but it exacted a cost as well. Or, as Robert Hooker put it over two centuries ago, "Change is not made without inconvenience, even from worse to better."[17]

For those who have never experienced the maelstrom of massive social change, have never lived in the vortex of an institutional storm, have never spent their adult life at the ground zero of organizational meltdown, it may come as a shock to realize that "change" and "renewal" are not the same things. Though Vatican II called the religious orders of the church to "renewal," it took a great deal of "change" to tap into the marrow of the process. And it is change that can both obstruct and impersonate renewal. In the end, it has been an unending struggle to reconcile the two. The fact is that it is not possible to have renewal without change, but it certainly is possible to have change without renewal.

The changes in religious life that had been spurred by Vatican II brought personal maturity, new creativity, and transition from the mindset of one century to another. They also brought high expectations, personal confusion, spiritual disease, and lack of clarity of purpose.

Maturity, long denied to women religious in the name of obedience, came with relief, but not without some angst for women whose entire personal lives had been choreographed by people euphemistically called "superiors." Finally, faced with making decisions common to teenagers—with whom to travel, where to go, what to do, when to be back—women religious integrated the two disconnected dimensions of their lives: the personal and the professional. Having been for long years highly developed professionally, they were now able to grow into the kind of adulthood that went with it. They began to make ministry decisions based on personal interests, public needs, and particular talents rather than simply on the institutional identities of the congregations to which they belonged. They began to take public positions in non-church institutions—as administrators of welfare centers or soup kitchens or women's shelters, for instance—in order to serve humankind in general, not simply the descendants of the Catholic immigrant population that had prompted their congregation's historic move to this country in the first place. They made public statements, in the manner of any concerned citizen. They took public interest in public situations. They marched in

Selma and were arrested in antiwar demonstrations. They moved beyond the denomination to the universal. They grew up and they grew into the world around them. They became a bridge between the strictly spiritual life and an avowedly secular one. They became voices of the gospel in the public arena.

But they also did more than serve established institutions around them. They began to create new ones. They closed old academies to open education centers for the poor. They phased out orphanages to open hospitality houses for the destitute. They formed civil rights groups and began peace and justice centers. It was a heady time. Creativity, the right to have new ideas, to suggest new approaches to old problems, to make life new—exhilarating as the possibility may have been—was, at the same time, awkward, even frightening for some. Individual religious—whole congregations—quavered between these realities, fixated on the danger of leaning too far, too long, in either one direction or another if the best elements of the past were to be preserved and the most imperative dimensions of the future were to be addressed. Congregations moved in small steps to deal with cosmic questions: they left schools one person at a time, they experimented with schedules one tiny house at a time, they launched new inroads with the new poor, one small soup kitchen at a time, while the rest of the congregation tried to go on attending to the internal questions of new prayer styles, new schedules, new clothes. And one at a time they had to struggle with it. A woman at a parish church with me broke into tears over a run in her hose. Another one got angry because, after fifty years in a convent, she didn't know how to style her hair anymore. A novice set her jaw and said, "I can't wait around here any longer for this to change." Young nuns left religious life in large numbers, disillusioned by the slowness of the small changes and the amount of personal energy that had to be expended over what were to them minuscule issues in apparent danger of never being resolved.

Social transition from the mentality of past centuries to integration into this one—in dress, in ministry, in lifestyle, in personal interactions—took a heavy toll. What was really true and permanent, stable and real, if things once defined as permanent, invariable, and of the essence of religious life were no longer immutable? The major restructurings Vatican II required in the name of "fidelity to the charism of the founder, the signs of the times, and the needs of the members" broke the hardened shell of religious life into shattered glass.

For many, as a result, religious life as they had lived it was forever over, and with that realization came deep personal despair and a kind of institutional depression. For others, religious life as they envisioned it had only just begun, and with that realization came high energy and new commitment to the worthy, the noble, the necessary.

The teeter-totter on which these two elements balance has not completely stabilized yet, a good forty-five years after the fact. Nor perhaps should it if the ancient values on which religious life have been based are to fuel the new directions in which it must develop if it is to have anywhere near the social impact of its origins. If the ancient takes over again, religious will be nothing but museum pieces in a surging new world, the dinosaur survivors of a life that is fascinating but irrelevant. If the tradition is lost completely, religious will be nothing but social service workers who make their work their lives. The tension between the two is clearly the very lifeblood of renewal. It was not easy to come by.

The maturity, creativity, and social transition of religious of the period were easy to see. More difficult to understand, however, were the doldrums into which what seemed to be such positive activity was to cast religious life in general. After years of membership loss, especially among the newer, younger members of congregations who were disaffected by the control and routinization of a life they had expected to find charismatic or prophetic, even fewer women entered a developing Vatican II religious life, whatever its fledgling directions and its real but tentative developments. The question in the face of the new creativity, the clear maturity, and the necessary social transition was why? The answers may well be many. But there are at least two, which, in the climate of the time, may well deserve consideration. In the first place, the Catholic population itself, whatever its deepest attitudes toward Vatican I religious life, was not prepared for the changes sparked by Vatican II. In the second place, religious communities themselves, though awash in change, had yet to be able to ground change in renewal.

Vatican II was an event whose hour did not really come. Most pastors, formed in another council themselves, gave few homilies on the subject and provided even fewer programs. Lay people were left to cope with change altar rail by altar rail, hymn by hymn, liturgy by liturgy. There were few explanations given, little theology taught. Parishes simply implemented new formulas, accepted nuns in new habits—grudgingly in many places—said prayers in new translations, and watched in sullen sadness or deep resentment as the church as they had known it faded into oblivion.

Of all the church, the people most mobilized for change were women religious. Mandated to hold renewal chapters and write renewal constitutions, groups retrained their entire memberships in the theology of Vatican II in anticipation of what would of necessity be a community project. Change was impossible without the support of the entire group. Groups suspended their Vatican I constitutions and instituted experimentation in every area of religious life. The work moved quickly, but almost entirely internally. There was very little consciousness of the confusion it generated among a laity that had no idea whatsoever why the changes in process were historically sound, let alone necessary, and even less rehearsal for it.

It was an exciting time. It was also a dangerous time, a time of great personal tension and deep spiritual struggle. Religious themselves asked, Why stay when life here was just like life anywhere else? Why give up so much for nothing? Lay women and religious themselves asked, Why give yourself to a life so unlike any other if, in the end, they were all the same? No "higher" vocations? No hundredfold? No privilege or special treatment or public status? It was a question that begged for answers. It was the renewal question that no amount of change could supply.

The truth is that religious had been formed in the spirituality of the virgins and martyrs, of sacrifice and perseverance—virtues men had traditionally required of women—when what Vatican II called for was the spirituality of priests and prophets, of community-building and witness. It was, then, on the deepening, the broadening, of both personal development and spirituality that the transition to Vatican II religious life really depended. To bring the church into the modern world, it would take a spirituality far beyond docility and childlike obedience. It would take women committed to risk and with courage for the unknown. But prophecy and risk are not the hallmarks of large groups. It was not large groups who started religious life, and it is not large groups that will renew it now. Religious life must travel light into the future, burdened by nothing of its successes of the past, held down by none of its past goals but fresh in direction, vital in its meanings for the people of today.

A movement that loses its radical creative edge loses its vision and its reason for existence. A movement that is only radical can lose both its popular base and its stabilizing foundation. The continuing task of Vatican II is to sharpen the edge of religious life again. What religious did for past generations, they must now do for those forgotten peoples of our own generation. A whole new global population must be carried beyond the limitations of their lives, become visible to those who see them not, be heard by those who are deaf to their tears.

The truth is that out of this conflict between creativity and spiritual confusion has come something far more dynamic than either. The image of a religious life steeped in the prophetic dimensions of its founders and at the same time deeply immersed in the life of the spirit, the search for the holy, and the spiritual wisdom of the past is becoming ever more apparent. Lay people by the thousands are attaching themselves to the prayer life and ministry of women religious, who have found their old identity again in new ways. Associate, oblate, and lay membership programs are thriving. Women's centers and retreat programs are developing out of women's congregations all over the country. Women are entering religious life again: older now, yes, but totally committed in whole new ways to doing the new things that the new suffering need; they are being educated, formed, and directed by women's congregations everywhere. More than that, religious communities are beginning to realize that everyone who comes to a religious community does not want to stay forever, a principle of membership understood and integrated by Buddhist monasteries for thousands of years. Now, temporary membership is a developing dimension of religious life in a culture where few expect to do anything forever anymore.

Conformity is no longer the major religious virtue, togetherness masking as community, and the fear of change is no longer the agenda of religious life. Renewal of spirit, openness to new needs and depth, if not necessarily length, of personal commitment has become the new norm. "Why did you come here?" I asked a new applicant. "Because this is the only group of women I have been able to find that cares about exactly what I do—community, the gospel of Jesus, and a commitment to peace and justice," she said simply. Interestingly enough, I couldn't help but think that her answer sounded to me exactly like what Vatican II wanted from religious, too: that they would examine their life from the perspective of the "charism of the founder, the needs of society, and the gifts of their members." But if that's the case, religious life is not only new again, it is also a long way from being over.

MICHAEL NOVAK

The Rescue of Vatican II*

Theologian, author, and former U.S. ambassador, Michael Novak is a professor and a trustee of Ave Maria University in Ave Maria, Florida, and George Frederick Jewett Chair Emeritus at the American Enterprise Institute in Washington, DC.

Novak received the Templeton Prize for Progress in Religion at Buckingham Palace in 1994, and delivered the Templeton address in Westminster Abbey. He has also received the Boyer Award in 1999; with Milton Friedman and Vaclav Klaus the International Prize by the Institution for World Capitalism; the Anthony Fisher Prize for The Spirit of Democratic Capitalism *presented by Margaret Thatcher; the Weber Award for contributions to Catholic Social Thought in Essen, Germany; the Cezanne Medal from the City of Provence; the Catholic Culture Medal of Bassano del Grappa in Italy; the highest civilian award from the Slovak Republic in 1996; the Masaryk Medal, presented by Vaclav Havel of the Czech Republic, in 2000; the Gold Medal of the Pennsylvania Society in 2001; and the Medal of the Italian Senate from the Pio Manzù Centre, with a citation from its president, Mikhail Gorbachev.*

Novak's writings have appeared in every major Western language, and in Bengali, Korean, and Japanese. He has written some twenty-seven influential books on the philosophy and theology of culture.

His masterpiece, The Spirit of Democratic Capitalism, *has been reprinted often in Latin America, and was published underground in Poland in 1984, and in Czechoslovakia, Germany, China, and Hungary. One reviewer called it "one of those rare books that actually changed the world."*

---

* This reflection is an excerpt from the new introduction to the Transaction Edition of Michael Novak's *The Open Church* (New Brunswick, NJ: Transaction Books, 2001).

35

WE COME NOW TO AN aspect of church history that has been lost sight of since the council. Journalistically (I later worked for *Time* magazine, during the third session of the council), it was much easier to portray the sheer novelty of the council than to portray its continuities with the past. The news business is in the business of *news*—novelty—and the public does not go to the press for solid scholarship. In a delicious irony the media bring us the opposite of "nonhistorical orthodoxy," nonorthodox novelty. Important realities are often distorted, and history itself is significantly falsified. For instance, the era before the council was more like a golden age in Catholic history than like the dark age described to an eager press by the postconciliar "progressives." There were many glaring deficiencies in it, and yet it was in many respects healthier and more faithful to the gospels than much that came later in the name of "progress" and "openness."

Once the passions of those participating in the council rose, the victorious majority (the "progressives") acquired a vested interest both in stressing new beginnings and in discrediting the leadership and the ways of the past. That emphasis shifted the balance of power in the church into their hands. To them accrued the glory of all things promising, new, and not-yet-tried; to their foes accrued the blame for everything wrong. The more power wrested from the "old guard," the more massive the power acquired by the reformers. The more the past was discredited, the greater the slack cut for new initiatives and new directions. The politics of the postconciliar church in the United States and some parts of northern Europe became an unfair fight.

Within a decade of the end of the council, every major institution in the American church and in many others was dominated by the progressives, under the sway of "the spirit of Vatican II." That spirit sometimes soared far beyond the actual, hard-won documents and decisions of Vatican II. Some seized the right to go *far* beyond those. It was as though some took the church to be dis-incarnate, detached from flesh and history—detached, that is, from Rome and the Vatican, and so far as possible from any concrete local authority. Detached, too, from past tradition and the painful lessons of the past. It was as though the world (or at least the history of the church) were now to be divided into only two periods, pre-Vatican II and post-Vatican II. Everything "pre" was then pretty much dismissed, so far as its *authority* mattered. For the most extreme, to be a Catholic now meant to believe more or less anything one wished to believe, or at least in the sense in which one personally interpreted it. One could be a Catholic "in spirit." One could take Catholic to mean the "culture" in which one was born, rather than to mean a creed making objective and rigorous demands. One could imagine Rome as a distant and irrelevant anachronism, embarrassment, even adversary. Rome as "them."

It is not too much to say that John Paul II rescued Vatican II from disaster. His total awareness of the presence of the Holy Spirit at the council, the new Pentecost, suffused his every action as archbishop, then cardinal, of Krakow and later as Universal Pastor of the church. He brought back a sense of incarnation, concreteness, discipline, and practicality, and he was an indefatigable theoretician. He gave a thorough and authoritative interpretation of Vatican II.

Bishop Wojtyla wrote even before the Second Vatican Council assembled that the most important word for the council to tell the world concerns Everyman's answer to the question: Who am I? Who are we? What is the meaning and sense of the human project? In formulating this answer, three terms seemed to him crucial: freedom, the person, and community. These three are tied together by the active energy that drives through all of them: love of the truth about man.

Freedom is for truth, and is built up, constituted, by fidelity to truth. The search for truth is communal, not only personal, and it requires for its exercise the open society—open in its polity, its economy, and its culture. It is the vocation of the church to keep this vision before the human race, in part by living out this vision in advance of the human race, through its own constant repentance, reform, and starting again.

All these points Vatican II wrestled with, for instance in its debates about the meaning of the liturgy (public worship) of the church, its most vital, inmost source of connection with God's action in the world, for this connection is at once communal, personal, and free. And then wrestled with them again in its discussion of the meaning of the church. *Person, community,* and *freedom* were important red threads coursing through all its debates. They were woven into worldly contexts in the later debates in later sessions, first raised in the second session, in such documents as those on "Religious Liberty" and, as it was at first called, "The Church in the Modern World." In both these documents, Wojtyla played leadership roles in committee, not always in the very front rank, but by making intellectual contributions at crucial intersections.

Although he was only forty-two when the council opened, Wojtyla made eight oral interventions in the council hall, a rather high number, and often spoke in the name of large groups of bishops from Eastern Europe. (Altogether he made twenty-two interventions, oral and written.) He was an unusually active member of various official drafting groups for *Gaudium et spes,* and even a chief author of what was called the "Polish draft." His voice was crucial to the passage of the document on religious liberty and to the deepening of its philosophical and theological dimension, in line with the necessities of the non-free nations behind the Iron Curtain. No one, perhaps, was more influential in persuading the Americans and Europeans that their own views on liberty needed to be deepened in order to account for questions arising from other cultures. In later memoirs about the council, such world-class theologians as Yves Congar and Henri de Lubac praised Wojtyla's acumen in committee work as well as his magnetic presence.

All in all, the council met for four sessions across four consecutive autumns from 1962 through 1965. It reached agreement on sixteen major documents. All these were published in official form in the languages of the nations and have been subjected to a stupendous amount of commentary. Still, it is sad how few Catholics, even well-educated ones, have actually spent time reading the documents themselves. (Those most fond of the "spirit" of Vatican II seldom sent students to study the "letter.") These "Declarations," "Decrees," and "Constitutions" are for the most part splendidly poised and balanced, and quite nourishing to the inquiring soul. They were written as if with devotional purposes in mind, to move the heart as well as intellect.

JOHN CATOIR

Cardinal Suenens Predicted a Third Vatican Council

Father John Catoir is the founder and president of St. Jude Media Ministries, a national organization that uses radio and TV to reach out to millions of Americans.

Born in New York City in 1931, Catoir graduated from Fordham University's School of Business in 1953. After two years in the Army, he entered the seminary and was ordained a priest for the diocese of Paterson, New Jersey, in 1960. He received his doctorate in canon law in 1964, and served as judicial vicar until the priests of his diocese elected him clergy personnel director in 1973. In 1978, he became the director of the Christophers, a Catholic multimedia organization based in Manhattan. He hosted a nationally syndicated TV series called "Christopher Closeup," for over seventeen years. From 1997 to 2000, Catoir was executive director of New Jersey's most comprehensive poverty program, called Eva's Village. This ministry feeds seven hundred free meals a day to the poor; it also runs separate drug and alcohol rehabilitation centers for men and women.

Father Catoir was the president of three national organizations: the Catholic Press Association (1988-1990), the Association of Catholic TV and Radio Syndicators (1983-1985), and the National Association of Church Personnel Administrators (1975-1977). He has written fifteen books and is a syndicated columnist for Catholic News Service. In 1993, Catoir received the St. Francis de Sales Award for outstanding contributions to Catholic journalism, the highest award of the Catholic Press Association.

CARDINAL LEON-JOSEPH SUENENS WAS ONE of the four moderators of Vatican Council II, appointed by Pope John XXIII. In his book *Memories and Hopes*,[18] he mentions me as his "occasional" secretary. I was honored to have traveled with him many times back and forth across the ocean during the 1980s and early '90s. The cardinal told me of his efforts during the council to get the bishops to empower the "sleeping giant" of the laity. He was convinced that the age of the laity had arrived. This idea met with fierce resistance.

Cardinal Suenens led the charge of the reformers against the traditionalists headed by Cardinal Ottaviani. Cardinal Suenens told me that he met Cardinal Ottaviani in a Vatican elevator after the council. The battle was over, or so it seemed. They both smiled and exchanged polite greetings. No other words were spoken. The reformers may have prevailed at the council, but their hopes have not yet been fully realized.

The following retrospective may be helpful in understanding the history of the two Vatican councils.

Pope Pius IX (1846-1878) was elected as a moderate progressive, against the reactionary Cardinal Lambruschini. His pontificate, the longest in history, soon became an imperial one. He centralized authority, and his encyclical *Quanta cura* (1864), with its "Syllabus of Errors," dealt a fatal blow to the nineteenth-century rationalist movement. He summoned the First Vatican Council (the twentieth general council, 1869-1870) to declare the infallible authority of the pope in matters of faith and morals. He wanted to cancel all conciliarist interpretations of papal authority. This awakened storms of protest. There was a great deal of unfinished business.

Eighty-eight years later, on October 28, 1958, Angelo Giuseppe Roncalli, the aging cardinal of Venice, was elected pope on the twelfth ballot. He was obviously a compromise candidate, chosen in his old age so as to have a short reign. He chose the name John XXIII. Within three months, on January 25, 1959, he captured the attention and the imagination of the world by calling the Second Vatican Council. He said it was in response to an inspiration of the Holy Spirit. His leadership met with strong opposition within the Holy See, but he stood his ground. His optimism was contagious. He disagreed with "those prophets of gloom, who are always forecasting disaster, as though the end of the world were at hand." In contrast to them, John believed that "In the present order of things, Divine Providence is leading us to a new order of human relations which, by men's own efforts and even beyond their very expectations, are directed toward the fulfillment of God's superior and inscrutable designs."[19]

John XXIII died in 1963, and Pope Paul VI was elected to finish the work of the council. Paul asked Cardinal Suenens to memorialize Pope John at the opening of the second session of the council. The cardinal told me it was an honor he would never forget. In his eulogy, Suenens declared:

> John XXIII was the pope of dialogue, and this has special reference to the men of our time. . . . The words of John awakened a response.
>
> Men recognized his voice, a voice speaking to them of God, but also of human brotherhood, of the re-establishment of social justice, of a peace to be established throughout the whole world.
>
> They heard a challenge addressed to their better selves, and they raised their eyes towards this man whose goodness made them think of God. For men, whether they know it or not, are always in search of God, and it is the reflection of God that they sought in the countenance of this old man who loved them with the very love of Christ.[20]

Cardinal Suenens told me that for Pope John the council was not merely a meeting of the bishops with the pope, a horizontal coming together. It was, first and above all, a collective gathering of the whole episcopal college with the Holy Spirit. It was a vertical coming together, with an openness to an immense outpouring of the Holy Spirit.

Paul VI (1963-1978) continued the work of the council, raising the hopes of progressives by his willingness to listen. They thought that henceforth church leaders would be willing to discuss problems more openly before arriving at unilateral decisions. However, when Paul VI issued his encyclical *Humanae vitae* in 1968, condemning artificial contraception, he ignored the advice of his own consultants. Thousands of priests resigned in protest, and a multitude of laity left the church. I asked Suenens if Paul VI really believed in collegiality, a concept he formally approved. He said that Pope Paul was a holy man, but his many years as an official of the Roman curia shaped his thinking. He was by training a product of the curia.

When Paul VI died in August of 1978, John Paul I was elected on the first day of balloting. This is a rarity in the history of the church. The cardinals said they wanted a pope who had no past connections with the curia. John Paul I, who was dubbed "the Smiling Pope," in contrast to his predecessor, who was always frowning, immediately took steps to shed the traditional pomp of his papal coronation. He even held press conferences. His sudden death on September 28, 1978, however, shocked the whole world and disappointed millions of Catholics.

Karol Wojtyla of Krakow, Poland, was elected shortly after, and he chose the name of John Paul II. However, he soon began calling himself a restorative pope, indicating his view that the Second Vatican Council had gone too far. It wasn't long before he became a great disappointment to many progressives. Many bishops thought that he paid only lip service to the idea of collegiality. Within the Holy See there was a common opinion that the word "collegiality" should only apply when there was a true ecumenical council. The many synods called by John Paul II were an exercise in Vatican control.

This pope was the first non-Italian to be named pope since Pope Hadrian VI in 1523. He was not, however, an outsider. His ideas were more in line with the curia than anyone expected. Nevertheless he won worldwide acclaim for his part in bringing about the collapse of Soviet communism.

I once asked Cardinal Suenens what he thought of Pope John Paul II. He replied, "In the middle of a storm, one does not comment on the cleanliness of the captain's uniform." When I asked him about the future of the church, Suenens was optimistic. He predicted, "There will be a Third Vatican Council in the twenty-first century because so much more needs to be done to realize our goals, and complete the work of renewal. We still have to awaken fully the sleeping giant of the laity."

Cardinal Suenens's own efforts to awaken the laity are reflected in the FIAT movement that he inspired. He asked me to head it up in the United States and Canada. The idea is based on the centrality of evangelization in the life of the church. Suenens wanted the laity to take more responsibility in spreading the faith. "We can no longer depend on a handful of missionaries to pass the faith along to the next generation." Perhaps evangelization will be a theme in the next ecumenical council.

Suenens asked the laity to turn to Mary for guidance. Her words *Fiat mihi*—"Be it done unto me according to your word" (Luke 1:38)—were spoken to the Angel Gabriel. This disposition is a spiritual model for all Christians. Mary taught us how to interact with the Holy Spirit. The cardinal often called Mary the secret of Pentecost. She was with the twelve frightened apostles when the Spirit descended. She taught them how to pray and be open to the Spirit. The apostles emerged from that room, awakened and emboldened to carry the Good News to the four corners of the world. Based on this model, Cardinal Suenens envisioned a network of prayer meetings where the laity would imitate Mary, invoking the Holy Spirit for strength to go forth and make Christ known and loved. This dream of his remains to be realized through the FIAT movement, which is alive and well, having chapters in eighty countries worldwide. The headquarters of the movement is in Brussels, Belgium, under the supervision of Cardinal Danneels.

PART TWO

VATICAN II AND THE LITURGY

Liturgy: The Church Praying Is the Church Believing

Michael J. Daley

As I entered the church, I remember it being very quiet, almost silent. This was a place where, if your child cried, you took him or her out with you. Things were very serious. Statues and candles abounded. Combined with the Stations of the Cross, the ornate reredos behind the altar, and the like, one's senses were challenged, perhaps somewhat distracted. The women, of course, were veiled (St. Paul would have been proud). The men, for the most part, were nicely dressed. An air of formality, as well as transcendence, pervaded the place. When the opening song began, there was no singing. It was more like liturgical muzak with sounds coming from the organ.

After the initial greeting, the priest conducted the Mass in Latin, with his back to the people. His movements were very measured with a concern for the rubrics. Even when he had to face the people, he was instructed not to make eye contact with them. The rationale was that you didn't want to disrupt anyone's prayer. The server, his constant companion, was busy genuflecting and ringing bells. It was, however, hard to hear either the priest or the server. The best one could do was to follow along in one's missal and hope to keep up.

The sermon had no reference to the scripture of the day. Its theme was one of suffering. The world, according to the priest, was full of temptation. It was both to be avoided and converted at the same time. Limbo was spoken of. It was real to him and to these people. At communion one encountered the solid, imposing rail that separated the lay people from the sanctuary. The Eucharist was given to you there, on your tongue, with the server holding the paten ever so attentively.

As Mass ended and I was walking out, I said to myself, "Thank God for Vatican II!" The unfortunate thing, however, was that I had just been with a group of people who cursed Vatican II, who saw the reformed liturgy as the cause of utter ruin for the Catholic Church. This was a story not of yesteryear, though, but of somewhat recent vintage. What was it about Vatican II and the change in the liturgy that so offended these people? Why was their pain my joy?

Granted, this liturgical experience of mine predated Pope Benedict XVI's 2007 *motu proprio Summorum Pontificum* which permits wider use of the Tridentine liturgy. Still the group of people attending Mass that day were Traditionalist Catholics (out of union with Rome; sede-vacantists, in fact, arguing that the chair of Peter has been vacant since Pope Pius XII) strongly supportive of the Tridentine liturgy. One of the purposes of Benedict's *motu proprio* was a desire for unity with Tradi-tionalist Catholics, who, initially led by the now-deceased Archbishop Marcel Lefebvre, rejected the liturgical reforms of the council.

The Cart before the Horse

Of all the conciliar decisions that have most affected people, it could be argued that the ones instigated by "The Constitution on the Sacred Liturgy" (*Sacrosanctum concilium*) have had the most concrete and, in some circles, contentious results. As Mark Massa notes in his book *Catholics and American Culture*, "perhaps more dramatically than any other decree issuing from the council, the decree on church worship touched the 'folks in the pews' in immediate and understandable ways."[1] A great liturgical scholar, Austrian Jesuit Josef Jungmann, said that it was this constitution "more than anywhere else that the aggiornamento which John XXIII had demanded of the council assumed visible and incisive forms."[2]

Put into its proper context, however, the changes evidenced in the decree weren't anything revolutionary, but more the seeds of years of liturgical scholarship beginning to bear fruit.[3] Many place the begin-nings of the liturgical movement at the feet of Dom Prosper Guéranger, who, in 1833, reestablished the Benedictine Order in France at the Abbey of Solesmes. There he devoted the resources of the abbey to the study of the church's liturgical traditions. The abbey's influence eventually spread to other monastic centers in Europe, most notably Maria Laach

(Germany), where historical scholarship was combined with a desire for translating liturgical reforms to a more general audience.

Godfrey Diekmann, O.S.B., long-time editor of *Worship* magazine and one of the architects of the council's document on the liturgy, further pinpoints the movement's development to August of 1924. It was then at Maria Laach, through the initiative of Father Lambert Beauduin, that the first dialogue Mass was celebrated. Diekmann says "people gathered around the altar and everyone played a part. The worshippers realized that day that the roles in ritual were meant to be distributed. They discovered that the laity had a role in worship and in the church. . . . Rome was very, very nervous about it for quite some time. But the church has never been the same since."[4] Diekmann's own monastery, St. John's Abbey in Collegeville, Minnesota, became a leader in the American liturgical reform movement under the direction of Virgil Michel. In 1926 he began the Liturgical Press and published the first issue of *Orate Fratres* (today known as *Worship*), a periodical devoted to liturgical practice and pastoral ministry.

Since the early twentieth century, there was hesitant but encouraging papal approval of the initiatives of the liturgical reformers. One increasing concern on the part of the popes was that the laity were being relegated to observers during the Mass. This prompted Pius XII, in 1947, to issue *Mediator Dei*. This encyclical was devoted entirely to liturgical matters. For those who previously had been resistant to the liturgical movement, it gave encouragement; for those who had long labored in the forefront of the movement, it gave cautious support.

As the council approached, then, much of the legwork had already been done. The challenge was to make the council fathers aware of these developments and see the benefits of renewing the liturgy.

The Council's First and Foundational Document

Many consider *Sacrosanctum concilium*, the first document promulgated by the council, on December 4, 1963, to be Vatican II's most important one. Diekmann, speaking shortly after the council to an international group of theologians gathered at the University of Notre Dame to examine its significance and progress, saw its choice as the first matter to be discussed as "felicitous." He went on to remark that "[i]t was not the theological construct of the post-Constantine or post-Tridentine eras, but the living Church describing her self-discovery in liturgical action that to a very large extent determined the ecclesiology basic to all subsequent documents, including the great Constitution on the Church."[5]

Echoed in the refrain of the document's words "full, conscious, and active participation" (no. 14), the image of church as the People of God emerged. This image stressed over and above the long-standing hierarchical understanding of church that we are first and foremost a community of disciples charged by baptism to participate in Jesus' threefold office of priest, prophet, and king. In more general and musical terms, as has been illustrated by Kenneth E. Untener, former bishop of Saginaw, Michigan, the concert of the priest became the sing-along of the people.[6]

Perhaps just as challenging, if not more so, than the call to a participatory liturgy and church was the council's admission of change. If anything illustrated the church's absolute and timeless traditions, it was the Latin Mass. Since the Council of Trent (1545-1563), it had experienced little change and acquired a uniformity that it had not possessed in the past. With this in mind, the constitution realized the need for revision:

> The rite of the Mass is to be revised in such a way that the intrinsic nature and purpose of its several parts, as well as the connection between them, may be more clearly shown, and that devout and active participation by the faithful may be more easily achieved.
>
> To this end, the rites are to be simplified, due care being taken to preserve their substance. Duplications made with the passage of time are to be omitted, as are less useful additions. Other parts which were lost through the vicissitudes of history are to be restored according to the ancient tradition of the holy Fathers, as may seem appropriate or necessary.[7]

The impression that the church had always done things the same way was broken. This admission was carried throughout the other documents as well. Commenting on this circumstance, Diekmann concluded that "[o]ne of the great achievements of the Council is its demolition of the image of the monolithic Church, of the de facto canonization of uniformity in the name of unity. . . . And because this canonization of uniformity had obtained so triumphantly in the liturgy, and for so long, its firm rejection in the liturgy Constitution set a liberating precedent for the following documents."[8]

With the desire that the liturgy truly be experienced as "supremely effective in enabling the faithful to express in their lives and portray to others the mystery of Christ and the real nature of the true church" (no. 2) and "the summit toward which the activity of the church is directed" (no. 10), the council fathers engaged in a process of making the liturgy more intelligible, relevant, and participatory for all. Physically, the priest turned around to face the people, and with him the altar was placed closer to the people. In many places the communion rail was taken down. Lay people were allowed to enter the sanctuary and exercise the ministerial roles of lector, server, and, eventually, extraordinary minister of communion (no. 29). The vernacular, the language of the people, became the order of the day, replacing Latin (nos. 36.2, 54). Commenting on Latin's supposed unifying aspect for the church, more than one person has observed that you could go anywhere in the world and not understand the Mass. In defense of the staunch supporters at the council who desired to retain Latin, however, it must be admitted that Latin served as a powerful symbol uniting the church in all places.

Theologically, for a people who had been used to so emphasizing the presence of Christ in the Eucharist, "the Sacrifice of the Mass," it was both inviting and challenging to allow them to see that Christ was also present in the minister, the other sacraments, the proclaimed word, and the gathered community (no. 7). The constitution further instructed that liturgical studies be promoted in seminaries and other institutions of learning (nos. 15-19). Having long played second fiddle to the Eucharist, the document said, "it is essential to promote that warm and lively appreciation of sacred scripture to which the venerable tradition of both eastern and western rites gives testimony" (no. 24). Admitting the true catholicity of the church, the constitution called for adaptation of the liturgy to various traditions and backgrounds of people (no. 37). Additionally, the catechumenate, also known as the Rite of Christian Initiation of Adults (RCIA), was restored, and the council fathers expressed the desire to revise the rites for the celebration of the other sacraments (nos. 66-82); the divine office (nos. 83-101); the liturgical year (nos. 102-111); sacred music (nos. 112-121); and church architecture (nos. 122-130). An adage that guided the council fathers through these changes could be well summarized in a statement attributed to Cardinal Montini, the future Pope Paul VI, who during the debate on liturgy remarked, "The liturgy is for men, not men for the liturgy."[9]

Looking back at the council and the succeeding years of the council's liturgical implementation, long-time Catholic journalist Arthur Jones asks people to "look for a moment at what didn't happen in the 1960s. Millions of Catholics did not abandon the church. Even in the earliest post-Vatican II days, for all the public tumult, millions upon millions of American Catholics still went to Mass on Sunday, and now they heard it on a repeated basis in a language they could understand. Not only that, the scripture readings and prayers were heard to be relevant to the struggles in the street, in the home, in the soul."[10]

As I said earlier, "Thank God for Vatican II."

KATHLEEN HUGHES, R.S.C.J.

Mystery at the Heart of Worship

Kathleen Hughes, R.S.C.J., was born in Cleveland, Ohio, and entered the Society of the Sacred Heart after graduating from Newton College of the Sacred Heart. She was the first woman to receive a doctorate in Liturgical Studies from the University of Notre Dame (1981). She served as a professor of Word and Worship at the Catholic Theological Union in Chicago for nineteen years (1980-1999) and also served a term as academic dean. In 1999 she became provincial of the United States Province of her order.

Sister Hughes was a member of the Advisory Board of the International Commission on English in the Liturgy (ICEL) for nineteen years and chaired the subcommittee that prepared original texts for worship among English speakers across the world. She has written eight books, including The Monk's Tale: A Biography of Godfrey Diekmann, O.S.B. *(1991), and* Saying Amen: A Mystagogy of Sacrament *(1999). She has lectured widely in the United States and abroad and has published several hundred articles and reviews demonstrating a broad range of interest in worship, sacraments, preaching, language, feminism, and spirituality.*

Sister Hughes received the Frederick R. McManus Award from the Federation of Diocesan Liturgical Commissions (2004) and the Jubilate Deo award from the National Association of Pastoral Musicians (2010) for her contribution to the pastoral liturgical life of the United States church.

I BEGIN WITH A STORY that goes back to the days of the Second Vatican Council, a story told to me by Godfrey Diekmann, O.S.B., a patristic scholar, a charismatic speaker and teacher, and an indefatigable promoter of the liturgical movement from the late 1930s forward. Godfrey and Monsignor Frederick McManus were the two Americans invited to assist with the liturgical preparatory commission of the council and to stay on during the council to serve as expert consultants for the U.S. bishops. Godfrey remembered the day when the "Constitution on the Sacred Liturgy" was presented for a vote, chapter by chapter. He watched proceedings from the balcony in St. Peter's. And the votes were virtually unanimous. Godfrey told me of his euphoria that day—there was more lay involvement, more liturgical participation, more use of the language of the people, more than all the early liturgical reformers had ever dared dream.

That evening Godfrey and Fred went to dinner with some of the American bishops. They were gathered at the Cavalleri Hilton outside Rome toasting this amendment and that compromise in the document when a woman leaned over from a neighboring table and said: "Aren't you all Americans? Don't you know your president was shot today?" They went out into the night, looking for a church where they could celebrate a requiem Mass.

That story has touched me so much because it speaks of an amazing conjunction of events. The election of President Kennedy signaled that the Catholic Church had come of age in the United States. The church moved out of the ghetto and into the mainstream. And this momentous event converged with the Second Vatican Council, which promoted rapprochement with the modern world, identification with its joys and its sufferings, interreligious dialogue, a language of tolerance and understanding, a church opening its windows so that the Spirit could blow through. Truly the spirit of *aggiornamento* was in the air. And I contend that nowhere across the world were the reforms of the Second Vatican Council received with as much delight and implemented with as much relish and competence as in the United States of America. There was new life and there was energy and there was an outpouring of hope. But that energy and life, that fresh vision of ourselves as church, that great awakening to the mysteries we celebrate, begun more than fifty years ago, is languishing in our day. Why?

In the church, just as in our country, there is a great hardening of ideological positions and an astonishing lack of civility among us. There are different camps on almost every issue of any import, and there is a fair amount of distrust and fear. We are mirroring the political culture in our country, the inability to communicate, the shift from dialogue and debate to diatribe.

And all of our divisions are played out when we gather for worship. The liturgy is, of its very nature, a perfectly condensed statement of our identity and our beliefs as the Body of Christ. When we gather for the liturgy we bring to public ritual expression our understanding of—and relationship with—God, our understanding of the community and how we relate to one another, our understanding of the holy, of authority, of inclusion, and a host of other core beliefs. All of it is enacted in the choices we make, the arrangement of space, the ways and times we sit and stand, the ministers who stand before us, the focus of the homily, the music we select, the amount of liturgical participation we promote, how we receive communion, even the register of the language that we select.

I would venture to say that *what* we gather to celebrate is beyond dispute. We gather for the praise and glory of God, to enact the saving mystery of Christ's death and rising, in the power of their abundant and life-giving spirit. But while *what* we celebrate is generally beyond dispute, *how* we celebrate it is the subject of wildly divergent and divisive choices.

This past year I was present for the daily Eucharist in a retirement center for my order. I was sitting in front of a woman whose speech has been virtually nonexistent until very recently. Now she will ask, "Who are you?" or, "Are you okay?" That is the extent of it. But just after the words of institution and the presider's invitation: "Let us proclaim the mystery of faith," this woman said, loud enough for me to hear, "What do you suppose he means by that?" I was deeply moved by that question, and I thought to myself, "I don't know, not really. It *is* a mystery." Her question has stayed with me.

Have we lost sight of the blessings we have been given?

Have we lost sight of the mystery?

Have we been so preoccupied with the surface issues that we have missed the real reasons we gather in the first place?

A few years ago a brilliant little book by Mark Searle was published posthumously by Anne Koester and Barbara Searle, Mark Searle's widow. The title is *Called to Participate: Theological, Ritual and Social Perspectives*. Searle revisits the meaning of "full, conscious and active participation," that form of participation demanded by the very nature of the liturgy, and he distinguishes three levels of active participation that are progressively deeper and more demanding.

There is, first of all, the ritual level: the greetings and singing, the acclamations, the various postures and gestures of prayer—all the stereotyped forms of social interaction, all the written rubrics and unwritten patterns and expectations of a local community, which constitute our worship. Searle contends that most of us became preoccupied with this first level. Yet ritual participation is always in virtue of something else, something deeper, something more.

The second level of "active participation" is involvement in the liturgy as the work of Christ. In the Eucharist we enter into Christ's liturgy, the endless self-giving of Christ into the hands of the One he called *Abba* from whom he receives back his life. Human worship is an offering of our whole selves with and in Christ to God. That is our participation in the paschal mystery of Christ's obedience unto death, our identification with Christ in his radical obedience to God.

The third and most demanding form of "active participation" is our participation in the Trinitarian life of God. The sacraments are the means by which those who entrust themselves to God are drawn into the divine life. Participation in the Trinitarian life is a mystery beyond telling; it is participation in the communitarian life of Father, Son, and Spirit. It is life lived as sons and daughters of the Father in the Word who was begotten of the Father from all eternity and is forever of one being with the Father. It is life whose very form is the Spirit of the Holy God, poured into our hearts, flooding their depths, to draw us into the depths of God. (Searle, *Called to Participate*, passim.) Three levels of full, conscious, and active participation—participation in the ritual, participation in Jesus' death and rising, participation in the mystery of the Trinity—three progressively deeper invitations into mystery, three heart movements from the visible to the invisible, from the human to the divine. We participate in ritual prayer in order to participate in the priestly work of Christ on behalf of the world, and we participate in the Trinitarian life of God and thus in God's work in human history. Full, conscious, and active participation has a scope and a breadth and a depth that is breathtakingly beautiful. It also makes enormous demands on us!

I believe we have too often been preoccupied with level one, the level of the exterior ritual. And here's the result. Our energies are drained and our communities are divided by superficial choices that happen to be the least important aspect of our participation. I also believe we would advance a long way to hope and harmony in our communities if people were invited into the ever deeper mystery of participation in Jesus' death and in the mystery of being joined to the triune God—that's where we are bound together with one another; that's where we share a common mandate to lay down our lives for the life of the world.

When we gather for worship we rehearse the vision and the values of the reign of God. Each liturgy is a dress rehearsal for the great end-time banquet. And we have to rehearse again and again, over a lifetime, until we get it right, until that great day when we enter fully into the Mystery. But meanwhile, we live in hope.

For those who weary of the journey here's a helpful reminder captured in a cartoon image. It is a cartoon of a Bedouin family riding across a vast desert on camels. Picture them: the father in front on a very large camel, then the mother on a camel more her size, then three children, graduated in size, the youngest at the tail end. And the youngest calls out in that whiny voice every parent knows from car trips: "Are we there yet?" And the father turns around in exasperation and says: "No, we're not there yet. We're nomads for God's sake!"

JOSEPH A. BROWN, S.J.

Preparing the "Welcome Table": Reflections on Fifty Years of Black Catholic Liturgy

A native of East St. Louis, IL, Joseph A. Brown was born in 1944. He entered the Jesuit novitiate, in Minnesota, in 1962, just before the Second Vatican Council began. After graduating from St. Louis University (1968) with a degree in Philosophy and Letters, Brown then received an M.A. from the Writing Seminars, Johns Hopkins University (1969). Around this time, he became active in the National Black Catholic Clergy Caucus and participated in workshops sponsored by the National Office of Black Catholics (1970-1984).

Ordained to the priesthood in 1972, Brown taught theater and poetry at Creighton University (1973-1979). Then he went to earn degrees in Afro-American Studies (M.A., 1983) and in American Studies (Ph.D., 1984) from Yale University. Brown has taught at the University of Virginia, Xavier University (New Orleans), and Saint Joseph's University, where he held the MacLean Chair of Jesuit Studies in the College of Arts and Sciences. Presently, he is a professor and director of the Black American Studies Program at Southern Illinois University (Carbondale, IL).

Brown's writings include works of poetry such as Accidental Grace *(1986) and* The Sun Whispers, Wait: New and Collected Poems *(2009) and other works that address issues of black Catholic spirituality such as* A Retreat with Thea Bowman and Bede Abram: Leaning on the Lord *(1997);* To Stand on the Rock: Meditations on Black Catholic Identity *(1998); and (with Fernand Cheri)* Sweet, Sweet, Spirit: Prayer Services from the Black Catholic Church *(2006).*

MUCH OF THE WORK OF the Second Vatican Council seems to me to have been the articulation of common wisdom already circulating in the world. When I think of my place in the Roman Catholic Church, in the middle of the twentieth century in the upper Midwest of the United States, the effort toward inculturation of the liturgy was already a part of my ritual understanding. By the time the conciliar decree *Sacrosanctum concilium* was promulgated (December 1963), my fellow-teenage choir members had been performing selections from the widely popular "Missa Luba" for several years. In 1958, when the Congolese children's choir recorded the "Missa Luba," our high school choir learned the "Kyrie" and "Sanctus" for our spring concert. In a small Catholic high school, in Beloit, Wisconsin, the world of worship was irrevocably challenged.

In those same years before the opening of the council, the great liturgical pioneer and prophet, Father Clarence Rufus Joseph Rivers, Jr., was adapting the melodies of the Negro Spirituals into liturgical-service music in his parish in Cincinnati. What Father Rivers was composing between 1956 and 1964 became part of the liturgical repertoire for our Jesuit House of Studies in St. Bonifacius, Minnesota, as early as 1964— within months of the first Eucharistic liturgy in English, celebrated at the Annual Convention of the Liturgical Conference, in August of 1964.[11] Rivers understood that African Americans had a culture rich in the theology of perseverance, transcendence, and liberation; and possessed an equally rich tradition of symbols that allowed them to be fully engaged in their worship. But he was adamant in his challenge to U.S. Catholicism that African Americans were second-class citizens (if that) in the general culture and even less respected in the church of their birth or choice. Before the black Catholic bishops wrote their pastoral letter in 1984, Rivers and many others of us criss-crossed the country presenting workshops developing liturgical practices that were "authentically black and truly Catholic."[12]

During those years (1964-1984) the first priority for the liturgical pioneers within the black Catholic Church was to introduce elements of black Christian worship practices to the vast majority of Catholics who were black, as a sort of internalized evangelization. Decades, if not centuries, of conditioning had alienated many of them from much of the culture that was their birthright. Rivers reflected on his mission, thus:

> . . . within the general context of the Church's groping to integrate the music with the rest of worship that I came to understand that it was not enough for us to introduce black music into the liturgy but that it was necessary to bring the whole range of black culture to bear on our worship efforts.[13]

In order to make this catechesis effective, much learning and research and ecumenical dialogue had to be initiated. Replacing familiar but culturally unconnected music with songs that were often judged to be "secular" or "Protestant" or "embarrassing" was not progress. The work had to affect the soul, in myriad ways, if the renewal of worship was to be solidly conceived. Much attention was paid to discovering the spiritual gifts that had "no north, no south, no east or west." The bishops presented characteristics of black spirituality that have deep resonance in the work of the best of the theologians working in the black Catholic Church these last fifty years: "Black Spirituality has four major characteristics: It is contemplative. It is holistic. It is joyful. It is communitarian."[14]

What is remarkable in this listing is the first element: it is contemplative. Almost by instinct the authors of the pastoral letter focus on one of the great requirements of liturgy. They echoed Rivers: "it should help people reach beyond the here and now beyond the status quo. Beyond the finite boundaries of this world, to reach the transcendent; to be in touch with God." The great songs of African American culture, the so-called Negro Spirituals have been the strategies for our cultural transcendence, for as long as they have been sung. For a people abused by unspeakable oppression to be able to imagine a world in which they are free, safe and beloved by God, and for them to live as if that world is real is to live by faith that brings the kingdom into the here and now, if only for the duration of the performance of the song. So it is not surprising that Rivers would use these songs and other compositions inspired by these songs to become the midwife of the birth of black Catholicism. He taught us to sing our song in a strange land; and by using our voices to make this land a home.

In 1972, when I was very young and he was even younger, Father J-Glenn Murray, S.J., assisted me in preparing my ordination liturgy. To be inclusive, to be hospitable, and to be truly Catholic and authentically black, I focused on giving the people of East St. Louis, Illinois, the best possible experience of how a dream could be fulfilled. Presiding was the Most Reverend Harold Perry, SVD, at that time the only black bishop in the United States. A neighbor who provided the music for the largest black Baptist church in the city was the main organist. The men who had just become the St. Louis Jesuits provided some of the service music. From the Spirituals to traditional Gospel music to the universal classic "Amazing Grace," we created something new and viscerally understandable. The sacrament allowed the people, for the first time in their believing lives, to enter into an experience that was anything but a mystery. It was theirs.

When Sister Thea Bowman, F.S.P.A., Ph.D., addressed the National

Catholic Conference of Bishops in 1989, she became a sacramental moment in the development of black Catholic liturgical life. Asked to talk about being "black and Catholic," Sister Thea began her remarks (delivered from a wheel-chair), by singing, "Sometimes I feel like a motherless child." Reaching back into black tradition she herself was the lesson she taught. Her great challenge to the bishops can be considered a watershed for not only her primary audience (the bishops) but also for those "listening in" (the thousands of black Catholics who have made her remarks part of the black Catholic "canonical" literature). Born in the black Baptist church, trained in Roman Catholic traditional religious practices, Sister Thea announced, as a representative of all those who had never been asked to speak truth to power in such a setting, that she —and we—

> come to my church fully functioning . . . I bring my black self, all that I am, all that I have, all that I hope to become, I bring my whole history, my traditions, my experience, my culture, my African-American song and dance and gesture and movement and teaching and preaching and healing and responsibility as gift to the church.[15]

This declaration outlines what anyone should be able to say as they enter into every liturgical movement as called for by the Second Vatican Council. Sister Thea provides the outline of where black Catholic liturgical thought and practice have joyfully labored these last decades. Bringing song and dance and preaching and praying and teaching as gifts to the universal church, black Catholics have often found themselves being called to be evangelizers to the once-dominant church that formerly did not have room for them at the "welcome table."

When the National Black Catholic Congress gathered in New Orleans in 1992, the participants engaged in notable liturgies that reflected much of what Rivers and Bowman and others had called for during the previous decades.

> Semi-darkness. A nearly bare space, surrounded by bleachers for four thousand delegates and guests. In the clear center of the room, three turned-over iron pots. The choir began chanting, "Hush, Hush, Somebody's Calling my Name," and twelve women came out and swept the space clean, using large palm branches. Then, in keeping with southern traditions of housekeeping, they "tamped" down the dust, by sprinkling water all around the space. When they had finished, six men came into

the space and constructed an altar—over the iron pots. When the preparations were complete, the twelve black Catholic bishops of the U.S. came into the room and made a circle around the altar. The women blessed them with water and the eucharist proceeded.

Layer upon layer, from the whispering chant announcing that in the Kingdom of God, each of us is known and sought out by God, even in the wilderness where we find ourselves. The iron pots had been used by the enslaved Africans when they slipped into the wilderness to pray. They believed that the pots would contain their voices so that no one but God and the ancestors would hear them. And then, when the assembly had built a church that honored its past, the men who had been set apart to lead that church came into the circle of faith and hope and were blessed by all who had gathered.

Then the lights came on, the choir got "happy" and the time of jubilee commenced.[16]

This surely fulfilled the call of the council:

It is very much the wish of the church that all of the faithful should be led to take that full, conscious, and active part in liturgical celebrations which is demanded by the very nature of the liturgy, and to which the Christian people, "a chosen race, a royal priesthood, a holy nation, a redeemed people" (1 Pet 2:9, 4-5) have a right and to which they are bound by reason of their Baptism.[17]

The people who had been the oppressed race, the despised nation, the orphans of their own history and cultures, not only found a seat at the "welcome table"; they finally understood that they had to build the table for themselves. Remembering their good manners, and the instruction of Sister Thea Bowman, the black Catholic bishops and Father Rivers, these same redeemed and restored children of God have made their gifts available to the church universal. And that is good.

BRUCE T. MORRILL, S.J.

Change as the Norm

Bruce Morrill grew up in northeastern Maine, where he graduated from public high school in 1977 before heading to Massachusetts to attend the College of the Holy Cross. After a postgraduate year in the Jesuit Volunteer Corps working as a youth minister in a remote Alaskan Eskimo village, he entered the Jesuit novitiate in Boston. In addition to completing required Jesuit studies in philosophy at Fordham University and divinity at the Jesuit School of Theology in Berkeley, he obtained an M.A. in anthropology at Columbia University and a Ph.D. in religion at Emory University.

Father Morrill currently holds the Edward A. Malloy Chair in Catholic Studies at Vanderbilt University, where he is professor of theology in the Divinity School and Graduate Department of Religion. He previously was a faculty member at Boston College and has occupied visiting fellowships and chairs at Saint Joseph's University (Philadelphia), the Milltown Institute (Dublin), Seattle University, and Holy Cross. In addition to dozens of articles, book chapters, and reviews, he has published eight books, including Encountering Christ in the Eucharist: The Paschal Mystery in People, Word, and Sacrament *(2012),* Divine Worship and Human Healing: Liturgical Theology at the Margins of Life and Death *(2009), and* Anamnesis as Dangerous Memory: Political and Liturgical Theology in Dialogue *(2000).*

WHEN JOHN XXIII ANNOUNCED HIS plans for an ecumenical council in January 1959, I was gestating in my mother's womb. When Paul VI closed the final session of Vatican II nearly seven years later I was in first grade. I can still remember in those childhood years the thick little paperback book with the red cover featuring a gold coin struck with the heads of those two popes, *The Documents of Vatican II*, sitting on the desk of one of my teenaged brothers. I doubt he read it much and suspect it landed there via either the parish curate responsible for the altar boys and CYO or my father, who, as one of the first members of the newly formed parish council, would most likely have gotten it from our pastor. While the print packed into those pulpy pages was beyond my ken, I did enjoy the glossy, colorfully illustrated new catechism books my class was receiving at the start of each school year, the first group not to be administered the *Baltimore Catechism*.

Change was the order of the day during my early school years in that parochial school and church, just as it was in our declining mill town of South Brewer, Maine, where the small shoe factory and the large paper mill along the river were each shutting down. Whereas my sister's first-grade class had received their first communion as a group, decked out in white dresses and suits, mine was the first for whom no such communal pageantry would take place. Rather, once our teacher judged a student ready, she arranged with the parents to present their child at the altar rail at a regular Sunday Mass. Recognition came in the form of an announcement during the Mass, asking that all wait to form the communion line until the child with his parents came up to receive first. In my case the accompanying party was my father and godmother, while my devout Russian Orthodox mom watched from our pew. Confirmation, of course, was still a corporate event, administered in the Portland diocese to children who had reached the age of reason. The bishop made his way to the parish every three years, at which time were presented to him the first through third graders, both the parochial students and the Sunday-school-educated public school children, who mostly lived in the "New Development" of modest ranch and cape-style houses built in the fields above the old river town.

When confirmed in 1968 I was among the newest group of altar boys, the first to memorize the (formidable!) responses in English rather than Latin. The 1962 Order of Mass was nonetheless incomprehensible to my eight-year-old mind. I can remember being scared to death as I kept track of what to do next, whether at Mass or the Sunday evening Benediction service. Within just a couple months of getting the knack of it all, however, changes started coming nonstop. A Sunday evening Mass option replaced Benediction, and it seemed like every few weeks we were getting new instructions on what to do and say and when. Most notable was the installation of an altar table facing the people and with it, the demise of the old prayers at the foot of the altar (to my great relief).

Change was happening in the nave and wider church community as well. Whereas I can recall in third grade the church being nearly full for the daily 5:30 p.m. Mass during Lent, and then standing room only for the services of Holy Week, just one year later, in 1969, Lenten Mass attendance had collapsed and the numbers at the Triduum thinned. The

parish school closed that June, with the total enrollment having dwin-
dled to just over 100 (my fourth-grade class down to nine, from some
twenty as kindergarteners). I later learned the diocese closed on average
four schools per year, as large numbers of the Sisters of Mercy quit the
convent. My sister and I attended public school thereafter, and within
just a couple years convinced our parents that the weekly CCD classes
(conducted by volunteer parishioners) were a waste of time. By then the
pastor had long been promoted to a big parish in Portland and the curate
reassigned, replaced by a solitary pastor. Today that church is one of
eight parishes served by a regional team of just three priests—for now.

The story of my post-Vatican II years, then, is one of having grown and
eventually come of age amid great liturgical and parochial change, not
only in the style and content of the rituals but also the decline in priestly
and religious vocations and the emerging role of volunteer lay ministers
in liturgical and other capacities. I now realize how great were the socio-
economic and cultural transformations that, combined with the impact
of *Humanae vitae*, no doubt contributed to the parish's diminishment
in that period. But at the time I experienced ongoing change through
the lens of adolescent protestation. My political sensibilities had taken
liberal contours, as I'd looked up to my teenaged (draft-eligible) brothers
reacting to the events of 1968 and then the debacle of Vietnam. They had
gone away to college and moved out of state by the time I was watching
the Watergate hearings in eighth grade and Nixon's resignation in the
summer after ninth. By the time I headed away for college in the latter
1970s, I had come to consider change a constant, and change for the
better always in terms of progressive social causes, transparent structures, and accountable leaders. As for the church, in which my participation and interest had grown, my enthusiasm was with ecumenism, the
advancement of the laity and women, and social teaching, all in concert
with participation in the reformed liturgy, which had gradually come
into its own in the local parishes (as had myself, serving as a lector).

Little wonder, then, that I found my way to Jesuit-run Holy Cross,
where I majored in religious studies. The department was chaired by
John Esposito, who was turning out noted publications on Islam and
politics while also expending enthusiastic energy on his students. I found
in a young Jesuit professor, just arrived with his Vanderbilt Ph.D., the
eventual mentor of my honors thesis, while in my junior and senior years
Piet Schoonenberg, S.J., served on the faculty and Bernard Cooke joined
it permanently. The latter two I recruited in my senior year to give key-
note addresses for an inaugural student lay liturgical ministries weekend
I founded along with others in the Committee for Campus Ministry.
While the weekend attracted more than 150 clearly engaged partici-

pants, I doubt many of those Catholic college kids realized the stature of the two theologians addressing them. It was more a matter of what they had come to expect. The Jesuits had formed a Vatican II ethos at Holy Cross characterized by robust Sunday and weeknight liturgies, extensive service involvement in the parishes and among the needy in Worcester, and a silent Ignatian retreat that roughly a quarter of the students would make sometime before graduation.

Thirty years have passed, and my recent college reunion gave many of my classmates and me pause to reflect on the conventional Catholic culture we had known on campus those years and how different we find the ethos of the church today, including the attitudes of their children. Scientific polling data on the now steady decline in American Catholic liturgical attendance, including the especially sharp drop among youth and young adults, points to a combination of wider socio-techno-cultural factors (disabling the rhythms of civic and religious ritual, fragmenting social bodies) and alienation from or disinterest in the official church (both its internal and external politics).

Increasingly I consider myself witness to a progressive, ecumenical liturgical-theological movement that blossomed in the wake of Vatican II, enjoyed a springtime (with a bow to Lucien Deiss) in the 1970s, then a brief summer in the 1980s, before autumnal decline into the present wintry season (another nod, to Karl Rahner). True, a small vanguard of young people seeking identity in traditionalism are embracing the type of church and liturgy emerging from the Vatican's reassertion of hierarchical and narrowly Roman power through the implementation of *Liturgiam authenticam* (2001), *Redemptionis sacramentum* (2004), the 2002 General Instruction of the Roman Missal, and the 2011 English translation of the Mass. I cannot help but wonder, however, whether much of American Catholicism will end up like my mother's Orthodox parishes, which by the 1980s found few regularly attending the mystical liturgies members nonetheless expected clergy and cantors to execute, but then saw an infusion of participation with the arrival of new immigrants from the former Soviet Bloc. The center of American Catholicism in the twenty-first century may well be comprised of immigrant, notably Hispanic, groups for whom parishes will, as they did for Euro-immigrants a century earlier, provide social bonds in place of the families left behind. Still, this will take a different popular-religious shape, as these immigrants come without numbers of their own priests and sisters ready to anchor ethnic parishes but, rather, with a propensity for the biblical-evangelical Christianity great numbers of Latinos are finding attractive. If graced with a long life, I shall with fascination watch the unfolding of these new seasons.

BILL HUEBSCH

The Church on the Eve of Vatican II*

Bill Huebsch was born in 1951 and raised on a family farm near Perham, Minnesota. He and his family were from Perham, but they belonged to St. Lawrence Parish. It was at the parish church that major moments in his life were celebrated. It was there that he learned the prayers at the foot of the altar; there that he memorized the answers in the Baltimore Catechism, *and there that he first heard about a great council of the church that would be held in Rome, beginning in 1962.*

Huebsch began his years at Crosier Seminary prep school just as Vatican II was winding down. Later he earned a B.A. in religious studies at the University of North Dakota, and, in 1981, an M.T.S. from the Catholic Theological Union of Chicago. He spent five years each on the diocesan staff in Crookston and New Ulm in Minnesota, and many years on the pastoral staff of St. Stephen Parish in suburban Minneapolis. For the past two decades he has worked in Catholic publishing, and now directs an online pastoral center for Twenty-Third Publications, which is found at PastoralPlanning.com.

In 1990 Huebsch established The Vatican II Project, which contributes to the effort being made within the church to keep alive the spirit and energy of Vatican II.

He has published nearly twenty books in recent years, along with numerous booklets, articles, and screenplays. One of his books, Grace: God's Greatest Gift *(1988), was named in* U.S. Catholic *among the top seven most influential books on spirituality for today's world. One of his recent books is* Dreams and Visions: Pastoral Planning for Lifelong Faith Formation *(2009).*

I WAS RAISED IN THE 1950s. We were American Catholics. We were from the immigrant working class of the nineteenth and early twentieth

---

* This reflection appears in modified form in *Vatican II in Plain English: The Council* (Allen, TX: Thomas More Publishing, 1997).

century. We never had a lot of money or prestige or social power. But none of that really mattered then because our faith—the center of our lives—was *certain* for us. The Protestants may have had the presidency. They had Billy Graham and Norman Vincent Peale. But we were Catholics; we had the Mass. On our altars, Christ became real. We were certain. Presidents and preachers be damned. No one could top the Mass!

So when Vatican II reformed the Mass, a sea change occurred in Catholic self-understanding. The council unwittingly tinkered with far more than the liturgy of the church when it did its work. It also tinkered with a huge, collective, unconscious Catholic memory that prevailed in the church on the eve of the council.

This is a memory of dark, heavy church aromas—incense lurking about the pews and beeswax candles burning silently at the tabernacle, leaving ages of sulfur behind them. A memory of sacristies, redolent with the fragrance of spilled wines and the after-shave lotions of the priests. So many priests then. Altar servers playing with fire, lighting candles and charcoal, fumbling with the chains of the thurible, tripping on the hem of life.

It's a memory of faithful masses, kneeling in the pews: patient, silent, waiting. Genuflection was serious. Doubles during Benediction of the Blessed Sacrament. God was watching. This was *His* place (and there was no doubt about God's gender then). The high ceilings and unseen crosses at the tops of the steeples made God larger than life, than the very life created by God.

It's a memory of Benediction: a brief ceremony of songs, poems, and silence accentuated with incense, holy water, and gold monstrances. The monstrance: the most holy object at the parish church, the place where the priest put the host, larger than the ones you received, white, crisp, the Body of Christ. Round like the moon, rising above the kneeling congregation, "exposed" for all to gaze upon in absolute reverence. The Body of Christ was "exposed" in benediction, a vaguely, deeply sensual act. I think I remember being taught that you weren't even supposed to move while it was visible. Catholics fell to their knees to adore the sacred sacrament. The heart and soul of being Catholic was believing that this, indeed, is the true and absolute flesh and blood of God's own Son. As the *Tantum ergo* came to a close, a clear and palpable sense of blessing descended on the congregation: Blessed be God. Blessed be His Holy Name. Blessed be Jesus Christ, true God and true Man . . . blessings, praises. A sweet beatitudinal sense of well-being and honor fell upon everyone.

And, of course, it's a memory of Latin. Memorized by priest and altar server alike, it added a surreal dimension to all the devotions. God, we might have believed, understood our prayers better when they were uttered in Latin. *Introibo ad altare Dei. Ad deum qui laetificat juventutem meam.* ["I will go to the altar of God. To God who gladdens my youth."] Could that have been true? Did God understand Latin better?

It's a memory of Gregorian chant being sung to us by distant choirs huddled in lofts at the back of the church. We didn't want to sing. We wanted to be *sung to by the choir.* Protestants sing; Catholics listen. That's how it'd been since the sixteenth century.

Attending Mass and contributing money were the measures of being a good Catholic. The money we gave was spent for buildings, by and large: bricks and mortar. The buildings were ours; pastors would come and go, traveling missionaries would come through town, leaning out of pulpits, spinning stories about the horrors of life on the other side of the world, but the *building* was our foundation. It belonged to us. We built it.

It's a memory of Catholic devotional life. You could spot a Catholic car from fifty feet because there was a statue of a saint, normally Christopher, on the dashboard. Devotion to the saints and devotions in general were what we did. We used the saints to find lost things (St. Anthony), to bless farm fields (St. Isidore), and to protect us from harm (all the rest).

I knew a woman once who believed firmly in spontaneous combustion, not of her or of anyone she knew, but of her house. She was convinced that at any time her attic might burst into flames! Because of this fear, she developed a staunch devotion to St. Florian, patron against home fires, and she gradually filled her attic with St. Florian medals and holy cards. She would occasionally go up there, sprinkle the place with holy water, and read a prayer to St. Florian, who, apparently, helped her, since the attic survived. During these little prayer services in the attic this same woman would, of all things, *light a candle*! Florian protected her from all harm.

It's a memory of Mary. Mary, of course, was more. She wasn't "just another saint." She was the Saint of the saints, the leader. She offered Catholics a sort of female version of the deity, a place near God where power and glory were apportioned almost equally. After all, what decent fellow would not want his own mother to have as much glory as himself? There's really no basis for comparison among the holy men and women of the church: Mary was The Greatest, The Queen. "Holy Mary," we prayed. "Mother of God, pray for us sinners [she wasn't one herself, after all] now and at the hour of our death."

We knew she would if we asked sweetly. What a blessing to have Mary praying for you. Devotion to Mary, alone among devotions, sometimes even rivaled the Mass for its place in our Catholic lives. It was, after all, something we could do without a priest. When someone died, the first thing a family did was to pray a rosary. When bad weather blew in from the west, Catholics headed to their basements, Rosary cases and blankets in hand, to sit among the vegetables in the root cellar and pray to Mary for protection.

She wasn't our only source of blessing, of course. There was also a jar of holy water standing on the banister in most Catholic houses with which we blessed ourselves and our homes. Every night after our bedtime prayers, Catholic moms moved quietly through their houses with the holy water jar, blessing each child and, finally, herself and Dad. What a lovely gesture, what a loving, gentle way to enter sleep. Each year we waited in the car after the Easter Vigil, the memories of those solemn ceremonies still fresh while the Easter bunny was on his way, as Mom obtained a new supply from the parish crock. The parish moms seemed to like this moment in the year, standing among the lilies with one another, dressed in pink and yellow spring dresses, putting all their hopes for the blessing of their families into mayonnaise jars.

Catholic boys, the preseminarian ones, kept extensive holy card collections like others did baseball cards, except our cards were blessed, powerful in some important, invisible way. They had pictures of the saints on them, but they also had "ejaculations." Holy card ejaculations were brief prayers one memorized and, periodically, spontaneously uttered. "All for the honor and glory of God and for the poor souls in purgatory!"

These holy cards were icons of our Catholic devotional identity. They carried an energy all their own, and those prayers printed on them merited indulgences for the user. Catholics could build up an "account" of these indulgences counted as "days off in purgatory," 500 days for this, 1,000 days for that. It was all rather like a frequent flier club for Catholic souls who were willing to sacrifice themselves for God. There were *Catholic* holy cards and *Catholic* indulgences. No one else had them.

It would be inaccurate to paint too romantic a view of life in the church on the eve of the council. There were also terribly fierce, inflexible rules that, when enforced, caused great harm. Families expelled their own children for marrying improperly, for divorcing, and for failing to follow the rules exactly. "Fallen away" Catholics were treated harshly and excluded from Catholic circles, left to roam among Protestants. And Protestants were considered apostates and heretics, people who had left the one true church and who now would not see heaven. The unbaptized of the world, including all the Jews, Buddhists, and others, were simply targets for conversion to Catholicism. Their failure to convert sentenced them to Limbo, at best, and to Hell, at worst.

The huge, collective Catholic consciousness that existed on the eve of Vatican II consisted of an odd mixture of love and fear. It was both sublime and harsh. It was Benediction and Bingo.

Then, rather suddenly it seemed, Pope John XXIII was elected to the papacy. He was funny! He was plump! He was welcoming to Protestants and Jews. He was absolutely extraordinary! We'd never seen a Catholic, much less a pope, like him. And soon thereafter, Vatican II got under-way leading us to a Catholic Church we'd never seen before either.

OWEN CAMPION

Human Experience and Liturgy

*Owen Campion was born in Nashville, Tennessee, on April 24, 1940,
and was educated there through the secondary level. He received his
bachelor's degree in United States history and psychology from St.
Bernard College, Cullman, Alabama, and his graduate theological
training at St. Mary's Seminary and University in Baltimore, Maryland.*

*On May 21, 1966, he was ordained a priest of the diocese of Nashville.
After five years in pastoral ministry, he became editor-in-chief of
the* Tennessee Register, *the Catholic weekly newspaper then serving
all Catholics in Tennessee. He held this position until 1988, when he
became associate publisher of* Our Sunday Visitor.

*From 1981 to 1984, Monsignor Campion served as treasurer of the
Catholic Press Association of the United States and Canada, and from
1984 to 1986 he was president of the Association. In 1989, the Holy See
named Campion its ecclesiastical adviser to the International Catholic
Union of the Press (UCIP, using the initials of its French name). He
served the maximum number of terms in this capacity, leaving it in
1998. The International Union named Campion a member for life of its
governing council in 2001.*

*In 1988, the Catholic Press Association conferred on Campion the St.
Francis de Sales Award, for contributions to Catholic communications.
The University of Dayton presented him with its Daniel J. Kane Award
in 1997, also for contributions to Catholic communications.*

I WAS A FRESHMAN IN college when the recently elected Pope John XXIII
announced that he wished to convene another ecumenical council. At
the time of his announcement, very few persons alive had memories of
such a council, the First Vatican Council having closed about ninety
years before.

The processes of councils were unknown. Even more unknown was
the pope's reason for summoning a new council. It was said, accurately

or not, that John XXIII wanted "to open the windows" of the church. However, no one knew what this meant. My recollections of the council center not on its birth, but upon the fact of the council itself, and its aftermath.

By the time the council actually convened, I was a graduate student in theology, preparing for the priesthood. Certainly the Catholic academic world was attuned to developments at the council. The Catholic press reported it extensively, and no other Catholic event since that time has generated as much coverage in the commercial media.

Coincidentally, for me the council occurred when profound, and at times deeply divisive, conditions were happening in American society. I was a son of the South, descended from generations of Southerners, and I was very much familiar with the attitudes and realities in Southern life surrounding race. Earlier, I had been in the first secondary school class in Tennessee to be desegregated. I remembered the energetic, and not uncommonly angry, discussions that had accompanied racial integration. Over the years, those discussions had led to a great national effort, historically now called the civil rights movement, and a countereffort with considerable strength itself.

President John F. Kennedy had been assassinated, and dark rumors of conspiracy and disloyalty were in the air. It is true that many Americans learned from the president's murder how far hatred could go.

The Vietnam War was beginning to take its toll in lives. It also was taking a toll on the collective American mind and heart.

The days were stormy in many respects.

From this perspective, I heard with the strictest attention and the greatest delight the council's expressions of the church and of where the church stood in the entire human experience.

The great "Constitution on the Church" and on the "Church in the Modern World" created within me a peace and furthermore an enthusiasm. I saw the church, described in the eloquent words of the council and in definitions drawing so heavily from the scriptures and the most majestic sources of Christian theology, as possessing the answer even to the most troubling of human problems and worries.

It was a feeling that has remained with me for forty-five years of priestly service. Most of my priesthood has been spent in the Catholic press, and every day for almost a generation and a half I have been expected to look at problems, great or small, confronted at the very moment by people with a thought toward relief. My excitement about the church, realized years ago as I read about the council, has never failed me.

Because of this excitement, I have never felt overwhelmed or defeated, even as causes in which I believe, such as human rights, perennially seem here and there to meet their match. My hope for a world of human opportunity and dignity, with God and under God, is as vivid as ever. I thank the council.

In another personal sense, but equally as compelling, the council's steps to reform the Roman liturgy greatly have benefited me.

Here I must be clear. I loved the drama and elegance of the older liturgy, when it was done well, of course. But, the reformed liturgy has allowed me greater personal participation in the formal worship and a much greater insight into the realities behind the symbols.

As time has passed and as my opportunities and responsibilities have broadened, I have on many occasions been in the company of Catholics from cultures quite distant and different from my own. For my perception, the use of the vernacular, a reform advocated by the council, has very strongly reminded me of the universality of the church and of the gospel that the church proclaims. It is more than the mere mechanism of language. It is that, through the use of languages and gestures most profoundly rising from the heart, the church is enabling people, through formal, public liturgy, to express to God their deepest beliefs and thoughts. Nothing could be more universal, and indeed more Catholic, than the enablement of this expression.

The council produced a new day for the church through so many statements and reforms. It also prepared for the church three marvelous pastoral leaders at the highest level, Popes Paul VI, John Paul I, and John Paul II.

Paul VI probably is best recalled for his many efforts to put into practice the mind of the council. These efforts deserve to be recalled. For me, in my vision of the church and humanity, an equally great contribution by Paul VI to the human experience was his sense of human dignity, individually and collectively. He splendidly guided the church through the demise and aftermath of colonization and through the anxiety of nuclear war. Even in his controversial encyclical, *Humanae vitae*, he taught the world the great Christian understanding of human relationships and of human cooperation in the divine act of creation.

While destined to guide the church for only a month, Pope John Paul I gave the world a full picture of joy and hope when life stands on the gospel.

And of course, Pope John Paul II, for a generation, has become the boldest and most frequent advocate for human rights and for theism itself.

Would I wish to have lived in any other period of time? God has always been with us, and God was with those who preceded us. I would not have feared in other times. But I thank God that I have lived in the era of the Second Vatican Council, because the council so magnificently has given me, through the message of the church, a glimpse of the loving God we cannot see.

JOSEPH H. CHAMPLIN

Reflections on the Constitution
on the Sacred Liturgy

Father Joseph Champlin was born on May 11, 1930, and educated in the public schools of New York State before graduating from Phillips Academy at Andover, Massachusetts, in 1947. After studying at Yale and Notre Dame, he began and continued his journey to the priesthood at seminaries in Rochester, New York. He was ordained for the diocese of Syracuse in 1956. During fifty-plus years of priestly ministry, Father Champlin served as pastor in three parishes within his diocese, but also held the post of associate director for the Liturgy Secretariat, National Conference of Catholic Bishops in Washington, DC, from 1968 to 1971.

Over the years Father Champlin traveled more than two million miles here and abroad, lecturing on liturgical and pastoral matters as well as conducting retreats for priests and missions for parishes. He also wrote fifty books, with over twenty million copies of his publications in print. For many years he wrote a weekly column on the liturgy and worship distributed by the NC News Service. In addition, he appeared in about a dozen videos and made numerous television appearances. His most popular book, Together for Life *(1970; rev. ed. 1988), continues to be used by two-thirds of all couples being married in the Catholic Church.*

Champlin served as rector of the Immaculate Conception Cathedral in Syracuse, New York, until 2005, but continued to write and lecture around the country. He died on January 17, 2008.

At the time of the Second Vatican Council, Father Champlin was serving as associate pastor of the cathedral in Syracuse and as secretary for the then recently established diocesan liturgical commission.

MY REMOTE PREPARATION FOR THE Second Vatican Council and its "Constitution on the Sacred Liturgy" took place as a youngster during the 1930s in a small southern tier New York State village. My instructors were three maiden aunts who walked a few blocks to daily Mass and prayed that either my brother or I would become a priest. The other instructor was my devout single-parent mother, who, burdened by a divorce, heart disease, and the Depression, drew great strength and wisdom from frequent participation in the Eucharist.

My proximate preparation for the council occurred during the 1940s and '50s in another small village, but now in central New York. My guide was the pastor of the local parish in the town where I attended public high school. A musician who taught teenagers to play the pipe organ for daily Masses, Father Harold Quinn loved the liturgy, read everything available about it, and guided me through a tumultuous adolescence to the priesthood. He also changed my life forever by taking me as a seminarian to the Liturgical Conference in Grand Rapids, Michigan. I never missed one of those conferences over the next two decades.

It was at those sessions that I met some great giants in the church and in the field of worship. Two of these individuals, Benedictine Father Godfrey Diekmann and canonist Father Frederick McManus, were to become consultants at the council. I also listened to, spent time with, and was greatly influenced by Monsignor Martin Hellriegel, the visionary pastor of Holy Cross Church in St. Louis. Those conferences and these people introduced me to the historical perspective of liturgical reform. Maria Laach, Solesmes, and Pius Parsch in Austria, St. John's, St. Meinrad's, and Dom Damasus in New York—all these became familiar names and places.

I also began to understand a nearly century-old pattern of renewal in the liturgy: the double impact of, from the top, official changes, and, from the bottom, advocacy recommendations. Thus, there were Vatican directives like St. Pius X's decree on communion, music, and participation; and there were the unofficial movements urging vernacular in the liturgy, restored Holy Week services, and Mass facing the people. Later, we received the papal documents in the 1940s on the Mystical Body, the liturgy, and biblical studies; at the same time, others from below urged a richer appreciation of Baptism, involvement of lay people, and a deeper understanding of the Mass. Just prior to the council, the church issued several small, but radically transforming ritual changes—mitigation of the Eucharistic fast, introduction of evening Masses, and several rites in the vernacular.

As we know, these decades of liturgical research, advocacy, and change meant that when Pope John XXIII convened the Second Vatican Council the only topic with significant background material ready was the liturgy. This subject consequently became the first under discussion and the first approved.

Many viewed that timing as distinctly providential. They saw the sequence in this fashion: the bishops having studied, debated, and voted on worship matters, returned home and lived the renewed liturgy for almost a year before returning for the subsequent sessions. They then did discuss the theology of the church, the priesthood, the modern world, but only after having experienced what the church at worship could or should be.

During those 1960s, I was full-time at a busy center-city cathedral, but working as the part-time secretary for the recently formed diocesan liturgical commission. That meant writing, lecturing, and meeting about these liturgical renovations. I also witnessed and personally suffered through the complexities and the pain of the change process.

In 1968 another development occurred that also was to change my life forever. Father Frederick McManus invited me to Washington to work as his associate in the liturgy secretariat for the National Conference of Catholic Bishops. This proved to be a radical shift for me. An individual with great love for the liturgy, but without formal education in it, and an experienced parish priest, but with no "office" background, now instantly becomes a national expert, working with highly detailed materials in a complex structural setting.

During the following three years, there were, in addition to work with the new liturgical books or directives, several developments flowing out of the liturgy constitution that directly impacted me.

Father McManus asked that I organize a national conference in Chicago for church leaders on the U.S. document *Music in Catholic Worship*, which was then in development, and on the recently approved eucharistic prayers, one of the first fruits of the "Constitution on the Sacred Liturgy." The participants were mostly church musicians and chancery office personnel (there were few trained liturgists on a bishop's staff at that time). As a result of the conference, many of these diocesan officials were anxious to have especially the new eucharistic prayers explained to their clergy. My official status, parish background, and plain talk apparently appealed to them. Invitations to address the clergy multiplied. For the next three years, I criss-crossed the country, conducting workshops on all of the current and impending liturgical changes.

During that time, I wrote two books that grew out of the directives from the Second Vatican Council. *Christ Present and Yet to Come* provided guidelines for the priest presider in the revised liturgy. The second, *Together for Life*, offered to clergy and engaged couples a practical vehicle for implementing those many rich options contained in the new Rite of Marriage. The success of both texts indicated that they fulfilled a real need.

During those three years, the seeds were being sown and the foundations being established for a semi-official liturgical organization and for centers of graduate liturgical study. The Federation of Diocesan Liturgical Commissions emerged from these efforts, and opportunities for such advanced degrees opened up in places like Catholic University, Notre Dame University, and St. John's in Collegeville, MN.

In 1971, my bishop called me home to become pastor of Holy Family Church in Fulton, New York, a small-size central New York city. I thought this shift would end my lecture journeys, but that did not happen. My position and experience as a pastor added credibility to those lectures in the 1970s and 1980s, while we introduced additional liturgical changes and integrated more fully the spirit and principles of the liturgy constitution.

I knew from my Washington experience that a revised order of penance would soon be released. With this in mind, I converted, aided by a liturgical artist and local contractor, a church room into a reconciliation chapel, one that would accommodate the alternatives of the new ritual (e.g., biblical readings, extension of hands, face-to-face confessions), yet retain the traditional elements (e.g., privacy, anonymity, kneeling). A local photographer made slides of the room, and I published a lengthy article about the revised rite. Armed with the slides and copies of the essay, I spoke over the next few years to clergy and lay people in about sixty U.S. dioceses, explaining this restored ritual for penance, reconciliation, and confession.

Throughout the last decade, while still speaking and writing about the implementation of the liturgy constitution, I have observed the efforts of two groups at the opposite ends of the liturgical spectrum: those who judge that changes of the Second Vatican Council, including the worship revisions, have gone too far, too fast, and those who judge that they have not gone far or fast enough. In between are those many people, the majority, who have quite warmly welcomed the documents of the Second Vatican Council in general and the "Constitution on the Sacred Liturgy" in particular. This corps of Catholics believes that these documents and their implementation, despite limitations, have significantly enriched the church.

CYPRIAN DAVIS, O.S.B.

The Liturgy, Inculturation, and the Renewal of Religious Life

Cyprian Davis was born September 9, 1930, in Washington, DC. He attended the public schools in the same city. When he was fifteen, he was received into the Catholic Church. His freshman year of college (1948-1949) was at the Catholic University of America. The following year he entered St. Meinrad Seminary, where he received an A.B. degree in 1953. He entered St. Meinrad Archabbey (St. Meinrad Abbey at that time) in 1950 and made the first vows of a Benedictine in 1951. Davis was ordained to the priesthood in 1956 and received an S.T.L. degree from the Catholic University of America the next year. He pursued advanced studies at the Catholic University of Louvain in Belgium, where he received a license in historical sciences in 1963 and a doctorate in historical sciences in 1977.

Currently Davis is emeritus professor of church history in the St. Meinrad School of Theology, having joined the faculty in 1963. He is also adjunct professor of history in the Institute of Black Catholic Studies, a summer institute at Xavier University in New Orleans. In addition, Davis serves as archivist for St. Meinrad Archabbey and the Swiss-American Benedictine Congregation, as well as archivist for the National Black Catholic Clergy Caucus, of which he was a founding member.

Davis has written very extensively in the area of monastic history, black Catholic history, and black Catholic spirituality. In 1990 he published The History of Black Catholics in the United States, *which was awarded the John Gilmary Shea Award in 1991. He co-edited with Diana Hayes* Taking Down Our Harps: Black Catholics in the United States *(1998). At present he is working on the life of Henriette Delille, a woman of color, who founded the Sisters of the Holy Family.*

Davis served on the subcommittee for the preliminary drafts of the U.S. Catholic bishops' pastoral letter "Brothers and Sisters to Us," published in 1979, and the black Catholic Bishops' pastoral letter "What

We Have Seen and Heard" in 1984. Between the years 1994 and 2000, he served as visiting lecturer in history and archival management in several Benedictine and Trappist monasteries of monks and nuns in the West African countries of Senegal, Togo, Burkina Faso, Benin, Ivory Coast, and Nigeria.

IN THE SUMMER OF 1958, I was sent to the University of Louvain in Belgium to get a degree in history. I had been ordained only two years. I found a home at the Benedictine Abbey of Keisersberg (at that time Mont César). I was one among several young monks from all over Europe who came to study at what was one of the most prestigious Catholic universities in the world. The monks of Mont César were established scholars, men such as Abbot Bernard Capelle, Dom Bernard Botte, Dom Odon Lottin, Dom Hildebrand Bascour, and others.

Shortly after my arrival, Pope Pius XII died on October 9, 1958. His death marked the end of an era. The election of Angelo Roncalli as John XXIII a few weeks later was to have a tremendous impact on us all, collectively and as individuals. This impact, of course, was the Second Vatican Council, which John XXIII announced in the year following. The professors at the University of Louvain would play important roles in this council.

Historically, Louvain had acquired the reputation of being a center for relentless scholarship and "cutting edge" research in theology, scripture, and history. Certain of my fellow students in theology, liturgy, and other sacred sciences had a ringside seat at history in the making because their professors were involved in the preliminary work of the council. One of those involved with the preliminary commissions on the "Constitution on the Sacred Liturgy" was Bernard Botte, a monk of Mont César, one of the foremost scholars in liturgical history and founder of the Liturgical Institute in Paris. Later, over a glass of wine, he would regale us students, monks, and others with stories about the committee meetings both before and after the council.

I remember the day when John XXIII died, June 3, 1963. The first session of the council had been concluded that winter. The entire world had literally watched at the pope's bedside. A fellow student, a friend, told me that he was so moved by John's death that he came back to the practice of the faith—he needed to be again one with those who were members of the church that mourned him.

I returned to the United States in August of 1963. Pope Paul VI had been elected a few weeks before. I had been absent from the United States for five years. I had left the country with a view of Catholicism that was somewhat triumphal and narrow. I returned with a heightened sense of the Catholic Church's history, a sense of the breadth of Catholicism, and the richness of its past and its present. It was this view of the church that would enable me to understand and accept the tide of change that would sweep over the ecclesiastical landscape after the council.

Before returning to my monastery, I visited with my parents in Washington. I had arrived just in time to participate in the "March on Washington" and to be present on the Mall when Martin Luther King, Jr., delivered his "I Have a Dream" speech. During my absence, the civil rights movement had begun a new day for black Americans. While in Europe, I had experienced my own black consciousness. The marchers walked in groups to the Monument Grounds. I marched with the Benedictine monks from St. Anselm's Abbey in Washington. Before the council there would never have been this open display of Catholic priests marching for justice and an end to racial discrimination. The Catholic Church in America was reticent about open participation in protests or "political" movements. The council, on the other hand, reminded us that the church was present in this world and that the church had to speak out against injustice with a prophetic voice.

Today we speak freely about inculturation. It was the council, however, with its teaching on the liturgy and on missions that made it possible for Africans and African Americans to re-introduce the drum and other African musical instruments into the liturgy. Today in almost every African American Catholic parish, the people sing Gospel music, clap their hands, and sometimes dance because of the encouragement given by the council for adaptations in the liturgy by the local church. Perhaps even more telling is the increase of musical compositions by black Catholic composers such as Clarence Rivers, Rawn Harbor, and Grayson Brown. Returning to St. Meinrad was a return to a monastic community that was in transition. In the next few years there would be dramatic changes in our monastic way of life. The celebration of the liturgy is the center of any Benedictine monastery. It was after the close of the council in 1965 that the implementation of the liturgical decrees was carried out. Since the liturgy has such an important place for Benedictines, any changes are fraught with tension and insecurity. In December of 1964, St. Meinrad was designated as one of the places in the archdiocese for liturgical experimentation. The altar was moved to face the people. The priest-monks began to concelebrate at the conventual Mass. By 1966 the nonordained monks began receiving communion under both species. At first Vespers for the Feast of All Saints in 1967, the monks of St. Meinrad began celebrating the Liturgy of the Hours in English. It was a little like a minor earthquake. The Monastic Breviary, which contained the Divine Office for monks and nuns of the Benedictine Order, had ceased to be used in this monastery where it had been used from its foundation. It had profound implications for our spiritual life and our monastic discipline. What is more, it meant that we needed to translate into English many ancient liturgical texts, compose new prayers and antiphons, or rewrite old ones when needed. We needed a new lectionary and a new ordering of scripture readings for the Office of Vigils. Finally, we needed more musical compositions. Thanks to the talents of many monks within our community, and with the collaboration of monks and nuns elsewhere, within a year or so we had created a very beautiful Office.

The conciliar document on the renewal of the religious life called each religious community to return to an understanding of the original charism of one's order or community. For monks, this meant serious research into the Rule of St. Benedict and into the historical development of each monastic house. This resulted in regular meetings and lengthy discussions on how to bring our monastic way of life into line with the spirit of the council. Here again there were real tensions and some bitter discussions regarding clerical monasticism and nonclerical monasticism and between professionalism and manual labor. Every monastery knew these tensions. St. Meinrad was no exception.

Life in a monastery is structured by a certain formality. Much of it is based on seniority according to profession. Traditionally, priests and clerics preparing for priesthood took precedence over brothers. In keeping with the demands of the council, this sort of distinction between clerics and lay changed. In 1968 the order of precedence was no longer based on ordination or lack of ordination. From now on the monks would take precedence according to the year of one's profession of vows.

This really meant a shift in the status of brothers. It meant a realization that the monastic charism was the focal point of our life, not priesthood. We no longer considered the Order of St. Benedict as a clerical order. There was a corollary. Before the council, only those in solemn vows belonged to the chapter and had the right to elect the abbot. Brothers made perpetual vows, not solemn vows. As a result of the conciliar document on the renewal of the religious life, "all brothers were to be brought into the heart of the religious life" (see *Perfectae caritatis*, "Decree on the Sensitive Renewal of Religious Life," no. 15). Everyone in the monastery now has solemn vows and a place in chapter meetings. Today, every member of the community with solemn vows has the right to elect the abbot.

In the period that followed Vatican Council II many religious communities underwent the struggles of internal division and dissension. This was certainly the experience of my own community, although less so than in other communities. Yet for most the council brought an opportunity for renewal and restoration. It brought about a deepening of faith and a greater understanding of the tradition. Let me close this reflection with the words of a Benedictine monk, Bernard Botte, who left such an important imprint on the liturgical renewal at the Second Vatican Council.

> In spite of the scandals and abuses the church of Christ is the guardian of the deposit of faith. It's the church of the apostles, of the martyrs, and of the saints of all times. During the Council the Holy Spirit visibly inspired in the church the desire to purify itself and to return to its ideal. We should believe that the Spirit is still there, according to Christ's promise, and that he will complete the work he began.[18]

Now some fifty years after the convening of the council, I, as an African American, am struck by the increasing cultural diversity of the Catholic Church. The Jesuit theologian Karl Rahner, in fact, noted that at the council the church was indeed actualizing itself through its attendees gathered from throughout the globe as a world, or global, church for the first time.

In a variety of ways, the council made us more conscious of the demographic differences within the Catholic Church. These differences have made the church more complex as we come to respect the culture of the different peoples that make up the universal Catholic Church. The monocultural church of the past has given way to the recognition that we are a multicultural, Catholic faith community. Distinctions not considered for generations are celebrated today. We are Hispanic or Latino. We are both Puerto Rican who are Spanish speaking but also black. African Americans are Caribbean or Haitian. On May 6-8, 2010, there was a convocation of a Catholic Cultural Diversity Network at the University of Notre Dame. Though we were many, we were all Catholic. Though diverse in our history and culture, we were all Catholic.

This diversity has also created some suspicion in our differences. African American Catholics are very sensitive to the fact that many dioceses have moved the Catholic schools to the suburbs. African Americans remember that the parochial schools provided education for the sons and daughters of many different immigrants. In many places, the nuns are still teaching African Americans and West Indians, Hispanics, and Latinos. But in many places today the teachers are no longer in inner cities.

For blacks and browns and those of color the nomination and election of Barack Obama was a victory for us all—he is one of us. Many black Catholics see Obama in Africa and in Asia. In the morning after his nomination, the streets in the Caribbean broke out in song and in carnival. In the Bahamas, it was Junkanoo, a spontaneous celebration of new hope and freedom. So it was with the church fifty years ago. Vatican II ushered in a sense of hope and greater freedom as the church embraced both diversity of its people and a renewed commitment to a "preferential option for the poor."

M. BASIL PENNINGTON, O.C.S.O.

Liturgical Moments

Father M. Basil Pennington, O.C.S.O., was a Cistercian (Trappist) monk who served a variety of roles—professor, vocation director, and abbot—over the years at St. Joseph's Abbey (Massachusetts), Assumption Abbey (Missouri), and Abbey of Our Lady of Holy Spirit (Georgia). He was born on July 28, 1931, in Brooklyn, New York. After graduating from the seminary there, he joined the monastic community in 1951. After his ordination on December 21, 1957, he studied in Rome, obtaining degrees in theology from the Pontifical University of Thomas Aquinas (1959) and canon law from the Gregorian University (1963).

Father Pennington served as a peritus *in the Second Vatican Council and collaborated in the preparation of the new Code of Canon Law and the new constitutions of his Order. In 1968, in collaboration with Thomas Merton, he founded Cistercian Publications and fostered the work of translating the Cistercian Fathers into English. Three years later he collaborated in the establishment of the Institute of Cistercian Studies at Western Michigan University, Kalamazoo.*

In 1971 in response to Pope Paul VI's request that the Cistercians help the church renew the contemplative dimension of life, Father Pennington began teaching—through retreats and workshops, articles and books— the simple, ancient method of entering into contemplative prayer found in their tradition. It soon became popularly known as Centering Prayer or Prayer in the Heart. He was on the advisory board of Contemplative Outreach, an international lay movement to foster Centering Prayer among the laity. He was also one of the founders and the chairman of the Mastery Foundation, an interreligious outreach that seeks to help those in sacred ministry to empower their ministry through Centering Prayer.

Pennington taught Centering Prayer in over fifteen countries, including China, and published some fifty books and one thousand articles in twenty-five languages. His primary books are Centering Prayer: Renewing an Ancient Christian Prayer Form *(1980), and* Lectio Divina: Renewing the Ancient Practice of Praying the Scriptures *(1998). He died on June 3, 2005.*

It was an unforgettable moment in world history, a moment whose impact only the centuries will fully reveal. The river of white miters flowed steadily out of the bronze doors and across the square toward the great open portals of the largest basilica in Christendom, St. Peter's. At the end was the pontiff, the incarnation of tradition, so it appeared, sitting on his portable throne, riding above the crowd on the shoulders of the handsome men in rose brocade. Tradition was about to blossom forth in an unprecedented way: The Second Vatican Council convoked by Blessed John XXIII.

For so many of us gathered on that day, an ecumenical council was something that sort of descended from heaven, bearer of infallible truth. How often had we heard in the course of our theological training: the Vatican Council [i.e., Vatican I] said this; Second Lateran declared; Trent anathematized. . . . And now suddenly here we were in an ecumenical council. Like most of the American contingent, we pretty much expected to simply have a presentation of the schemas that had been prepared by the preparatory commissions, then a great signing, and home we would go. I suspect we were as shocked as anyone when Cardinal Liénart claimed the council for us. Soon enough we began to learn the lessons of incarnation as the negotiations for the council commissions got under way.

The one preconciliar schema that survived with any fullness was that on the liturgy. As I look back on the council now, I wonder how much myth has grown up even in my own mind, history embellished to bring out more fully the reality of days and events that were too full of the transcendent to be contained in the narrow confines of definable concepts.

Certainly Father Cyprian Vagaggini has become a mythical master. The story is that after ordination he spent five years studying sacred scripture, then five years studying the fathers of the church. With this background, comparable to that of the great medieval scholastics who studied *sacra pagina* [literally, the sacred page; that is, scripture] for years before beginning their own masterly lectures, Father entered into a five-year study of scholasticism, largely under the tutelage of Thomas Aquinas. Finally came the years of liturgical study that gave birth to his own two-volume work, *Theological Dimensions of the Liturgy*, and the subsequent preconciliar schema.

In that first session of the council, there was a rather superficial study of the lightweight schema on communications. The Spirit seems to have helped them to realize that it was not the time to say much about a field that was shortly to explode. Fortunately, this decree left the way wide

open for the church to embrace all the potential that today's developments offer us to fulfill Christ's mandate to bring the Good News to all
nations. Sad to say, as with all the inspired documents of the council, the
potential has hardly begun to be realized.

Then the real work began with the schema on liturgy. The possibilities were very exciting. Among all those wondrous happenings, there are
two that stand out for me personally: one because with all its simplicity
it has had a profound effect on my life, the other because of my personal
involvement with it and its potential significance.

It was a rather ordinary session and things were going along in a rather
ordinary way when a bishop—I don't know just who, one of the multitude (this was one of the profound learning experiences for the bishops,
so used to being the center of everything back home: to find themselves
just one of the "school boys" seated in the bleachers)—stood up and
made a very simple, apparently prosaic statement. But it was one of those
moments of grace in the council, a moment greeted by a profound and
profoundly aware silence. The bishop simply said: When the gospel is
proclaimed at the liturgy, Jesus Christ proclaims his Good News.

It seems so obvious. Look what happens at the liturgy. The priest
or deacon prays over us: "The Lord be with you." And we pray over
him: "And also with you." Then he proclaims: "The Gospel according
to . . ." And what do we respond? "Glory to you, O Lord." And at the
end? "Praise to you, Lord Jesus Christ." The priest or deacon has disappeared. It is the Lord. No wonder we stand, as it were, at attention. The
Lord himself is speaking to us. Each day at the liturgy I eagerly await
this moment when the Lord is going to speak to me and give me a word
of life for the day, a word I can bring to others, even as it enlivens my
life. In this simple way, my being as a disciple of Jesus Christ has been
tremendously and constantly nourished through all the years since that
seemingly very ordinary but very special day at the first session.

The second happening came about when the very gentlemanly and
gentle bishop from Brooklyn, Charles R. Mulrooney, asked me to
help prepare an intervention. His proposal was in effect that national
hierarchies should be able to make national or local "feasts," such as
Thanksgiving in the United States, to be full-fledged liturgical feasts. As
a monk, living the liturgy is a very big part of my life. It had long seemed
to me most incongruous that, while we as a community, along with the
rest of America, celebrated Thanksgiving abundantly in the refectory,
in church, apart from a "votive" Mass of thanksgiving, we were able
to give the feast little attention. Indeed, we usually were required to
celebrate the Office with the somber tones of a ferial day. The bishop's

proposal, which was substantially incorporated into the "Constitution on the Sacred Liturgy," while it satisfied a liturgical need, actually had more far-reaching significance. It affirmed that liturgy and life should be closely and coherently one, that liturgical prayer should be an expression of the life of the people. What a people believe and live should guide the way they pray. It was a clear, concrete expression of indigenization. The universal liturgy of the church was to make room to take on the color and spirit of the people who were celebrating it. But perhaps more significant for the future of the church was that this proposal sought to return to the bishops, the national or regional or local hierarchy, their authority to decide a matter that affected their people pastorally.

I do not know how many in the *aula* realized the full implications of what was being proposed by the apparently very quiet and gentle American bishop. Some certainly did, so that, while the idea of allowing space for local feasts was granted, the mode of the proposal, giving authority to the local episcopate, was sidestepped. This remains an area of struggle if not strife, in an ongoing tug of war between Roman authorities and national conferences of bishops in the area of liturgy as well as in many other areas of church life.

Exciting moments, moments of growth, of deeper realization of who we are as church, what it means to be church: the People of God, Christ's people guided by him to express who we are in prayer and praise and bring that Good News to the people among whom we live. Praise and glory to the Assumed Queen of Heaven and Earth!

PART THREE

WHAT IT MEANS TO BE CHURCH

Formulating a New Understanding of Church

WILLIAM MADGES

I WAS BORN DURING THE final third of the pontificate of Pope Pius XII (pope from 1939 to 1958). As I entered Catholic grade school, it was customary for me to be told, "The church believes this" and "The church teaches that. . . ." Of course, it was clear to me who "the church" was. It was the pope, the bishops, the priests. What they taught is what I must believe. (My instruction in the faith, however, didn't come directly through bishops or the pope, but through the nuns who taught at my school. Their trustworthiness to communicate accurately what "the church" taught was always beyond question for me.) The point is that, although I "belonged" to the church (that is, was baptized, accepted the church's teaching, received the sacraments, etc.), I wasn't *really* an essential part of the church. The *essential* part of the church was the clergy—in particular, the hierarchy. I was part of what was called "the faithful." Our job, as the name itself suggests, was simply to follow faithfully the guidance and the teaching of the clergy (aka the church). It was not our job to take the initiative in any aspect of the church's life; rather, it was our task to follow the clergy's lead. All that began to change in the wake of the Second Vatican Council.

The nature and structure of the church had been one of the two topics considered at the First Vatican Council (1869-1870), the first Roman

Catholic council to be held since the Council of Trent responded to the Protestant Reformation. The council had been called by Pope Pius IX to address some of the pressing challenges posed to the traditional beliefs and practices of the church by the development of modern culture. In particular, the council felt compelled to defend certain basic convictions of Catholic faith: that God exists and can be known by reason, that divine revelation is credible, that faith elevates reason, that faith and reason can never be at odds with each other. The council also felt it was necessary to defend the primacy and authority of the pope.

This defense seemed necessary in light of the developing trends in modern thought and culture. Enlightenment philosophers had, in the words of Immanuel Kant, encouraged people to think for themselves. "Enlightened" individuals should not hold something as true simply because the church or the state taught it. Dramatic discoveries and theories in science also challenged the authority of the church. Charles Lyell's geological discoveries and Charles Darwin's theory of evolution challenged the veracity of traditional and biblical beliefs concerning the age of the world, human origins, and God's providential role in the unfolding of cosmic and human history.

The nineteenth century was also an age of revolution in politics. After the upheavals of the American and French revolutions, the political scene continued to be unstable. People rebelled against systems of absolute monarchy and governments that ignored their wishes, as evidenced by the political turmoil in Europe in 1830 and 1848. By mid-century Karl Marx had called on the workers of the world to unite to create a classless society, in which religion would evaporate because the economic and social conditions that brought it into existence would have been transformed. People everywhere wanted greater freedom. Traditional authority in its different forms was under attack.

In response to the revolutionary political changes and the anti-Catholic policies of a number of European governments, many Catholics, including bishops, wanted to see the power of the pope not merely maintained but increased as a counterbalance to the power of nation-states. The Italian occupation of Rome and the attack on the Papal States in the final third of the nineteenth century appeared to severely threaten not only the political, but also the spiritual authority of the pope. It was believed that without the Papal States the pope would no longer have the independence necessary for the exercise of his spiritual authority.

Vatican I was in session when its work was cut short by the invasion of nationalist military forces seeking to unify Italy and by the Franco-Prussian War. The bishops completed only four of the anticipated fifteen chapters of the "Dogmatic Constitution on the Church of Christ" (*Pastor aeternus*). These four chapters described the establishment of the apostolic primacy of St. Peter, the continuation of Peter's primacy in the Roman pontiffs, the power and nature of the pontiff's primacy, and the infallible teaching authority of the Roman pontiff. In these chapters, the council fathers affirmed that Jesus had placed St. Peter at the head of the other apostles so that the unity of bishops, the apostles' successors, and the unity of faith of all believers might be maintained. They identified the primacy of the pope as the bulwark and firm foundation of the church.[1] Moreover, the bishops affirmed that the pope has full and supreme power of jurisdiction over the entire church, not only in matters that pertain to faith and morals but also in matters that pertain to the discipline and government of the worldwide church.[2]

With regard to faith and morals, the bishops of Vatican I declared that "when the Roman pontiff speaks *ex cathedra*, that is, when, in the exercise of his office as shepherd and teacher of all Christians, in virtue of his supreme apostolic authority, he defines a doctrine concerning faith or morals to be held by the whole church, he possesses, by the divine assistance promised to him in blessed Peter, that infallibility which the divine Redeemer willed his church to enjoy in defining doctrine concerning faith or morals. Therefore, such definitions of the Roman pontiff are of themselves, and not by the consent of the church, irreformable."[3]

This emphasis on papal primacy and authority, understandable as it is within the nineteenth-century context, permitted misconceptions about the nature of the church in the decades following Vatican I. It appeared to some that all that really needed to be said about the nature of the church had been contained in what was said about the pope. And the pope's role and authority were described in such a way that the church appeared to be a society of unequals, governed by an absolute papal monarch. In such a perspective, for example, the bishops appear only as deputies or representatives of the pope, rather than as successors of the apostles in their own right. And the laity appear as faithful subjects, but not really active participants in the mission of the church.[4]

When Pope John XXIII announced his intention on January 25, 1959, of convening an ecumenical council, many concluded that its primary goal would be the completion of Vatican I's work of describing the tasks of the church. Few initially expected that the upcoming council would ultimately situate papal primacy within a much broader and a more biblical understanding of "church" than had been the case in the nineteenth century. A strong and vocal minority of bishops and cardinals consistently supported a scholastic, juridical, and hierarchical definition of the church, in keeping with the lines laid out at Vatican I. The majority, however, argued for a more biblical, inclusive, and pastoral definition. The clash between these two different approaches was evident from the very first session of the council.

The initial draft (schema) of Vatican II's statement about the church, entitled *De Ecclesia*, outlined an understanding of church that was consistent with the then-standard emphasis on the hierarchical and juridical aspects of the church. This draft had been prepared by the Theological Commission, headed by Cardinal Alfredo Ottaviani. When first presented to the council fathers toward the end of the first session of the council (December 1-7, 1962), it was roundly criticized. Emile Josef De Smedt, Bishop of Bruges (Belgium), criticized the schema for triumphalism, clericalism, and juridicism. Instead of speaking of the church as the "church militant," with its members lined up in battle array prepared for victory, De Smedt advocated a more pastoral and humble description of the church as Christ's flock. Instead of regarding the church as a pyramid of people, priests, bishops, and pope, De Smedt emphasized that the church was essentially the People of God, who shared the same fundamental rights and obligations of being part of Christ's Mystical Body. Finally, in place of a juridical concept, De Smedt declared that the church should be presented to the world as the "mother" of humankind, who were all brothers and sisters to one another. The initial schema was similarly criticized by others, including Cardinal Döpfner of Munich, Cardinal Frings of Cologne, Cardinal Suenens of Maline-Brussels, Cardinal Bea of the Secretariat for Christian Unity, and Cardinal Montini of Milan (the future Pope Paul VI). But the schema was also defended by Cardinal Ottaviani, Cardinal Siri of Genoa, Cardinals Bacci and Browne of the curia, and others.[5]

Between the first and second sessions of the council, Pope John XXIII died and Cardinal Montini was elected Pope Paul VI. The intersession was dominated by bitter clashes within the various commissions. As the council made a new beginning in September 1963, it also had to consider an entirely new document on the church, with an entirely new name, *Lumen gentium*.[6] The new draft, however, was subjected to revision, in light of the debates at the second (1963) and the third sessions (1964). Finally, the "Dogmatic Constitution on the Church," in its present form, was overwhelmingly approved on November 21, 1964, by a vote of 2,151 bishops in favor and only five opposed.

The document finally approved in November 1964 was significantly different in content and tone from the original draft of the text that had been prepared two years earlier. The reorientation of the document becomes apparent even in a cursory comparison of the chapters of the draft constitution considered by the bishops during the first session of the council in 1962 and the final constitution approved two years later. The 1962 draft contained the following chapters: (1) the nature of the church militant; (2) the members of the church militant and of the need for them to be saved; (3) the episcopate as the highest degree of the sacrament of order and of the priesthood; (4) residential bishops; (5) states of evangelical perfection; (6) the laity; (7) the magisterium of the church; (8) authority and obedience in the church; (9) the relations between church and state; (10) the necessity of the church to proclaim the gospel to all peoples everywhere; (11) ecumenism.[7] The 1964 approved text contains the following chapters: (1) the mystery of the church; (2) the People of God; (3) the church is hierarchical; (4) the laity; (5) the universal call to holiness; (6) religious; (7) the pilgrim church; (8) Our Lady. The final draft supplements the first draft's juridical and hierarchical emphasis with the inclusion of more pastoral and communitarian elements.[8] In particular, the final draft, with its chapters on the "People of God" and the universal call to holiness, revised the first draft's understanding of the church and the role of the laity and bishops within it.[9] The revised understanding of church is most evident in three areas: the relationship of clergy and laity within the church; the relationship between the Catholic and other Christian churches and communities; and the relationship of the bishops to the pope.

At least since the time of the Reformation in the sixteenth century, it had been commonplace to think of the church, first and foremost, as the clergy and, in particular, as the hierarchy. Vatican I had further highlighted and emphasized the focal position and authority of the hierarchy, especially the pope. Therefore, it came as no surprise that, in the first draft of the "Dogmatic Constitution on the Church," the role and power of the bishops is presented before the exposition of the role of the laity and that the issues of authority and obedience receive special emphasis. In the second draft of the constitution, a single chapter was devoted to the People of God and the laity. Cardinal Suenens from Belgium proposed dividing this chapter into two chapters, and he recommended that the separate chapter on the People of God be placed before the respective chapters on the hierarchy and the laity. The final draft of the constitution did exactly that. Moreover, the final document affirms the "priesthood" of all believers, laity as well as clergy. The issue whether the clergy and the laity constituted two separate spiritual estates or only one was a central, divisive issue at the time of the Reformation. Now four centuries later, Vatican II declared that all the baptized, "by regeneration

and the anointing of the holy Spirit, are consecrated as a spiritual house
and a holy priesthood" (*Lumen gentium*, no. 10). Although the council
continued to distinguish the "common priesthood" of the laity from the
"ministerial priesthood" of the clergy, the acknowledgment of the laity's
share in Christ's priesthood was a significant reorientation. In addition,
the final version of the constitution affirmed that the laity participates
not only in Christ's priestly office but also in his prophetic office.[10] This
means that all of the baptized faithful, and not only the hierarchy, can
possess a sense of the faith that has been inspired and sustained by God's
Spirit. Although the hierarchy possesses the ultimate authority to interpret the meaning of the faith, all of God's people share in the possession of the faith and in helping to penetrate its depths. With confidence,
therefore, the constitution declares:

> The whole body of the faithful who have received an anointing
> which comes from the holy one (see 1 Jn 2:20 and 27) cannot be
> mistaken in belief. It shows this characteristic through the entire
> people's supernatural sense of the faith, when, "from the bishops
> to the last of the faithful," it manifests a universal consensus in
> matters of faith and morals. By this sense of the faith, aroused
> and sustained by the Spirit of truth, the People of God, guided
> by the sacred magisterium which it faithfully obeys, receives not
> the word of human beings, but truly the word of God (see 1 Th
> 2:13), "the faith once for all delivered to the saints" (Jude 3). The
> people unfailingly adheres to this faith, penetrates it more deeply
> through right judgment, and applies it more fully in daily life.[11]

A second area in which *Lumen gentium* reoriented Catholic teaching
concerns the relationship between the Catholic Church and other Christian communities. Although the constitution re-affirms the traditional
teaching that the "one, holy, catholic, and apostolic" church was handed
over to Peter and the apostles to be shepherded, *Lumen gentium* backs
away from the simple identification of the Roman Catholic Church with
the Mystical Body of Christ, which the original draft of the constitution
had endorsed.[12] In its final version, *Lumen gentium* declares:

> This church, constituted and organized as a society in the pres-
> ent world, subsists in the Catholic Church, which is governed
> by the successor of Peter and by the bishops in communion with
> him. Nevertheless, many elements of sanctification and of truth
> are found outside its visible confines. Since these are gifts belong-

ing to the church of Christ, they are forces impelling towards catholic unity.[13]

Instead of asserting, in an unqualified way, that Christ's church or mystical body is the Catholic Church, the constitution acknowledges that Christ's church subsists—exists or lives—in the Catholic Church and that elements of truth and sanctification can exist outside of its visible structure. This statement was not an endorsement of "indifferentism," the term used in the nineteenth century to characterize the belief that it doesn't really matter whether one is a Catholic Christian or a Protestant or Orthodox Christian. Vatican II, however, does move away from the nineteenth-century, Catholic position that all elements of truth and sanctification are to be found in the Roman Catholic Church and none is to be found elsewhere. Vatican II affirms that some elements of truth and sanctification are to be found in other Christian churches and elsewhere, while the Roman Catholic Church possesses those elements in their *fullness. Lumen gentium* offers a more inclusive understanding of church. Thus it asserts that the church "has many reasons for knowing it is joined to the baptized who are honored by the name of Christian, but do not profess the faith in its entirety or have not preserved unity of communion under the successor of Peter."[14] In addition, *Lumen gentium* affirms that Jews and Muslims have a special relationship to the People of God. In fact, even those who know neither the gospel nor the Christian church, including atheists, can attain salvation. The constitution declares:

> Those who, through no fault of their own, do not know the Gospel of Christ or his church, but who nevertheless seek God with a sincere heart, and, moved by grace, try in their actions to do his will as they know it through the dictates of their conscience—these too may attain eternal salvation. Nor will divine providence deny the assistance necessary for salvation to those who, without any fault of theirs, have not yet arrived at an explicit knowledge of God, and who, not without grace, strive to lead a good life. Whatever of good or truth is found amongst them is considered by the church to be a preparation for the Gospel and given by him who enlightens all men and women that they may at length have life.[15]

The third area of significant reorientation has to do with the relationship of the bishops to the pope. Here too, *Lumen gentium* exhibits both continuity with past declarations about the nature of the church and new emphases as well. On the one hand, for example, the constitution reiterates the teaching of Vatican I concerning the primacy of the pope and his infallible teaching authority (*Lumen gentium*, nos. 18 and 25). On the other hand, it also emphasizes the principle of collegiality, whereby bishops, together with the pope, share in exercising supreme power over the entire church (*Lumen gentium*, nos. 21-22).

From the very beginning of the council, the bishops assembled for Vatican II struggled to find a way to affirm the authority of bishops without separating it from the pope's authority.[16] Pope John XXIII signaled his own collaborative style already in the preparations for the council's first session. Instead of having the bishops from around the world respond to an agenda established in Rome, he wanted his fellow bishops to be actively involved in setting the council's agenda.[17] When John died on June 3, 1963, it was left to his successor, Pope Paul VI, to oversee the continuing discussions concerning the nature of the church and the relationship between pope and bishops. Two related points became central in those discussions: the effects of episcopal consecration and the meaning of episcopal collegiality. The latter notion was particularly contested, and a vocal minority of council fathers exerted steady pressure on Pope Paul to excise the notion of collegiality from conciliar documents.

Critics of collegiality argued that the doctrine has no basis in either scripture or tradition and is opposed to Vatican I. If nonetheless endorsed, collegiality would, in the words of Brazilian Archbishop de Proença-Sigaud, "give rise to a lack of discipline in the Church, whether with respect to the bishops and the Pope, or priests and bishops. . . . Bishops would be subjected to episcopal conferences, that is a collective authority, the worst kind there is. . . ."[18] In a letter to Pope Paul VI prior to the vote on the final draft in 1964, Cardinal Arcadio Larraona made this argument pointedly explicit, stating that if the council approved the novel idea of collegiality, the church would not only deny the doctrine it had held up to now, but also, in the process, would reveal that it had "for centuries acted against the divine law" by not previously operating in a collegial fashion. If the church had been mistaken in not previously endorsing episcopal collegiality, the door would now be open to claims that the church was mistaken on other issues as well.

How contentious Chapter 3 of *Lumen gentium* was is revealed by the plan for voting on it. Whereas for Chapters 1, 4, 5, and 6, there would be one vote by the council fathers on the chapter as a whole, for Chapter 3 there would be 39 votes on alternative wording of specific sections and only then a vote on the chapter as a whole. As John O'Malley points out, Chapter 3 "would be scrutinized like no other part of the document."[19]

Ultimately, Pope Paul VI felt compelled to intervene in the resolution of this issue in order to ensure the constitution's ratification at the council. He ordered the Doctrinal Commission to write an Explanatory Note to be added to Chapter 3 that would define the sense in which collegiality was to be understood.[20] The secretary general, Archbishop Felici, solemnly read the note in council on November 16, 1964, and he made it clear that the final, formal vote on *Lumen gentium* a few days later was to be governed by this interpretation. Paul VI apparently intended the note as his final attempt to win over those who had ceaselessly opposed the doctrine of collegiality ever since the second session (1963). In the speech (September 14, 1964) with which he had opened the third session of the council, Paul had identified the nature and function of the episcopate as "the weightiest and most delicate" of the important topics the council was to treat.[21] The Explanatory Note clarifies that "college" does not denote a group of equals who transfer their powers to their chairperson, but the body of bishops who are in communion with the pope and with one another. The bishops act as a college only when acting together with the pope and never independently. On the other hand, the pope's headship of the college does not preclude his acting on his own. This explanation was sufficient to re-assure the critics of collegiality that the doctrine would not contradict the church's tradition or undermine the pope's authority.[22] The supporters of collegiality were content that, although the note distinguished the powers a bishop receives through sacramental consecration (i.e., teaching, sanctifying, governing) from the exercise of those powers that requires a juridical determination by hierarchical authority, the constitution clearly affirmed that in the college the bishops, "while faithfully upholding the primacy and pre-eminence of their head, exercise their own proper authority for the good of their faithful, indeed even for the good of the whole church, the organic structure and harmony of which are strengthened by the continued influence of the holy Spirit."[23]

Although no document of Vatican II experienced more thoroughgoing revision between its first draft and the final approved document, *Lumen gentium* has been regarded as "the most momentous achievement of the council, both because of its important contents and because of its central place among the council documents."[24]

LADISLAS ÖRSY, S.J.

A Lesson in Ecclesiology*

Ladislas Örsy was born in Hungary on July 30, 1921. He entered the Society of Jesus in Budapest (Hungary) in 1943 and was ordained to the priesthood in 1951 in Louvain (Belgium).

Father Örsy earned a licentiate in philosophy at the Gregorian University in Rome in 1948, followed by a licentiate in theology at the Jesuit College at Louvain in 1952. Five years later he obtained his doctorate in canon law at the Gregorian University. In 1960 he earned an M.A. degree in civil law, which is equivalent to the J.D. degree in the United States, from the Honours School of Jurisprudence at Oxford University. Father Örsy taught at the Gregorian University from 1960 until 1966, when he came to the United States. In addition to being a visiting professor at the Graduate Theological Union (Berkeley, CA), the University of Fribourg (Switzerland), and the Pontifical Oriental Institute (Rome), Örsy taught at Fordham University (1967-1974) and at the Catholic University of America (1974-1991). Since 1991 he has been a professor of law at the Georgetown University Law Center, teaching philosophy of law, Roman law, and canon law.

Internationally respected as a leader in canon law, Father Örsy has written hundreds of articles in a variety of journals. His books include Marriage in Canon Law *(1986),* The Church: Learning and Teaching *(1987),* Theology and Canon Law: New Horizons for Legislation and Interpretation *(1992), and* Receiving the Council: Theological and Canonical Insights and Debates *(2009).*

During the Second Vatican Council he worked as a peritus *for participating bishops.*

---

* This story is an excerpt in modified form of the speech Örsy gave in 1999 at the Catholic Theological Society of America annual meeting, when he was awarded the John Courtney Murray Award.

94

It was through the council that I got my most important lesson in ecclesiology, and in particular that I learned about the hierarchy of truth and the role of the magisterium.

I did my theological studies before the council at the Jesuit Theological School in Louvain from 1948 to 1952. It was the time of the "new theology": its newness consisted in fresh approaches to the old mysteries. It promised well; it brought forth insights in abundance. The leaders were Henri de Lubac, Teilhard de Chardin, Yves Congar, M.-D. Chenu, Karl Rahner, Edward Schillebeeckx, John Courtney Murray, and many others. There were exciting exchanges. Disputations enlivened the investigations. We, mere students, watched and sensed that there was good wine in the making. At some point, however, the movement ground to a halt. A cold air of suspicion swept over the church; alarms were heard; censors and "visitators" were named and sent. They acted dutifully. They meant to preserve the tradition. In the name of the magisterium, and always for "prudence's sake," one outstanding theologian after another was removed from his chair or was ordered to keep silent on some issues, or quite simply in the name of obedience, was given a new job. Then the encyclical *Humani generis* was published. Its aim was to protect the Catholic community from error; it brought no inspiration for a new understanding of the old mysteries.

Once again, it seemed that there were no prophets in Israel; there was sadness in the land.

Then—who could have foreseen it?—an ecumenical council was called by the newly elected pope, John XXIII.

By those years, I was already teaching at the Gregorian University in Rome. We watched the preparations for the council. Over seventy documents were drafted covering the whole field of theology. Archbishop Felici (later cardinal), the secretary-elect of the council, foresaw one session, lasting at the most for two months, at which the episcopate of the world assembled in Rome would approve all that had been diligently prepared (mostly) under the direction of the Roman experts.

The council opened. And, lo and behold, theologians who a few years before were officially condemned, or effectively silenced, or discreetly transferred, were arriving in the Eternal City. They held seminars for bishops and gave lectures for all who cared about the great synod. That was just the beginning. As the council progressed, the very same theologians were helping the bishops to draft constitutions, decrees, and declarations. The once-exiled experts were offering new wine to the shepherds, and the shepherds liked it.

There I was, and I saw, and I watched. Through the deliberations and decisions of the council, the magisterium was correcting the magisterium. That is, the extraordinary magisterium of the council was supporting much of the new theology. It kept completing, rectifying, even reversing what was presented earlier as the "official teaching of the church." The council proclaimed not only a new hierarchy of truth but also showed in a practical way how the authority of day-to-day official teaching of the Holy See ought to be understood.

Thus, I received an existential training in the interpretation of "official teachings"—a training that has served me well to this day.

The Conversion of a Pope

Another event in my theological formation is difficult to classify. I had the grace to watch what might be termed the "conversion of a pope." Let me explain what I mean.

The council came to a critical point during the first session when the council fathers turned to the discussion of the Sources of Revelation. The draft was untouched by any new theology. In its paragraphs condemnations abounded. The discussion soon revealed that the majority of the bishops were against the draft. When the first "indicative" vote was taken, some 60 percent of the council fathers opposed its further discussion. By the rules of the council, however, two-thirds were needed to take the document off the floor. As the results were announced, the absurdity of the situation became manifest. The council had to go on discussing a document that the majority wanted to reject.

On that day, I happened to have dinner at the English college. A bishop from Down Under was another guest. He just arrived from the session at St. Peter's. He was upset and told me (there are words once heard that you never forget): "I am going home. This is a farce, not a council."

He did not leave. What he saw as a farce was turned into a council by Pope John XXIII.

By evening the Vatican Radio announced that the draft on the Sources of Revelation would be taken off the floor by the pope's order and sent back to a committee newly constituted. Moreover, so decided the pope, the council would have for all issues its own committees, each consisting of twenty-four members, eight appointed by the pope, sixteen elected by the council fathers. These new drafting groups would have the authority to change prepared texts and the power to propose new ones.

We know what those committees ultimately did: they quietly rejected nearly all the material studiously prepared and created the documents that brought the church into our modern world.

While the organization of the committees was under way, a story circulated in Rome. It was reported that a small deputation went to see the pope, a deputation consisting of persons of power and dignity from the Roman curia. They carried a warning to the supreme pontiff: "Holy Father, there is a danger. You must be careful. If you give that much freedom to the bishops, they will run away with the council. You will not be able to bring them back." It was reported that Pope John replied: "They too have the Spirit."

There was a magisterial statement, if ever there was one! The successor of Peter perceived the presence of the Spirit in the successors of the apostles and was willing to trust them. Out of this trust, the real council was born and produced plentiful good wine.

Of course, there is no way to know if Pope John XXIII really made that utterance. *Si non e vero, ben trovato* ["If it isn't true, it's well put"]. Whether he said it or not, the events proved that he created a climate of trust. But why do I speak of the "conversion of the pope"? Because before the opening of the council, it was well known that John XXIII was fully satisfied with the preparatory documents. He approved each one of them. Indeed, he was delighted with them. After all, he named the commissions that drafted them; he presided in person over the whole process. In all probability, he too expected their swift approval by the bishops at the council. Yet when the signs of the times warned him that his expectations were misplaced, he responded with humility and was willing to enter into new horizons with all the risk that such a step entailed. Yes, John XXIII had the greatness to learn from his bishops—without ever losing his effective leadership and apostolic authority. The pope called the council, and the bishops created the vision of the council.

The lesson? It is in that simple sentence: "They too have the Spirit." Creativity flourishes in a climate of trust.

MARTIN E. MARTY

Certainty and Condemnations

Martin E. Marty was born February 5, 1928—three hours before his fellow-Chicagoan Father Andrew Greeley—in West Point, Nebraska. He attended Lutheran seminaries, was ordained in 1952, and served as a parish pastor for eleven years. Meanwhile he received the Ph.D. at the University of Chicago, where he taught (the Fairfax M. Cone Distinguished Service Professor) from 1963 to 1998, chiefly in the Divinity School, where the Martin Marty Center for advanced studies has since been founded.

He was a columnist and senior editor at the Christian Century *for decades after 1956 and now is a writer for its blog. Marty was also founding president of the Park Ridge Center for the Study of Health, Faith, and Ethics. Among his many boards has been that of the Regents at St. Olaf College, Northfield, Minnesota (1988-2001), where he was chair and where he served as interim president late in 2000. He holds eighty honorary degrees. Among his other honors are the National Humanities Medal, the National Book Award, and the Medal of the American Academy of Arts and Sciences. He has been president of the American Catholic Historical Association, the American Society of Church History, and the American Academy of Religion. The Martin Marty Center at the University of Chicago, the Martin Marty Prize of the American Academy of Religion—both devoted to a concept that has concerned him for decades, public religion—and the Martin Marty Chair at St. Olaf College honor his themes.*

His recent books include Dietrich Bonhoeffer's "Letters and Papers from Prison": A Biography *(2011);* Building Cultures of Trust *(2010); and* The Christian World *(2009).*

At the time of the council he had just moved from parish ministry to his teaching role at the University of Chicago. He has written more than fifty books, including the three-volume Modern American Religion *(1997). He edited* Second Opinion *and the newsletter* Context. *Marty now shares a studio/study with his photographer son, Micah, with whom he has collaborated on five books. He enjoys and shares the interests of his musician-wife, Harriet, and the company of their extended family and does regular lecturing and consulting.*

MY JOURNALISTIC ASSIGNMENT WAS TO cover the latter part of the third session of the council in autumn 1964; a different *Christian Century* editor reported on each session. Members of the press ordinarily did not have a seat in the *aula*. But it happened that Bishop Peter Bartholome of St. Cloud, Minnesota, inspired by the fact that the first bishop of his diocese had been named Martin Marty, generously provided a courtesy pass. So for six weeks this unofficial observer enjoyed the rights, privileges, and perspectives of both press and observers.

That first October day was one of the two most memorable and decisive council moments for determining an aspect of my vocation. (The other was the day when Pope Paul VI frustrated the efforts of those who were writing and promoting the "Declaration on Religious Freedom," and when Chicago's Albert Cardinal Meyer and theologian John Courtney Murray rallied forces to project that debate into the fourth session.)

I arrived on October 29, 1964, the day four cardinals made tentative moves toward proposing a reexamination of the question of birth control as presently treated by the church. The story of how their move was also frustrated is not important for the lesson I drew from the occasion. And what I drew is based not on anything that appears in the council minutes or proceedings but on an anecdote passed on by the arch-anecdotalist among the observers, the late Professor Albert Outler.

As he heard and told it, there was much stir among the council fathers the evening of October 29 after the four speakers had shaken the serenity of many. The climactic encounter in Outler's hearing and telling occurred between an arch-conservative hierarch, who vehemently opposed the very idea of raising the question of reappraisal, and a more moderate one who thought it worth examining. If we change church teaching on contraception, argued the former, won't people expect other teachings to be changed? And what would now be the status of souls who we said had committed mortal sin by violating the church's norms concerning contraception?

This quandary was expressed again in dramatic form almost two years later. At the final meeting of the Papal Birth Control Commission on June 20-21, 1966, Bishop Carlo Colombo spoke vehemently against backtracking on contraception. Father Marcelino Zalba, a Spanish Jesuit, chimed in his support: If we change the church's teaching on contraception, what about "the millions we have sent to hell if these norms are not valid"? Patty Crowley, a married Catholic from Chicago, shot back: "Father Zalba, do you really believe God has carried out all your orders?"[25] Long after I lost the pounds I had gained while being entertained by various religious orders—Rome was a great place for Protestants to enjoy hospitality that year—and after the vivid recall of sights, sounds, smells, and textures of that halcyon autumn began to wane and fade, I have lived off the meanings of that kind of question. And I have carried it over into subsequent ecumenical and interfaith encounters or Christian-secular debates, where the temptation to be too sure about whom we save and whom we damn is strong.

I took from that little exchange not the notion that "we," in church and world, do not get to or do not have to make decisions. The council fathers and their *periti* had to deliberate and the bishops had to vote on important issues with which we, non-Catholics and Catholics alike, still live. But how they deliberated and what they have done since the council voting does matter.

Much of my work in recent years has had to do with militant fundamentalists, ethno-nationalists, uncivil citizens, and those who by actions and talk born of their cocksureness militated against ecumenical, reconciling, and civil speech and action. Often in their presence I have wanted to invoke the spirit of Oliver Cromwell, who wanted some opponents "by the bowels of Christ" to consider that they might be mistaken.

The need to ask whether God ratifies all our decisions is most appropriate when the deepest questions, the eternal puzzles, get deliberated. In the case of those two council participants the issue was eternity and destiny itself. Those in authority and those who gravitate to the viewpoints of the oversure church authorities are quite confident that they and God know and decide the same things, thanks to their interpretation of scriptures or of magisterial churchly teaching. So they can consign those with whom they disagree to hell, hereafter or now. Should the condemner be so sure about divine ratifications?

Martin Luther has sent shivers into the minds of some theologians who have read in the reformer's debates the shocking notion that *Deus absonditus* ["the hidden God"] is hidden not only in revelation (e.g., in bread and wine and water and grammar) but also behind revelation. "Now we know in part. . . ." The best book title this Lutheran has read on Luther's thought is *Let God Be God*, something that Luther, a regular consigner-to-hell of his foes, intended to do but often did not. Patty Crowley, who questioned Father Zalba in 1966, and the cardinal, who challenged the conservative hierarch in 1964, were both letting God be God.

From Protestant theologian Reinhold Niebuhr I have learned and adopted an ironic perspective. It is a biblically grounded awareness that inside our knowledge there is enough ignorance, inside our innocence there is enough guilt, along with our virtue there comes enough vice, that no matter what our actions, they will not always turn out to be as positive as we had designed and thought and hoped them to be. As one adopts this perspective there is a danger that we might retreat into cynicism and lapse into the expression of an "after all, everything has been tried, so why should we act," or a "what fools these mortals be" dismissive spirit.

Niebuhr went on to say that, in the spirit of Psalm 2:4, the same God who sits in the heavens and laughs at and holds in derision the prideful and cocksure also holds us responsible and does not dishonor human aspiration. So I took from the best of the council fathers and the most promising of their actions a sense that they must make decisions, but leave some of the consequences and judgment about their validity to the God in whose name the council was convoked. I hope my own life, work, and ministry were altered by a secondhand report of a second-level conversation at the council. I certainly intended it to, and have made decisions in the light of a calling reinforced in Rome. Whether or not God ratifies all those decisions . . . ? Read Psalm 2:4.

CHARLES E. CURRAN

The Church as the Pilgrim People of God

Charles Curran was born on March 30, 1934, the third of four children, to Gertrude Beisner Curran and John F. Curran. He went to the seminary in Rochester, New York, graduating with a B.A. from St. Bernard's College and Seminary in 1955 before going to study in Rome. After receiving a doctorate in sacred theology from the Gregorian University in 1961 and a doctorate in sacred theology with a specialization in moral theology from the Accademia Alfonsiana, Curran returned to teach moral theology at St. Bernard's Seminary in Rochester, New York, from 1961 to 1965. His teaching career at the Catholic University of America from 1965 to 1988 was marked by three significant events—in 1967 the faculty and students went on strike and successfully overturned the original decision of the Board of Trustees not to renew Curran's contract; in 1968 he was the spokesperson for a group of over six hundred Catholic scholars who issued a statement of dissent from the major conclusions of the encyclical Humanae vitae; *in 1986 after an eight-year investigation, the Congregation for the Doctrine of the Faith concluded that Curran was neither "suitable nor eligible to exercise the function of a Professor of Catholic Theology." After losing a lawsuit to retain his right to teach Catholic theology at Catholic University of America, Curran ultimately accepted the Elizabeth Scurlock University Professorship of Human Values at Southern Methodist University in 1991.*

Father Curran has served as president of three national academic societies—the Catholic Theological Society of America, the Society of Christian Ethics, and the American Theological Society. The Catholic Theological Society of America in 1972 named him the first recipient of the John Courtney Murray Award for distinguished achievement in theology. In 2010, he was elected to membership in the American Academy of Arts and Sciences. Curran has authored more than thirty books in moral theology. His 2008 Catholic Moral Theology in the United States: A History, *from Georgetown University Press, won the 2008 American Publishers Award for Professional and Scholarly Excellence in Theology and Religion.*

The diocese of Rochester, New York, sent me to live at the North American College and to study theology at the Gregorian University in Rome in September 1955 to prepare for ordination to priestly ministry. The vast majority of the Jesuit professors of theology at the Greg had been teaching there for twenty years or more. The professor's book in ecclesiology insisted from the very first thesis that the Roman Catholic Church was the kingdom of God on earth, founded by Jesus with a hierarchical structure emphasizing the role of the papacy. Such was my understanding of the church.

In 1958 my bishop informed me (that was the way things went before Vatican II!) that beginning in the fall of 1959 I should work toward a doctorate at the Gregorian in moral theology in order to teach moral theology at the diocesan seminary of St. Bernard's. In addition to going to the Greg, I also attended lectures and eventually obtained a second doctorate from the Accademia Alfonsiana, which specialized in moral theology. At the Alfonsiana I encountered a new approach to moral theology that emphasized the universal call of all Christians to holiness with a strong biblical and liturgical basis. Bernard Häring was the primary but not the only professor working in this direction. I invited many of my fellow graduate student priests to go over and listen to Häring's lectures.

From Häring I also learned a different understanding of the church. In a course on conversion, he insisted that the church too was in need of conversion. We are a pilgrim people. Likewise the church is the People of God with all, not just hierarchy, religious, and priests, called by God to holiness.

I left Rome in June 1961 to begin teaching moral theology and canon law at St. Bernard's Seminary. (Some of my students had already studied more canon law there than I had studied in Rome!) I left Rome with a different understanding of the church from what I had first learned there. But I also left Rome with the feeling that neither Pope John XXIII nor the future Vatican Council were going to bring about much change. Such a feeling needs to be explained.

I was in St. Peter's Square the early evening of October 28, 1958, when John XXIII was elected and came to the balcony to give his first blessing. In fact, on the basis of a tip I found in either *Time* magazine or the *New York Times*, I won five dollars by betting on Roncalli.

My first impression of the new pope was not positive. Pius XII was an aristocratic figure with a lean posture, who raised his eyes to God and blessed the crowd with three very precise signs of the cross. John was a rotund man who, before finishing the triple blessing, started waving to the crowd. This very young, impressionistic, newly ordained priest was somewhat taken aback.

However, John XXIII's unpretentiousness, gentleness, and pastoral concern scored high points. Some excitement accompanied his announcement on January 25, 1959, that he planned three works for the renewal of the church—a synod for Rome, the updating of canon law, and an ecumenical council.

I was doing graduate work during the Synod of Rome in the last week of January 1960. In my estimation it was a disaster. The 755 statutes were prepackaged and dealt primarily with insignificant things such as clerical dress and attendance at the opera and movies. The format was even worse than the content. The participants simply sat, listened to what was read out, and then all voted yes. There was no discussion of any kind. This was the old ecclesiology at work with no participation of those who were voting members of the synod. Such an approach did not augur well for the future ecumenical council.

In June 1960 the pope appointed the preparatory commissions to draft the documents for the council. The cardinals of the Roman curia chaired these commissions, and most of the members came from the Roman approach to theology. No one expected these curia officials to bring about much change.

I left Rome in late June of 1961. Just before leaving, Father F. X. Murphy, who had been a professor of mine at the Alfonsiana, invited me to a long lunch. F. X. regaled me with stories of the shenanigans and intransigent approach of the Roman curia, especially with regard to the upcoming ecumenical council. As a result of this conversation and my awareness that his mother's maiden name was Rynne, I knew who was the author of the famous "Letter from Vatican City" that appeared in the *New Yorker* at the very beginning of the first session of the council.

My first year teaching in the seminary (1961-1962) was very busy but most gratifying. The news I heard from Rome, however, was quite negative. Josef Fuchs, my moral theology professor at the Greg, was forbidden to teach undergraduate seminarians. Similar restrictions had earlier been placed on two professors at the Biblical Institute.

When Vatican II opened in October 1962, I was not expecting much. But things changed in a hurry. The opening address of John XXIII clearly indicated he saw the need for reform. He emphasized *aggiornamento* ["updating"], castigated the prophets of doom who saw nothing but prevarication and ruin in the modern world, insisted on the need for mercy and a positive presentation of church teaching rather than severity and condemnations, and distinguished between the substance of the deposit of faith and the way in which it is expressed and presented.

The first session proved that the curial agenda was not going to prevail. The more progressive draft on the liturgy, which providentially was the first one discussed, showed that the vast majority of the participants favored significant change in the church's liturgy, which had repercussions for a changed understanding of the church. The council participants rejected the prepared documents on divine revelation and the church that came from the curia-dominated preparatory commissions. The newer draft on the church prepared for the second session of the council emphasized the church as the People of God, a pilgrim church with a hierarchical structure. The subsequent sessions had their tense moments, but it seems after the first session that the general direction of the council and its understanding of church were now clear.

My assessment of John XXIII differs from that of others. I do not think he had a clear idea at all of what he wanted the council to do when he first called it. The greatness of John XXIII was that he was open to the call of the Spirit—both in the tradition of the church and in the signs of the times.

Over the years I have had my own tensions with the church, but the understanding of the church as the pilgrim People of God has always sustained me.

RICHARD ROHR, O.F.M.

Honesty and Creativity in the Church

Father Richard Rohr is a Franciscan of the New Mexico Province. He was born in 1943 in Kansas. He entered the Franciscans in 1961 and was ordained to the priesthood in 1970. He received his master's degree in theology from the University of Dayton and did further studies in Scripture at the University of Notre Dame and the University of San Francisco.

Rohr was the founder of the New Jerusalem Community in Cincinnati, Ohio, in 1971, and the Center for Action and Contemplation in Albuquerque, New Mexico, in 1986. After the initial founding periods, he handed both groups over to lay leadership and direction. New Jerusalem is still an alive community today in Cincinnati, and Rohr presently works with the Center in Albuquerque.

Rohr is probably best known for his numerous audio- and videotapes. Articles by Father Richard have appeared in numerous publications, many of his tapes have come out in fourteen books, and many of these have been translated into other languages. His recent books include Everything Belongs: The Gift of Contemplative Prayer *(2003),* The Naked Now: Learning to See How the Mystics See *(2009), and* Falling Upward: A Spirituality for the Two Halves of Life *(2011).*

Father Rohr now lives in a hermitage behind his Franciscan community in Albuquerque and divides his time between local work, the county jail, and preaching and teaching on all continents. He considers the proclamation of the gospel to be his primary call and uses many different platforms to communicate that message. Scripture, the integration of action and contemplation, community building, peace and justice issues, male spirituality, the enneagram, and eco-spirituality are all themes that he makes use of for the sake of the gospel.

I WAS FORTUNATE TO BE studying philosophy at Duns Scotus College in Detroit during the years of the Second Vatican Council. Because we had some very well-trained Franciscans at that time, they taught us how to think—how we know what we know instead of just what we should know, which seems to be more common today. Through phenomenology and what we called "philosophical psychology," we learned to assess and make use of our own "audio-visual aids," which developed a wonderful capacity for self-critical thinking and historical-critical thinking too. In short, we were taught an awful lot about our humanity before we piled too much divinity onto it.

By the time I moved to theology at St. Leonard's in Dayton in 1966, I was given a further gift. Our province had been wise enough to send a group of talented young friars to study theology in Rome during the very years of the council. They returned just in time to teach us! Again, we were not given simple doctrinal conclusions as much as the process of getting to those conclusions. We were not propagandized as much as educated. We were not formed into "system men" (a reasonable position for a Franciscan), although we were given a deep respect for how the system got to where it is, both its strengths and its weaknesses. As you would expect, it led us to know how to work within the historical situation with honesty and even courage because we knew we had been given the tools to do so with integrity. We had not been lied to. We had not been kept inside a closed system. The veil of the Wizard of Oz had been parted for us. We had nothing to hide from or to hide from others.

As wise people will know, this only gave us more self-confidence and more courage. We faced our questions and doubts in a faith-filled context, and with wise and educated men who could lead us through our doubts and criticisms. We did not have to spend the rest of our lives resolving or reacting or repressing. Only thirty years later do I know how unique and how blessed was that period. Most of my brother priests before my time were not given such an opportunity for honesty; many of my brother priests formed in the last fifteen years do not even want such honesty, or, worse yet, seminaries are afraid to give it to them. Yet, we are the very people who quote Jesus as saying that "the truth will set us free." I wonder if we believe it.

"Afraid" is the key word. Truth and gospel can flourish only in a situation where fear is not in control, or at least where our fears are faced honestly. Today we do not have such a safe harbor. It feels like everybody is afraid of everybody: seminarians of faculty and faculty of seminarians, priests of bishops and bishops of priests, Rome of bishops and bishops of Rome, laity of clergy and clergy of laity. Who would have believed that things could change so much in one lifetime?

We know from history that greatness does not emerge in times of mere survivalism. Greatness emerges when people are forced to think honestly and creatively. I thank God profoundly for the time in which I was educated and formed. I thank God for such wise and holy teachers as that period produced. I know now that I enjoyed both a safe harbor and a wonderful window of opportunity that few people have enjoyed in history. So sad that the window closed so quickly. So sad that the church cannot create a harbor in an unsafe world. It is the next generations of the church that will suffer. It is the gospel itself that is taking a back seat to fear, protectionism, and power.

We never seem ready for Jesus' great and self-effacing adventure.

ROSEMARY RADFORD RUETHER

The Conflict of Ecclesiologies
in the Legacy of Vatican II

Rosemary Radford Ruether was born in 1936 in Georgetown, Texas. She holds a B.A. in philosophy from Scripps College (1958), an M.A. in ancient history (1960) and a Ph.D. in classics and patristics (1965) from Claremont Graduate School (CA).

At present, Ruether is an emerita professor teaching feminist theological studies at Claremont Graduate University and Claremont School of Theology. She is an emerita professor at Garrett-Evangelical Theological Seminary in Evanston, Illinois, and at Graduate Theological Union in Berkeley, California.

Reuther is the author of forty-six books and numerous articles on theology and feminism, ecology, and social justice. Among her most recent books are America, Amerikka: Elect Nation and Imperial Violence *(2007),* Christianity and Social Systems: Historical Constructions and Ethical Challenges *(2009), and* Many Forms of Madness: Mental Illness and the Mental Health System *(2010).*

THE UNFOLDING OF THE VATICAN II ecumenical council was a very important event in the shaping of my thought and life. I was twenty-five when the council opened in 1962 and twenty-nine when it closed in 1965. During that time I was a doctoral student in patristics and the historical theology of Western Christianity at Claremont Graduate School in Claremont, California. In 1965 I completed my doctoral dissertation on the thought of the Cappadocian church father Gregory Nazianzus (Oxford Clarendon, 1969) and had also written my first book on ecclesiology, *The Church against Itself* (Herder and Herder, 1967), in which I explored the tension between historical existence and eschatological self-understanding in the life of the church.

My husband, Herman Ruether, and I were deeply involved in liturgical renewal as oblates of the Benedictine community at Valyermo,

California, and also attended what was then called the "Commonweal Club," which discussed progressive Catholic issues. I taught classes in church history and Christian thought at Immaculate Heart College in Los Angeles, a liberal college run by the Immaculate Heart Sisters, who were in deep conflict with the archbishop of Los Angeles, Francis Cardinal McIntyre. They would opt in 1969 to become a noncanonical order, selling their college and founding an autonomous master's program in feminist spirituality. Thus the things going on in Rome during the council were of intense interest and relevance to me and the Catholic circles of which I was a part.

What was evident to me, in following the progress of the council at the time (and still recognized today in historical accounts: see, for example, Giuseppe Alberigo's *A Brief History of Vatican II*, 2006), is that the decision-making process and the resultant documents were shaped throughout by a deep internal conflict between an aggressive faction representing the curia, accustomed to absolute centralized control and committed to a hierarchical ecclesiology, and the vision of John XXIII and his supporters attracted to a more democratic church open to the modern world and seeking renewal from its biblical and patristic roots.

Pope John XXIII had not consulted this curial group when he first announced the council. They sought to control it from the start, either to prevent it from happening altogether or else to define it as simply the completion of Vatican I. The pope in turn sought to impede their control and to open it to the free deliberation of the world's bishops, who were unaccustomed to being thinkers and actors in their own right. Once the more than two thousand episcopal delegates and their advisors arrived, this curial faction became a voting minority, but they remained very vocal and aggressive and sought to control the process and the ecclesiological perspective of the council and its documents at every turn. This effort had a quiet but consistent counterpart in the pope, while he lived. When he died, Pope Paul VI continued support for the council and its open process, but in a weaker and more ambivalent way.

The resulting documents reflect perspectives that are mixed and inconsistent, containing pieces of different ecclesiologies. They are also of uneven quality, some deeply informed by a renewed biblical theology of prophetic transformation and others, such as the document on the mass media, without innovative insight. The curial group made sure that the documents and public statements of the council continually reaffirmed that there was no departure from strict papal primacy over the whole church, while the reformers sought to balance this primacy with the new emphasis on the collegiality of the bishops. In the document on the church (*Lumen gentium*) and the "Decree on the Pastoral Office of the Bishops" (*Christus dominus*) these reformers sought to clarify an understanding of the episcopal office as a continuation of the college of the apostles within which the pope stands as a central member, making them not simply vicars of the pope but foundational representatives of both local churches and, together, of the universal church.

Most significantly, the document on the church also sought to ground its ecclesiology in a theology of the whole People of God. A very significant shift took place in the order of this document from its original prepared form to its final confirmation. Originally it began with a reflection on the "mystery of the church," followed by the hierarchical constitution of pope and bishops, then by a discussion of the laity. In the process of deliberation in the assembly this was decisively revised, placing the topic of the People of God immediately after the opening discussion of the mystery of the church. Thus, the shared baptism of all Christians (including members of non-Catholic churches) became the foundational ground of the church. The ordained hierarchy were situated within the whole People of God as servants of a common mission and call to holiness they all share, rather than outside and above them as their source.

This shift represents a decisive reorientation of ecclesiology. In the first "trickle down" view of the church, God the Father and Christ are seen as imparting redemptive power from above to the pope, who in turn imparts this to bishops, and they to priests. The laity fall outside the "perfect society" of the clerical hierarchy, ministered to but with no ministry of their own. The shift that took place in the document that put the People of God immediately after the discussion of the mystery of the church fundamentally recasts this ecclesiology. The primary reality that flows from the mystery of the church is the whole People of God born from baptism. The hierarchy then arises within this foundational reality as its self-articulation and servants. It is fair to say that the inconsistencies of the Vatican II documents reflect remnants of this older, top-down ecclesiology partly but not fully overcome by an entirely new vision.

The council closed on December 8, 1965, after no fewer than 168 assemblies over parts of four years, rushing in the last months to complete and confirm no fewer than twelve documents and decrees. This long process was an unprecedented effort to chart a renewed church in both its internal vision and structure and its relation to other Christians, non-Christian religions, and "the world." But it left a fundamental lacuna. While a new vision was at least partly laid out, no plan of implementation was defined, except for the decree on liturgy. After the departure of the voting majority of bishops, many of whom had been themselves partly transformed in their understanding of who they were within the church as baptized People of God and in relation to the pope, it was the curia, who had consistently sought to undermine this new vision, that were left in charge to implement the work of the council. Clearly their main intention was to minimize the new vision and return as much as possible to the trickle-down ecclesiology that they favored.

As long as Pope Paul VI remained alive, this reversion was partly impeded. But with his death and the quick demise of his successor, John Paul I, the curial conservatives had on their side a new pope, John Paul II, who largely favored their perspective. For the twenty-seven years of his papacy, followed by that of Benedict XVI, the Catholic Church has experienced a leadership dedicated to restoring top-down centralization. This has focused on many aspects of the institutional church. After Vatican II a number of progressive bishops were in power. Many of these had themselves been converted through the influence of the council to a more democratic, liberationist church. One thinks of figures such as Samuel Ruiz in Chiapas, Mexico; Helder Camera in Recife, Brazil; and Oscar Romero in El Salvador. Pope John Paul II systematically sought to rein in prophetic bishops and replace them, either by cutting short their reign or after their retirement, with conservative bishops submissive to Rome. Total control by the pope, as the one who alone selects bishops, with little or no local input, was reinforced.

The dominance of right-wing Catholicism was reconfirmed through a number of policies. One of these was the cultivation of Opus Dei as the favored way of Catholic spirituality, and the placement of Opus Dei bishops in key areas, such as Peru and El Salvador. The independence of theological teaching in Catholic colleges was reined in, demanding that theological faculties be made subordinate to ecclesiastical authority. Progressive seminaries favoring a liberation church were also either closed down or reined in to restore a conservative theology and way of life. Women's religious orders, especially in the United States, were viewed with suspicion, and continually "investigated" to put them back under hierarchical control. Women's ordination, not even imagined in the 1960s, became totally rejected, and any candidate for bishop or seminary leader banned who entertained its possibility. In short, the pope and his inquisitor in the Holy Office sought to systematically remove the institutional basis for a democratic, prophetic local church.

Has Vatican II died over the last fifty years? Its alternative vision remains still present in its documents. Many still cherish this vision, but feel increasingly marginalized in the church. We await a new birth in the Holy Spirit from the grass roots.

DANIEL E. PILARCZYK

Bringing Old and New Together

Daniel E. Pilarczyk was born in Dayton, Ohio, in 1934. He attended Catholic elementary schools and entered St. Gregory's Seminary in 1948. After high school and two years of college there, he studied philosophy and theology at the Pontifical Urban University in Rome. He was ordained a priest in 1959 and earned a doctorate in theology in 1961. Upon his return to the archdiocese of Cincinnati, he became assistant chancellor and began studies in classical civilization. He earned an M.A. from Xavier University and a Ph.D. from the University of Cincinnati. In 1963 he was assigned to full-time teaching at St. Gregory's Seminary, where he became rector in 1968. In 1974 he was appointed auxiliary bishop to Joseph Bernardin, then archbishop of Cincinnati. Pilarczyk was vicar for education in addition to being vicar general. He became archbishop of Cincinnati in 1982. During his years as archbishop he served as representative of the United States hierarchy to the International Commission on English in the Liturgy and chaired its episcopal board from 1991 to 1997. He served as vice-president (1986-1989) and president (1989-1992) of the National Conference of Catholic Bishops. He also chaired several committees of the conference, including education, liturgy, and doctrine. Archbishop Pilarczyk has received seven honorary degrees and published about twenty books, including Twelve Tough Issues: What the Church Teaches and Why (1988; rev. ed., 2002), and Live Letters (2002), a series of commentaries on the second readings for Sunday liturgies.

THE YEAR 1969 WAS A terrible time to be a seminary rector. Everything in the country seemed to be up for grabs, and much of what was in the church as well. Seminarians were demonstrating all over the country for greater freedom and greater say in their preparation for the priesthood. Nobody knew exactly what lay ahead, most certainly not the rector of St. Gregory's Seminary in Cincinnati.

I had been appointed rector the year before at age thirty-three in what was, as I learned later, a desperation move by our eighty-three-year-old Archbishop Alter. During my first year in office, I made some rather minor changes in the seminary program. These were greeted with enthusiasm by both students and faculty, and I thought that I had solved the seminary's problems for the foreseeable future. Toward the end of that first year, however, some faculty members came to me to say that, while things were pretty quiet for the present, there would almost certainly be big trouble unless further, more sweeping changes were made. In a state of chronic panic, I established a committee of faculty and students whose purpose was to build up anew from top to bottom the whole seminary program.

One aspect of the changes was the academic program. It had been clear to me for some time that the college "theology" program was inadequate. I put together another committee to deal with this particular question. I don't remember now what we did about most of the program, but I do recall that one of the committee's members, who had been a *peritus* at Vatican II, urged us to set up a course in the council's "Pastoral Constitution on the Church in the Modern World." He said it was the obvious way to introduce college freshmen to contemporary ecclesial realities.

I volunteered to teach this course. Although I had a degree in theology, I had never done any regular teaching of it before. I had to do lots of reading, since the kind of theology that I had studied in Rome before 1961 was not exactly the kind of theology that lay beneath the council's teaching. I also had to do lots of thinking, since the council's whole mindset was different from the mindset I had absorbed. In addition to that, I had to learn how to teach through lectures rather than through the analysis of texts that I had become proficient in as a teacher of Latin and Greek.

During the summer of 1969, I spent hours each day reading about the history of the council and about Christian secularity. Here in *Gaudium et spes* I was faced with a theological world that was concrete rather than abstract, practical rather than theoretical, oriented toward the world rather than heaven, toward the future rather than the past, toward the community rather than the individual. I remember walking around the seminary campus trying to figure out how all this new stuff fit in with what I had been taught. It was hard work, and sometimes frightening.

That autumn I taught the course for the first time to our college freshmen. Once they got the hang of my teaching methods and of what I expected of them, they loved it. *Gaudium et spes* spoke loud and clear to them. By popular demand, I offered the course again during the second semester of that year and four more times during the years I remained as seminary rector.

Meanwhile, there were suggestions from the students that other courses in the Vatican II documents be made available. Since I had come up with a method of study and presentation with *Gaudium et spes*, I was not unwilling to go a little further afield. I taught courses in *Lumen gentium*, *Sacrosanctum concilium*, *Dei verbum*, and several other council documents. These were electives and had to be taught in the evening so that students from several classes could participate. Eventually I set up a plan for studying and teaching all the council documents. This project had to be scrapped, however, when I was appointed auxiliary bishop and left seminary work.

In the process of responding to what my faculty colleagues and I had perceived to be the theological needs of the students, I had backed into a whole new theological specialty. It was hard work, not only because of the quantity of reading and study that it required, but also because of the effort to understand how these new approaches and new insights could be in harmony with what I had learned before. But it was a wonderful way to prepare to be a bishop. My work in the teachings of Vatican II reshaped my view of church and ministry and revelation and world and gave me excellent spiritual and intellectual equipment for the exercise of church leadership. Nobody planned it that way. Things more or less just happened. But that's the way God's providence often works.

As I go about my work in the archdiocese of Cincinnati, I often encounter priests who were my students in their seminary days. It's not unusual for us to trade memories about our time together with *Gaudium et spes* and *Lumen gentium*. I am grateful to them for their kind reminiscences, and grateful to the Lord for the way in which he has provided for all of us and for his church.

FRANCIS SULLIVAN, S.J.

Vatican II on the Charisms of the Faithful

Francis Sullivan was born on May 21, 1922, in Boston. After graduating from Boston College High School, he entered the novitiate of the New England Province of the Society of Jesus and was ordained to the priesthood in 1951. During his course of studies, he obtained an M.A. in philosophy at Boston College in 1945, an M.A. in classics at Fordham University in 1948, and an S.T.L. at Weston College in 1952.

After ordination he was sent to Rome for further study of theology at the Pontifical Gregorian University, where he obtained an S.T.D. in 1956. Although he had expected to return to his province to teach at Weston College, he was then assigned to teach ecclesiology at the Gregorian University. He continued to do this for the next thirty-six years, serving also as dean of the faculty of theology from 1964 to 1970. After being declared emeritus in 1992, Sullivan returned to New England, where, until 2009, he was an adjunct professor of theology at Boston College.

He has published seven books and numerous articles. His more recent important works include Magisterium: Teaching Authority in the Catholic Church *(1983),* Salvation Outside the Church? *(1992),* Creative Fidelity: Weighing and Interpreting Documents of the Magisterium *(1996), and* From Apostles to Bishops *(2001).*

For his outstanding contributions to theology, Sullivan was awarded the John Courtney Murray Award of the Catholic Theological Society of America in 1994.

DURING THE MONTH OF OCTOBER 1963, the bishops at Vatican II were discussing the draft of the "Dogmatic Constitution on the Church." This draft included a paragraph on "the charisms of the faithful." From time to time the bishops from the United States would meet at the North American College to discuss issues that were coming up at the council, and they would usually invite a theologian to give them his ideas on the issue and respond to their questions about it. It happened that I was the theologian who was asked to give a presentation on the question of the charisms of the faithful.

At that time I had been teaching ecclesiology at the Gregorian University for about six years, and I have to confess that this was the first time I had ever prepared a lecture on the charisms of the faithful. My study of the question led me to realize that there are two quite different notions of "charism" current in Catholic theology. According to the article in the *Dictionnaire de Spiritualité*, charisms are extraordinary gifts of grace, such as one finds in the lives of saints and mystics. However, A. Lemonnyer, author of the article on charisms in the *Dictionnaire de la Bible, Supplement*, drew quite a different notion of charism from an analysis of the teaching of St. Paul. According to this view, charisms are gifts of grace that equip people for the roles and ministries that they are to have in the Body of Christ. Some of these gifts are extraordinary, but many are not, and they are distributed widely among the faithful, in view of the contribution that each is intended to make to the life of the whole body. I also found that it was this notion of the charisms that had been affirmed in works by Yves Congar and Karl Rahner. This, then, was the view that I presented in my talk to the American bishops. I later learned that this was also the view that Cardinal Suenens defended in a speech that he gave at the council in response to Cardinal Ruffini, who had insisted that charisms were extraordinary gifts that one could not expect to find among the ordinary faithful.

After I had given my talk at the North American College, the thought came to me that the paragraph in the draft text that treated the charisms of the faithful could be improved, especially by making more ample use of the teaching and language of St. Paul. So I composed a paragraph that I thought was better than the one in the draft. But I was not a *peritus* of the council and did not have a way to submit an emendation on my own. However, a Jesuit from the New England Province, who had been my rector in the novitiate and subsequently my provincial superior, was now the Bishop of Kingston (Jamaica) and hence a member of the council. I had spoken with him a number of times during his stay in Rome, and now I recalled that he had once invited me to give him any thoughts that he might be able to use for an intervention at the council. So I told him about the paragraph that I had composed about the charisms of the faithful. The bishops were invited to submit in writing any emendations that they wished to propose for the improvement of the draft texts. Bishop McEleney graciously accepted my text and promised to submit it in his own name. When the constitution *Lumen gentium* was promulgated, I had the pleasure of seeing that the paragraph on the charisms of the faithful now corresponded substantially with what I had written. And when the *Acta Synodalia* were eventually published, I was able to verify the fact that in reworking that paragraph, the Theological Commission had accepted an emendation that had been proposed by Bishop John McEleney of Kingston, Jamaica.[26]

Impact on My Life and Ministry

The immediate impact that Vatican II had on me was on my ministry as a teacher of ecclesiology. Before the council began, I had been teaching the course on the church at the Gregorian for six years, and obviously I had been teaching pre-Vatican II ecclesiology. The conciliar decrees, especially the "Dogmatic Constitution on the Church" (*Lumen gentium*) and the "Decree on Ecumenism" (*Unitatis redintegratio*), had a significant impact on the course of ecclesiology that I offered to my students in the aftermath of the council.

About two years after the close of Vatican II, a development took place that in some respects was influenced by the council, and which eventually had a profound effect on my life and ministry as a priest. This was the entry of the Charismatic Renewal into the Catholic Church. I am convinced that Vatican II's positive teaching concerning the charisms of the faithful had a great deal to do with the acceptance of the Charismatic Renewal in the Catholic Church. I can hardly imagine that it would have met such acceptance if the council had adopted the view of Cardinal Ruffini that charisms are not to be found among the ordinary faithful. In any case, I think it unlikely that if the council had accepted Ruffini's view, I myself would have had an open mind about the claims that people were making about the charisms they had received through their participation in this movement.

I was not at all inclined to take part in it myself, but it excited my interest, and I took the time to become more informed about it. It was at least partly due to the positive teaching of Vatican II on the charisms of the faithful that I was able to come to the conclusion that many people could be experiencing genuine charisms as the fruit of being "baptized in the Spirit." That remained a theoretical judgment, with no basis in personal experience, until about five years after the council, when Father Carlo Martini, S.J., who at that time was a professor at the Biblical Institute, invited me to a meeting of a prayer group that had formed in Rome. Although my progress toward full involvement was hesitant and gradual, I continued to meet regularly with that prayer group until I left Rome twenty years later. Membership in "Lumen Christi" proved to be a great grace for my spiritual life, and also gave me new opportunities for ministry. Through the mysterious working of Divine Providence, the Second Vatican Council, and especially its teaching on the charisms of the faithful, has had a significant impact on my life and ministry.

LAWRENCE S. CUNNINGHAM

Tensions in Vatican II and How to Proceed Today

Lawrence S. Cunningham was born in 1935 and raised in Florida. He was educated both in Rome at the Gregorian University, where he received an S.T.L. degree, and in the United States at Florida State University, where he earned an M.A. in English and a Ph.D. in humanities.

After teaching at Florida State and the University of Scranton, he joined the faculty of the University of Notre Dame in 1988. Cunningham served as chair of the Theology Department there for six years. Currently he is the emeritus John A. O'Brien Professor of Theology at Notre Dame.

Cunningham lectures frequently here and abroad. He is the author or editor of over twenty books. Some of Cunningham's recent ones include A Brief History of the Saints *(2005);* An Introduction to Catholicism *(2009); and* Things Seen and Unseen: A Catholic Theologian's Notebook *(2010). Over the years, he has won three Catholic Press Association awards for his popular religious writing. Additionally, he continues to write the Book Notes column for* Commonweal *magazine.*

During his four years in Rome, Cunningham witnessed the death of Pope Pius XII and the election of Pope John XXIII, and, purely by chance, was present at the Basilica of Saint Paul-Outside-the-Walls when Pope John announced his decision to call an ecumenical council.

I REMEMBER QUITE CLEARLY RUNNING to a news kiosk near Saint Peter's Square to get a newspaper to read the biography of Angelo Roncalli, who had just been proclaimed pope from the loggia of the basilica by Cardinal Alfredo Ottaviani. Unknown to me at that moment, the new pope would quickly gain our attention both by his pastoral concerns and by his almost casual announcement at the Basilica of Saint Paul-

Outside-the-Walls, shortly after he attained the papacy, that he intended to (1) convoke a Roman synod (the first in centuries); (2) begin the revision of the Code of Canon Law; and (3) convoke an ecumenical council.

As a theological student at the Jesuit-run Gregorian University, I was well aware that many things were stirring in the Catholic world. The Assisi Conference had gingerly raised the issue of a vernacular liturgy. We were reading the hitherto suppressed works of Teilhard de Chardin (mailed from outside of Italy because his works were not easily found in the Roman bookstores). Josef Fuchs, who was newly appointed to the chair of moral theology at the Gregorian, was a fresh voice in the casuistic field of ethics, and Bernard Lonergan was opening for us new ways to think theologically. We also knew that in France, despite the heavy hand of the Holy Office, important reform movements were afoot. The first tentative steps toward ecumenical exchange were in process. I also began to read books that opened up a whole new way of thinking about theology. I still have on my shelf Bernard Häring's *The Law of Christ*, in French, and Edward Schillebeeckx's *Christ the Sacrament of the Encounter with God*—two books that gave me an entirely new way of thinking theologically.

When I look back to my hopes and dreams for that coming council, a few things stand out. In comparison to what the council actually did, our expectations were rather modest. Despite listening to lectures in Latin, reading texts in that language, as well as taking Latin oral examinations, hopes were raised that more vernacular would be permitted as a pastoral improvement. Would we at least get permission to celebrate the sacraments in the vernacular and, further, was it beyond possibility that some of the Mass would be in the vernacular? We thought that the proclamation of the scripture readings would make a good start.

While we were beginning to see the writings of theologians who provided a more holistic view of theology, as opposed to the desiccated neo-scholasticism still lingering at the Gregorian, it was clear that the gap between what the scripture scholars and the theologians were offering was wide. I still recall my uneasiness with the rococo Mariology handed to us, because it seemed that as a discipline Mariology was constructed independently of solid biblical or patristic foundations. But I still regard the decision to place the conciliar reflections on Mary within *Lumen gentium* as one of the best moves of the council. It had the twin benefit of articulating the Catholic sense of Mary's role in salvation, but it did so in a fashion that would not prove a stumbling block to either the churches of the Reformation or the Orthodox tradition.

By the time the council was actually convened, I was back in the

United States. How the council proceeded was a source of joy and gave me a sense, perhaps only half understood, that the conciliar fathers were putting into their decrees the thinking of our theological heroes: Yves Congar (who was, in my judgment, the theologian of the council), Henri de Lubac, Jean Daniélou, Bernard Häring, Edward Schillebeeckx, Karl Rahner, and those many others who were in the forefront of the liturgical movement (like the late Cipriano Vagaggini, O.S.B., and my own professor, Hermann Schmidt, S.J.), and the early pioneers of ecumenism.

The achievements of Vatican II cannot be considered an unqualified success, even though they did constitute a sea shift in church life and practice. Persons of a certain age speak of their experiences in terms of the pre- and postconciliar days. Such comparisons are a sure sign of impending old age, since descriptions of the "old" Catholic Church are meaningless to the students I teach today. The various documents coming out of the council ranged from the banal (the "Decree on Communications") to those that seem today somewhat safe and half-hearted. Even the crucial "Dogmatic Constitution on the Church" (*Lumen gentium*) shows an interior tension between an ecclesiology whose roots are in the older tradition of scholasticism and the newer thinking, whose roots are in Newman, Möhler, and whose fruition comes from Yves Congar. Even *Gaudium et spes* (the "Pastoral Constitution on the Church in the Modern World") presents a problem in that parts of it ring with the somewhat sunny optimism of the 1960s while not directly touching on issues that have come to the forefront of present-day discussions.

Whatever the tensions one sees in the conciliar discussions (and documents) of Vatican II, one does see a foundation on which we might advance. What needs to be advanced? Only the most naïve think that we have fully worked out the relationship between the local and the universal church. That relationship requires a balance between the bishop as pastor of the Catholic Church fully realized in its local instantiation and the claims of the papacy as the focal point of the unity of the church. The centralizing tendency of Rome is not only the result of the style of the current pontiff (although that is part of it, to be sure), but also the result of a deeper problem because the role of the local church has yet to be fully articulated, despite the efforts of some fine theological work like that produced by the late lamented Jean Marie Tillard in his brilliant book, *L'Eglise locale*.

A more "sociological" problem to be faced is the necessity of developing a concept of the church for that huge number of Catholics who have no experience of the church before Vatican II. What are we to make of those tendencies that, on the right, seek a kind of restoration, and, on the left, veer toward something like liberal Protestantism? How do we articulate and sustain that retrieval of the *fontes* ["sources" or "founts"] in a sane and nourishing fashion? That issue goes on apace while demographics herald what all of us know viscerally: the near collapse of traditional religious life (especially so among women), the rapid aging of the clergy, the rising number of Hispanic Catholics in this country, the polarization of Catholic intellectuals and those who would like to be so named.

These "crises," of course, are not unfamiliar to readers of church history, even though knowledge of the past is no excuse for complacency. If there was one creative tension found in the deliberations of Vatican II it was in the desire to affirm the transcendent force of Christian belief with a concomitant conviction that the deepest reality of the Incarnation is to be found in serving others and not being served. The sign value of the church is best illustrated in the (hundreds of) thousands of experiments in community outreach to the poor, in the witness of our contemporary martyrs, in the willingness to be countercultural witnesses to the worst excesses of the age. In a famous observation, written two generations ago, Karl Rahner said that the Christian of the future would either be a mystic or would not be a Christian at all. By "mystic" Rahner meant those who experienced something beyond the epiphenomena of church observance. That "something beyond," of course, is the reality of God in Jesus Christ. As long as there are Christians drawing on the ancient wisdom of the gospel, the passing of forms and the changing of ministries will be incidental to the authentic witness of the gospel.

What sustains me today? As a Catholic theologian with thirty years of teaching behind me, it is the edifying (I use the term technically!) image of the many students, past and present, who have left our university to do volunteer service here and abroad or those who have entered into forms of ministry or gone on to do advanced work in theology to teach or work for the church. I have devoted my life to form them, and they, in turn, have formed me in the adamantine conviction that this is gospel work.

RICHARD P. MCBRIEN

Renewed Commitment to Vatican II as Best Preparation for the New Millennium

Born on August 19, 1936, in Hartford, Connecticut, Richard McBrien was educated in public and parochial schools and at St. Thomas Seminary, Bloomfield, Connecticut. He did his major seminary studies at St. John Seminary, Brighton, Massachusetts, earning an M.A. in theology (1962). Ordained on February 2, 1962, for the archdiocese of Hartford, he served as a parish assistant and college chaplain (1962-1963), and then did doctoral studies in theology at the Gregorian University in Rome (1963-1965) during the Second Vatican Council, receiving an S.T.D. in 1967. McBrien served on the faculty and as Dean of Studies at Pope John XXIII National Seminary, Weston, Massachusetts (1965-1970), and then at Boston College (1970-1980), where he was also director of the Institute of Religious Education and Pastoral Ministry (1975-1980). He became the Crowley-O'Brien-Walter Professor of Theology at the University of Notre Dame in 1980 (changed to Crowley-O'Brien Professor in 2001), serving as chair of the department from then until 1991.

McBrien was president of the Catholic Theological Society of America in 1974-1975 and received its John Courtney Murray Award in 1976. His major publications include Catholicism *(1980; new ed., 1994) and* The HarperCollins Encyclopedia of Catholicism *(1995), for which he served as general editor. His most recent books are* Lives of the Popes *(1997),* Lives of the Saints *(2001), and* The Church *(2008).*

I HAD THE GREAT ADVANTAGE of doing my doctoral studies in Rome during Vatican II's second and third sessions (1963-1964). I had been released from my pastoral obligations in the archdiocese of Hartford at the request of Cardinal Richard Cushing, archbishop of Boston, to serve on the faculty of the yet-to-be-constructed seminary for so-called delayed vocations in Weston, Massachusetts. The original plan was to name the seminary after Pope Pius X, but Cushing later decided—to my great relief and satisfaction—to change the seminary's patron to John XXIII, in honor of the pope who had named him a cardinal. Cushing sent me to Rome to study for a doctorate in theology at the Pontifical Gregorian University.

Within a week of my arrival in the city, I was included in a private audience with the recently elected pope, Paul VI, in the company of Cardinal Cushing and several Boston priests and seminarians. (One of those Boston priests, Msgr. Daniel Cronin, was serving at the time in the Vatican's Secretariat of State. He would later become my archbishop in Hartford.) Soon thereafter, I managed to obtain the necessary credentials to attend at least one of the conciliar sessions in St. Peter's Basilica, and I also attended several press conferences that were held each day for the English-speaking media in one of the press offices along the Via Conciliazione. The panels included a few bishops and several *periti*. Their task was to describe and interpret the day's debates and votes (if any). These press conferences proved far more interesting and educationally fruitful than the Latin lectures to which we were exposed in the Roman universities.

I also served on the speakers committee at the North American College's graduate house, the Casa Santa Maria dell' Umiltà, where I resided during my two years in Rome. The Casa was situated between the Gregorian University and the Pontifical Biblical Institute (which was just out the back door), and the Trevi Fountain, a popular tourist attraction. Through my involvement in the lecture series, I had the opportunity to meet distinguished theologians and bishops, such as John Courtney Murray, who sat next to me at fellow Jesuit Gustave Weigel's lecture on ecclesiology, and Bishop (later Archbishop) Mark McGrath, C.S.C., of Panama, one of the chief architects of the "Pastoral Constitution on the Church in the Modern World" (*Gaudium et spes*), then known simply as "Schema XIII."

Because of our common association with the University of Notre Dame, where Mark served on the Board of Trustees, he and I would become good friends after 1980, the year I joined the Notre Dame faculty. I invited him to address my doctoral seminar on the council several years ago. The students were very much taken with him, in spite of his speech difficulties created by the onset of Parkinson's disease. I reminded them that they had the great privilege of hearing someone who not only attended the council, but also exercised a leadership role at it, particularly with regard to *Gaudium et spes*. Archbishop McGrath's participation in my seminar was later written up in Charles Morris's widely read book *American Catholic* (Times Books, 1997, pp. 334-35).

That the council made a profound and lasting impact on my work as a theologian, and as an ecclesiologist in particular, is self-evident to anyone who has read even a sampling of my monographs (especially *Do We Need the Church?* [1969], *Church: The Continuing Quest* [1969], *The Remaking of the Church* [1973], and *Catholicism* [orig. ed., 1980, 2 vols.]), and of the weekly columns I have written for the Catholic press since July 1966 (a selection of which were published as *Report on the Church: Catholicism after Vatican II* [1992]).

The general orientation of any Catholic theologian educated around the time of the council—either during it or just afterwards—was inevitably shaped and directed not only by the documents of the council but also by the whole conciliar event. And those of us who had the opportunity of doing our graduate work in Rome at the very time that the council was in session were privileged in a way that cannot easily be exaggerated. Undoubtedly, it is because I am such a grateful product of Vatican II myself that I may occasionally become impatient with a few younger Catholics who speak and act as if the council is, at best, an important historical event that is over and done with and no longer of continuing relevance, or, at worst, a mistake that a naïve Pope John XXIII perpetrated, with many harmful consequences to the life of the church—consequences that were made even worse during the allegedly indecisive pontificate of Paul VI.

In the minds of such observers, it has been John Paul II's special mission to undo whatever damage the council did, without ever faulting the council directly, and then to tighten the reins of discipline and to re-energize the church's spirituality. Such critics pay no discernible heed to John Paul II's own testimony of gratitude to the council in his *Sources of Renewal: The Implementation of Vatican II* (1979; orig. Polish ed., 1972), or to his calling of an extraordinary synod in 1985 to give tribute to the council as a work of the Holy Spirit, or to his insistence in *Tertio adveniente millennio* (1994) that the "best preparation for the new millennium . . . can only be expressed in a renewed commitment to apply, as faithfully as possible, the teachings of Vatican II to the life of every individual and of the whole Church" (n. 20).

Five decades after the council, I continue to think, and to teach, and to write under its positive influence. My large undergraduate Catholicism course, which I taught every fall semester at Notre Dame, had a significant component on the council, made all the more necessary in light of the fact that none of these students was even alive when the council adjourned in December 1965. A much greater portion of my M.A./M.Div. course on the church, which I taught every spring, was devoted to the council, and my doctoral seminar, taught every other fall, was devoted almost entirely to the ecclesiology of Vatican II. Finally, it is a relatively rare weekly column of mine that does not touch directly, or at least indirectly, on the abiding impact of Vatican II on the life, mission, and ministries of the church in our day.

While still archbishop of Krakow, Karol Wojtyla wrote his *Sources of Renewal* as an act of gratitude to the council, "to acquit himself of a debt" to it and to the Holy Spirit (pp. 9, 10). I, too, remain in their debt, and my whole life and work as a Catholic theologian can be seen as a way of rendering that debt, gladly and ever gratefully.

PART FOUR

REVELATION, SCRIPTURE, AND TRADITION

Introduction to Revelation

WILLIAM MADGES

I REMEMBER THE NEIGHBOR WITH whom my family shared a backyard fence in Detroit as I was growing up. He was a Lutheran. I can't recall exactly the circumstances, but I think the occasion for my speaking to him was that my grade school was selling candy as part of a fundraiser. He noted that he saw us go to church every Sunday, but he saw us also sometimes going to church in the evening during the week. He wanted to know if those weekday visits were for Bible study, as was the case in his church. I told him, "No, we go for a novena." He asked me to explain what a novena was. I tried to explain as best as I could as a fifth grader what this devotion to Mary, specifically Mary of Perpetual Help, meant. Our neighbor looked at me puzzled. He asked in response, "Where in the Bible do you Catholics find this notion that you should worship Mary?" At the time, I was not able to make the classic Catholic distinction between veneration of Jesus' mother and the saints, on the one hand, and worship of God, on the other. From my upbringing, however, I was convinced that our devotion to the saints and Mary was permissible because our parish priest promoted it. As I got older, I learned that these devotions were justified in terms of an appeal to the tradition of the church. That meant, even if the Bible didn't explicitly endorse some of our religious devotions—as our neighbor alleged—they were still permissible because God had revealed their goodness through the tradition promoted by priests and bishops, and taught to us children in Catholic parochial school.

This was the understanding of the authority of scripture and tradition that Catholics, young and old alike, had prior to the Second Vatican Council. Whereas Protestants believed that there was only one medium through which God communicated divine revelation, Catholics believed that there were two media, scripture and tradition. From the Catholic perspective, the scriptures were the written "source" for Christian knowledge about God, morality, etc., whereas tradition was the unwritten source, passed on orally from Christ to the apostles, and then from the apostles to their successors, the bishops. So Catholics were not dismayed if they could not produce conclusive evidence on the basis of scripture alone to establish the legitimacy of certain Catholic practices or beliefs (e.g., purgatory). This issue, the authority of the Bible and the relationship between scripture and tradition, had separated Protestants from Catholics since the sixteenth-century Reformation. It was revisited at the Second Vatican Council. The fruit of the lengthy debate concerning this topic and related issues was given expression in *Dei verbum*, the Council's "Dogmatic Constitution on Divine Revelation."

Dei verbum is one of the most important documents to be produced during the Second Vatican Council. At the time of the council, scholars such as R. A. F. MacKenzie and Francis X. Murphy hailed the document as equal in importance with the "Dogmatic Constitution on the Church" (*Lumen gentium*).[1] Looking retrospectively at the document decades later, Giuseppe Ruggieri largely concurs with MacKenzie's and Murphy's judgment. He writes:

> The common judgment is no exaggeration: the period from November 14 to December 8 [1962], and especially the week of November 14-21, which was devoted to discussion of the schema on the sources of revelation, represented a turning point that was decisive for the future of the Council and therefore for the future of the Catholic Church itself: the turn from the Church of Pius XII, which was still essentially hostile to modernity and in this respect the heir to the nineteenth-century restoration, to a Church that is a friend to all human beings, even children of modern society, its culture, and its history.[2]

The discussion of the first draft of the document on revelation, entitled *De fontibus revelationis* (On the Sources of Revelation), was heated and long. The draft or schema, which was prepared by the Preparatory Theological Commission under Cardinal Ottaviani, consisted of five chapters. The principal topics of these chapters were the "two sources" of revelation; the inspiration, inerrancy, and literary genres of scripture; the Old Testament; the New Testament; and holy scripture in the church.[3] From the very beginning debate centered on the notion of two sources of revelation. The Council of Trent (1545-1563) had applied the term "source" to the gospel. But in *De fontibus* the term was applied to scripture and tradition, which were regarded as the two "fountains" of revelation. This way of thinking about "two sources" had emerged in the context of Catholic apologetics vis-à-vis Protestantism. By regarding scripture and tradition as two separate, virtually independent sources of divine revelation, Catholic apologists could justify as authentically Christian those Catholic beliefs and practices that Protestants claimed had little or no basis in scripture. The wave of renewal that was coursing through some channels of theology in the first half of the twentieth century, however, challenged this idea of two sources. Instead of regarding scripture and tradition as two independent sources, this new theological movement spoke of them as a cohesive whole that transmits God's Word to successive generations in different ways. Scripture communicates in written form; tradition, in unwritten form. But neither is independent of or contrary to the other. Speaking from this perspective, Yves Congar declared: "There is not a single dogma which the Church holds by Scripture *alone*, not a single dogma which it holds by tradition *alone*."[4] Whereas the former, apologetic perspective presented a Catholic position clearly differentiated from, if not also antithetical to, the Protestant position, the latter perspective offered a Catholic position that displayed considerable common ground with the Protestant insistence on the authority and sufficiency of scripture. These two perspectives clashed at Vatican II.

As in the case of debates about other topics at the council, the *periti* or theological experts—such as Martelet (France), Schillebeeckx (Netherlands), and Rahner (Germany)—provided the council fathers with perspectives and conclusions drawn from recent scholarship that they could use to evaluate the cogency and appropriateness of the draft document they were now considering. Schillebeeckx's and Rahner's written critiques of the draft on revelation were particularly influential.[5] Although it is difficult to know which of their critiques had a greater impact, it is important to note that "nearly all of the arguments found in their texts would be used during the discussion in the hall."[6]

The debate concerning the original draft of *De fontibus* began on November 14, 1962, during the first session of the council. Cardinal Ottaviani spoke first. Anticipating criticism of the draft as neither pastoral in tone nor up-to-date in theological content, he declared that authentic doctrine was the firm foundation of pastoral theology and that the traditional content of the draft had been prepared by men who, although not sympathetic to the "new theology," were nonetheless scholars themselves. Monsignor Salvatore Garofalo, the official "reporter" for the draft, spoke next. He claimed that the primary goal of the council was to defend and promote Catholic doctrine in its most precise form. The draft on the sources of revelation, therefore, was clear in its condemnation of erroneous positions concerning the sufficiency of scripture and equally clear in its promulgation of the proper understanding of the relationship of scripture and tradition as two sources of revelation.[7]

Cardinal Liénart from Lille, France, rose at once to lead the opposition. He insisted that the draft needed to be completely rewritten because it did not deal accurately and well with the relationship of scripture and tradition. "There are not and never have been two *sources* of revelation," he claimed. There is only one source of revelation: the Word of God, announced by the prophets and revealed by Christ.[8] Cardinal Frings from Cologne, Germany, who followed Liénart to the podium, criticized the document both for its content and its tone. Contrary to Ottaviani's assertion, the document's content is not "traditional," but rather reflects the mentality of the anti-Protestant Catholic controversialists of the seventeenth to the nineteenth centuries. Their teaching corresponds neither to the understanding of revelation that patristic and medieval theologians espoused nor to the language of the Council of Trent. The tone of the draft, Frings declared, is not pastoral, and it is offensive to Protestants.

This exchange of sharply divergent judgments concerning the suitability of the draft continued as additional defenders and critics took the floor. Some bishops defended both the content and tone of the draft as necessary to prevent "modernist" biblical scholarship from infecting Catholic faith. Other bishops argued against the draft and in support of Catholic biblical scholars who were opening up new paths of investigation.[9] Cardinal Bea, one of the strongest advocates for renewal at the council and president of the Secretariat for Christian Unity, noted, for example, that of all the references in the draft to the work of biblical scholars, only one was a favorable mention. Bea, former rector of the Biblicum, stated that the schema must be made shorter, clearer, more pastoral, and more ecumenical. Bea's intervention gave clear expression to the orientation that Pope John XXIII wanted the council to have.[10] While some bishops called for amending the draft, others—such as Cardinal Ritter of St. Louis—called for its total rejection. Cardinal Ottaviani, however, challenged the notion that a draft document could be rejected outright. He and other defenders of the draft intimated that the document could not be rejected because it had been "approved" by the pope. In point of fact, the pope's consent had not been given to the content of this schema or the others, but simply to their being sent out for discussion in St. Peter's. Nonetheless, it became necessary to consult formally the regulations pertaining to conciliar procedures. Article 33.1 of the Rules of Procedure made it clear that schemata or drafts could be discussed, amended, or rejected.[11]

The see-saw debate continued over the next couple of days. Opposition to the schema was very fierce, however, not because of any individual point, but because of larger issues. "Specifically, leaders in the council saw the fate of Vatican II as hanging on the fate of this document. Would the council basically be a ratification of the status quo or would it be something other than that? The vote on *De fontibus revelationis* would tell."[12] By November 19, 1962, the eve of the vote on the schema, it was clear that an impasse had been reached. Although the majority of the bishops were not in favor of the draft, they were not convinced of the wisdom of rejecting it outright. And yet they also could not hope for significant changes if the document were simply sent back to the commission that had originally prepared it because that commission was headed by Cardinal Ottaviani and staffed by many people who supported the original draft. Bishop Joseph De Smedt of Bruges, Belgium, who was a member of the Secretariat for Promoting Christian Unity, insisted that the draft would have to be rewritten in a more ecumenical vein if the council did not want to destroy the great hope of Pope John XXIII and others, who were waiting for a significant step toward greater unity with non-Catholic Christians. De Smedt further noted that although the Secretariat for Promoting Christian Unity had offered to collaborate with the Theological Commission in preparing the first draft on revelation, the Theological Commission had declined the offer.[13]

On the next day, November 20, the secretary general of the council, Pericle Felici, told the council fathers that they were to vote on whether to table further discussion of the original draft. The question was formulated, however, in such a way that many bishops did not understand the meaning of the vote. Several clarifications were made. The result of the vote showed that 1,368 of the 2,209 bishops present were in favor of halting discussion of the present draft and in favor of preparing a new schema. Although a large number disapproved of the document, they were still 105 votes short of the necessary two-thirds majority required for such a decision. Thus discussion of Chapter 1 of the draft continued.[14]

On the following day, there was a dramatic announcement. Archbishop Felici announced that Pope John had decided that the schema should be withdrawn, even though the two-thirds majority required by the procedural rules had not been reached. This declaration took almost everyone by surprise. The pope's intervention made it clear that the Counter-Reformation attitude that had dominated the Catholic Church for centuries needed to be abandoned. Pope John gave the task of creating a shorter, more ecumenical and pastoral draft to a mixed commission, consisting of "liberals" (Cardinals Frings, Liénart, and Meyer), "traditionalists" (Cardinals Browne and Ruffini), and a centrist (Cardinal Lefebvre), with Cardinals Ottaviani and Bea serving as joint presidents.

As Francis X. Murphy (the pseudonymous Xavier Rynne) observed at the time, the most important single disclosure of this first session of the council was the great strength shown by the advocates of renewal and reform.[15] Previously it had not been known just how influential this tendency in the church really was. Among the members of the curia, the chief spokesperson for the new approach was Cardinal Bea. Under his leadership, the Secretariat for Promoting Christian Unity was able to evade domination by the Holy Office. The fact that Bea had been directed by papal decree to collaborate with Ottaviani in drafting a new schema on the sources of revelation meant that he now had the right to be heard on strictly theological matters, which, up to that point, Ottaviani had successfully retained within the exclusive control of the Holy Office.[16]

Although a revised version of the schema on divine revelation was ready for the second session of the council in the fall of 1963, this text was not presented to the council fathers for discussion until the following year. Between 1963 and 1964, the schema underwent further revision. When formal discussion of the text began during the council's third session, Pope Paul VI had been pope for about a year, having succeeded John XXIII, who had died on June 3, 1963. The revised text reflected a moderate position on many points, which modern biblical scholars found to be more satisfactory. Instead of identifying one fixed and absolute interpretative approach to the Bible, the revised document acknowledged that the church, under the inspiration of the Holy Spirit and conversant with the development of human knowledge, could grow in its understanding of revelation communicated through the Bible. Whereas the original draft had concentrated attention on the "sources" or "founts" of revelation and the relationship between scripture and tradition, the revised draft focused on the sacred scriptures themselves and their message. This new emphasis allowed for the validity of several modern theories concerning the biblical texts. It was precisely this moderate acceptance of pluralism that Cardinal Ruffini of Palermo, Sicily, opposed. During the debate on October 2, 1964, he repeated a point he had made previously: to encourage—as the present version of the text did—consideration of literary genres in determining the meaning of biblical texts was tantamount to admitting that the church had not properly understood the scriptures until quite recently. Pope Pius XII's 1943 encyclical *Divino afflante spiritu*, however, had given cautious endorsement to the consideration of genre and context in the determination of the meaning of biblical texts.

In the final speech of the day, Cardinal Koenig of Vienna, Austria, addressed the sensitive issue of the historical and scientific accuracy of the Bible. Koenig argued:

> Lest the authority of Scripture suffer, we must say sincerely and without fear that the sacred writer's knowledge of historical matters was limited according to the conditions of his time, and that God moved him to write in keeping with his background and education. In this way we see the complete condescension of the Divine Word, making Himself conform in all things to human conditions, including the limitations of human speech.[17]

This admission horrified those bishops who were convinced that every word of the Bible was true and that this truth was guaranteed infallibly. When discussion resumed at the beginning of the next week, the issue of inspiration and inerrancy was revisited. Although some bishops argued for a "looser" or more general understanding of inspiration, others argued just as vigorously for a concept of inspiration sufficient to preserve the historical veracity of the scriptures in their entirety. Bishop Philbin of Down and Connor, Ireland, for example, rejected the use of literary genres in exegesis because he feared it would undermine the historicity of the Gospels. And Bishop Carli of Segni, Italy, insisted that modern biblical methods, such as form criticism, threatened to undermine the faith of the church. Abbot Butler of Downside, England, tried to allay the fears of Philbin, Carli, and others by assuring them that the modern biblical movement did not intend to jeopardize the historical nature of God's revelation. Rather, it hoped to provide a wider and deeper appreciation of the biblical witness to God's Word.[18]

In light of the many suggestions for revision made by the council fathers, it was not possible to offer the entire text for a final vote before the close of the third session of the council. Therefore, final consideration of the text was carried over to the fourth and last session in 1965. Although the overwhelming majority of bishops were generally satisfied with the document as a whole, there was still some discontent about the document's treatment of the three issues that had provoked earlier debate. Those issues were the relation of scripture and tradition, the inerrancy of the Bible, and the historical nature of the Gospels. A significant number of revisions were proposed for each of the chapters when the document was considered in September 1965. These revisions were evaluated by the subcommission charged with preparing the final version of the text (headed by Cardinal Florit) and by the Theological Commission. Some council fathers, however, complained to Pope Paul VI that their recommendations were not receiving proper attention in the subcommission and Theological Commission. The pope, therefore, directed Cardinal Cicognani, the secretary of state, to send a letter to the commission requesting that the text be reconsidered with an eye to reaching a better consensus, especially with regard to the three disputed points. Paul VI also expressed his wish that Cardinal Bea participate in those discussions.

Those discussions yielded revisions of Chapters 2, 3, and 5 of the document.[19] Some wanted the text to state clearly that the Bible was not sufficient to convey all necessary Christian knowledge (as Protestants claimed) and, consequently, that not every Catholic doctrine can be directly proved on the basis of scripture alone. In response, the following sentence was added in section 9 of Chapter 2: "Thus it is that the church does not draw its certainty about all revealed truths from the holy scriptures alone." The section concluded with the same sentence as had been previously approved by the council fathers: "Hence, both scripture and tradition must be accepted and honored with equal devotion and reverence."[20] It is important to note the careful wording of this addition. It does not claim that the Bible is materially insufficient in conveying Christian knowledge, but leaves open the possibility that the whole deposit of Christian faith is contained in the Bible. It *does* insist that the church's certainty about the faith rests on both scripture and tradition, and for this reason both scripture and tradition must be revered.[21]

Concerning biblical inspiration, many bishops wanted to make clearer that the scriptural inerrancy that derived from the divine inspiration of the biblical authors was not restricted simply to matters of faith and morals. They wanted, therefore, to change the sentence in section 11 of Chapter 3 that stated that "the books of scripture completely and in all their parts must be acknowledged as teaching solidly and faithfully, fully and without error the truth of salvation." Many bishops simply wanted to drop the words "of salvation"; others wanted to substitute different wording so that there would be no doubt that the "truth" that scripture teaches would be understood to mean the *facts* mentioned in scripture that were connected with the history of salvation. After considerable deliberation, the text was changed to read: "Since, therefore, all that the inspired authors, or sacred writers, affirm should be regarded as affirmed by the holy Spirit, we must acknowledge that the books of scripture, firmly, faithfully and without error, teach that truth which God, for the sake of our salvation, wished to see confided to the sacred scriptures."[22] In order to understand scripture properly, this document asserts that we must determine carefully what truth God intended to communicate through the Bible. This way of understanding scriptural inerrancy has permitted Catholics, for example, to read the creation accounts in the book of Genesis as expressing that all things come from God and that everything God has created is good, without requiring the additional belief in the creation of the universe in seven days and the denial of evolution.

The final major area in which change was sought and approved was the historical character of the Gospels. Some bishops did not think it was sufficient for the text to state that the Gospel authors told the "honest truth about Jesus." They wanted the document also to affirm that the Gospels told the *historical* facts of Jesus' life and teaching. In response to these concerns, a phrase was added to underline the church's confidence in the *general* historical character of the Gospels, without insisting that every last detail of the Gospel narratives is factually true. The final revision of section 19 of Chapter 5 was made to read: "Holy mother church has firmly and with absolute constancy maintained and continues to maintain, that these four Gospels, whose historicity it unhesitatingly affirms [this was the phrase that was added], faithfully hand on what Jesus, the Son of God, while he lived among men and women, really did and taught for their eternal salvation, until the day when he was taken up (see Acts 1:1-2)."

The Theological Commission's handling of the desired revisions was overwhelmingly approved by the council on October 29, 1965. Out of 2,115 bishops voting, 2,081 approved the emended text as a whole. The formal promulgation of the "Constitution on Divine Revelation" took place on November 18.

AVERY CARDINAL DULLES, S.J.

Vatican II and Myself

Avery Dulles, S.J., an internationally known author and lecturer, was born in Auburn, New York, on August 24, 1918. He received his primary school education in New York City and attended secondary schools in Switzerland and New England. After graduating from Harvard College in 1940, he spent a year and a half in Harvard Law School before serving in the United States Navy, emerging with the rank of lieutenant.

Upon his discharge from the Navy in 1946, Dulles entered the Jesuit Order and was ordained to the priesthood in 1956. He received a Ph.L. degree in 1951 and an S.T.L. in 1957, both from Woodstock College in Maryland, and was awarded a doctorate in sacred theology in 1960 from the Gregorian University in Rome.

During the time of Vatican Council II Father Dulles was teaching at Woodstock College, a position he held from 1960 to 1974. He was a professor at the Catholic University of America from 1974 to 1988. From 1988 to 2008 Dulles was the Laurence J. McGinley Professor of Religion and Society at Fordham University, Bronx, New York. He had also been a visiting professor at universities and seminaries both in the United States and abroad. The author of over seven hundred articles on theological topics, Dulles published over twenty books, including The Catholicity of the Church *(1985),* Models of the Church *(1987),* Models of Revelation *(1992),* The Assurance of Things Hoped For: A Theology of Christian Faith *(1994), and* The New World of Faith *(2000). His collection of McGinley lectures,* Church and Society, *was published by Fordham University Press in 2008.*

Past president of both the Catholic Theological Society of America and the American Theological Society, Dulles served on the International Theological Commission and as a member of the United States Lutheran / Roman Catholic Dialogue. He also served as a consultor to the Committee on Doctrine of the National Conference of Catholic Bishops and as an associate fellow of the Woodstock Theological Center in Washington, DC. His awards included Phi Beta Kappa, the Croix de Guerre, the Cardinal Spellman Award for distinguished achievement

in theology, the Boston College Presidential Bicentennial Award,
the Religious Education Forum Award from the National Catholic
Educational Association, America Magazine's *Campion Award, the F.*
Sadlier Dinger Award for contributions to the catechetical ministry of
the church, and over thirty-five honorary doctorates.

In February 2001 Pope John Paul II made Dulles a cardinal, the first
United States-born theologian who was not a bishop to be so honored.
Cardinal Dulles died December 12, 2008.

I WAS NOT AT THE Second Vatican Council, but I feel almost as though
I had been. In January 1959, when Pope John XXIII announced that he
was convening an ecumenical council, I was in Rome, doing my doctoral studies in theology at the Gregorian University. Like everyone else,
I was caught by surprise. I had come to think that there would not be
any more ecumenical councils, since Vatican I's definition of papal infallibility gave the pope authority to do by himself all that an ecumenical
council could do.

There was much confusion in most people's minds about the purposes
of the coming council. Many, including highly placed curial officers,
seem to have thought that it would simply give conciliar authority to
the principal teachings of Pius XII and condemn positions that seemed
to be opposed to them. But John XXIII's statements about updating the
Catholic Church, avoiding condemnations, and promoting Christian
unity seemed to presage a more open type of council. Hans Küng in his
immensely popular *The Council, Reform, and Reunion* clearly favored
the latter alternative.

By the time Vatican II first assembled, I was back teaching at the Jesuit
theologate in Woodstock, Maryland. Two professors from our faculty—
Gustave Weigel and John Courtney Murray—were heavily involved
with the council: Father Weigel with the "Decree on Ecumenism" and
the "Declaration on the Jews"; Father Murray (from the second session
on), with the "Declaration on Religious Freedom." The two of them
shared drafts of various council documents with the Woodstock faculty,
sought out our reactions, and briefed both faculty and students on the
inner politics of the council. All of us were also avidly reading the spicy
reports by "Xavier Rynne" in the *New Yorker.*

Neither Father Murray nor Father Weigel was in good health. Father
Weigel came back gloomy and depressed from meetings of the Secretariat for Promoting Christian Unity and from the first two sessions of

the council. With his habitual pessimism, he was convinced that curial opposition would defeat all healthy initiatives from open and reform-minded bishops. He died of a heart attack shortly after the close of the second session, at the age of fifty-seven. Father Murray was ill at the fourth session and had to spend some time in a hospital in Rome. That may have been providential, because it gave European thinkers a better opportunity to offset what otherwise might have an excessively "American" tone in the document on religious freedom. Father Murray survived a year and a half beyond the council, and died of a heart attack in 1967 at the age of sixty-two.

Having written my dissertation on "Protestant Churches and the Prophetic Office," I was keenly interested in the documents on ecumenism and on the church. In effect, the council made my dissertation moot because the "Decree on Ecumenism" simply proclaimed what I had laboriously striven to prove about the Christian value of non-Roman Catholic bodies.

I did not carefully study the "Dogmatic Constitution on the Church" until just after the council, when Father Walter Abbott asked me to write the introduction and footnotes to *Lumen gentium* for his edition of *The Documents of Vatican II*. In studying that document, I was surprised by the ease with which it settled the long-standing disputes about the sacramentality of episcopal ordination and incorporated the relatively new theme of episcopal collegiality. In many respects *Lumen gentium* endorsed the results of the best theology of the past fifty years, with which I was somewhat familiar from my recent studies.

As a teacher of the seminary course on revelation, I was especially concerned with *Dei verbum*. It confirmed what I had already been teaching at Woodstock with the help of authors such as Romano Guardini, Karl Adam, Henri de Lubac, Yves Congar, and René Latourelle. I appreciated the council's understanding of Jesus Christ as "the mediator and fullness of all revelation." I was pleased that it treated scripture and tradition not as two separate sources but as two resources that must be used in combination to get at the word of God given to humankind in Jesus Christ. I liked the idea of treating tradition, as *Dei verbum* did, before scripture, and of seeing tradition primarily in active terms, as the process of transmitting the word of God to new generations. To my satisfaction, also, the council looked upon tradition as capable of progressively clearer articulation in the course of time.

The statements in *Dei verbum* on the inspiration and inerrancy of scripture harmonized excellently with what I was already teaching. I resonated with the council's nuanced view of the historicity of the Gospels and its reserve in identifying the human authors. I particularly relished the section on the interpretation of scripture, which distinguished between different levels of exegesis, from the historical-critical to the more ecclesial and theological.

In short, I found no difficulty but only support from the various council documents. My only worry was that in trying to speak to so many questions the council might trespass too much on theological territory, thus obscuring the necessary distinction between the roles of the magisterium and the theologians.

Almost immediately after Vatican II, and to some extent even before it ended, I became involved in trying to explain its achievements to various Catholic and ecumenical audiences in the United States—bishops, priests, religious, and laity. Father Murray, before he died, exhorted me to pursue this educational apostolate because he felt that the council could not achieve its proper effect unless its documents were rightly explained.

Most of us, in the first years, tended to place too heavy an accent on what was new in the teaching of Vatican II, thus casting the continuities in the shade. Without going to extremes, I sometimes overemphasized the novelties. With the election of John Paul II and the Extraordinary Synod of 1985, a more balanced interpretation has come to prevail, and I welcome this turn of events. We Catholics really need the magisterium.

PAULINE A. VIVIANO

Fighting Biblical Fundamentalism

Pauline A. Viviano was born in 1946, the seventh out of eight children. She is a true Midwesterner, having been born in Detroit, completed her graduate work in St. Louis, and is now living in Chicago, which she considers the greatest city in the world. She is the product of Catholic education from first grade through graduate school. She received her M.A. in philosophy (1971) and her Ph.D. in biblical languages and literature (1980) from St. Louis University.

Currently Viviano is an associate professor of theology at Loyola University of Chicago. Besides articles in academic and popular journals, her publications include a commentary on the book of Genesis in the Collegeville Bible Commentary series. She currently is completing a commentary on the books of Jeremiah and Baruch for the new Collegeville Commentary Series. In addition to university teaching, she often lectures at parishes and synagogues in and around Chicago.

She received the 2008 Mater Dei Award for outstanding contribution of a woman to the ministry of the church, from St. Joseph's Seminary, archdiocese of Chicago, March 2008, and the Chicago Medallion for Excellence in Catechesis for biblical catechesis of adult Catholics from the Office of Catechesis and Youth Ministry, archdiocese of Chicago, May 2008.

As a teenager when Vatican II was announced I had little interest in the council. I was consumed by what occupied most teenage girls in the late 1950s and early '60s: school, combating acne, and scheming to get the attention of my latest boy-of-the-month crush. Coming from an Italian Catholic family carried with it its own unique relationship to religion. In my mother's brand of Italian Catholicism there was a strong anti-clerical sentiment, expressed mostly in her antipathy for priests and nuns, coupled with an avid interest in religions of all kinds. She borrowed from the Rosicrucians, Norman Vincent Peale, Hinduism, and

140

Buddhism to shape her own rather eccentric belief system that included Jesus and, of course, Mary, especially Mary. My father had a much simpler faith, but he thought the involvement in religion should not be so demanding that it interfered with work in the family flower business, even on Sundays, and especially on holidays.

Vatican II became more of a reality in my college years, which coincided with the end of Vatican II and the beginning of the period of experimental liturgy. We went from silent observers at a Latin performance to participants in the vernacular of Christ's own prayer, but before we got there we had to endure some "hootenanny Masses" and "Bridge over Troubled Waters" type hymns. This transition was not without some resistance on my part, for I loved the Latin Mass; but in graduate school I ended up at a Sunday Mass whose celebrant was a liturgist, and he took it upon himself to explain to us the theology behind the "new Mass." I fell in love with this new Mass, with its rich theological underpinnings and have never missed the old Latin Mass of my youth.

But for my topic at hand, what was most significant from Vatican II in the late 1960s was my introduction to historical-critical interpretation of scripture in college—not that we called it that; it was just that the textbook did that. This method of interpretation had been around for a couple of centuries, but it had been "approved" for Catholics only since *Divino afflante spiritu* (1943). The approach was confirmed by Vatican II in *Dei verbum* and was now being taught in "progressive" Catholic colleges such as the one I attended—not that I knew at the time that it was "progressive." At the time I didn't know anything about *Divino afflante spiritu* or *Dei verbum*; all I knew was that I was learning about the world out of which the Bible emerged, and for the first time the Bible began to make sense to me. No longer did I have to believe that God literally "rode on clouds," which always conjured up in my mind "cloud races in the skies," or that God wrote with lightning on stone tablets at Mt. Sinai as imagined by Cecil B. DeMille. More important, it relieved me of the necessity of believing that God spent an evening killing off the firstborn of the Egyptians, including their livestock, or that God commanded the genocide of a people just to get Israel into the land of Canaan. Knowing the historical and literary context freed me from a simplistic understanding of the biblical text, but it also freed God from the limited perceptions of the deity held in bygone centuries.

My route to graduate studies in scripture was not a direct one. I pursued a degree in philosophy; but as I was completing my M.A., I realized what really interested me were theological issues, and so I decided to go on to study scripture, eventually getting a Ph.D. in biblical languages and literature with a specialization in the Old Testament. I studied scripture in those heady exciting post-Vatican II days when Catholic scholars such as Raymond Brown, Joseph Fitzmyer, Dennis McCarthy, and Roland Murphy were big-league players, not only in Catholic circles, but in the larger academic field. It was a time when lay Catholics discovered that they could become theologians without joining a religious community and even more surprising they could actually get a job "doing theology" upon graduation.

Immersed as I was in learning Hebrew and Greek, archaeology, ancient Near Eastern and Greco-Roman history and literature, and the myriad other areas of study one had to master to interpret the biblical text, I gave little thought to what the "people in the pew" were thinking about scripture. I was one of the "people in the pew," and I felt not just the excitement of learning new things, but also that my faith was being enhanced and deepened by my studies. I was becoming an adult believer. I assumed that other "people in the pew" would be as excited as I was about these new ways of coming to understand the biblical text. I did not know of the fights that went on behind the scenes. I did not know of those who continued to privilege the Vulgate of St. Jerome even though Pope Pius XII spoke of the necessity of studying the biblical text in its original languages (*Divino afflante spiritu* no. 15). I did not know of the attacks on the faith and orthodoxy of the biblical scholars that I was studying in newspapers and magazines that called themselves "Catholic." I learned of these things only much later.

When I moved from being a student to being a professor I brought with me my enthusiasm for the Bible and studying it from historical- and literary-critical perspectives, and most students responded with an enthusiasm of their own. I began to lecture in parishes and to teach in various diocesan programs. I conducted workshops on the Bible and taught at various summer Bible institutes across the country; and audiences responded by saying that for the first time the Bible came to life for them, but whether in the classroom or parish, a few took great offense at this "new" way of interpreting the biblical text. I was accused of "taking sadistic delight in chopping apart the biblical text" and even of teaching heresy; these attacks were few and far between, but the tide is shifting.

I suppose it was inevitable that the backlash against Vatican II, which has a stranglehold on some sectors of the Catholic Church, would also make its appearance with respect to biblical interpretation. Some prefer the seemingly simple approach of fundamentalism. Although this approach to the Bible is condemned by the Pontifical Biblical Commission in *The Interpretation of the Bible in the Church* (1993), it has been making an inroad into the church among those for whom everything is black or white, true or false. Fundamentalism doesn't allow for nuance, or indeed, for mystery. Some complain that biblical scholars are needlessly confusing "the people in the pew" and shaking up their faith, a complaint for which I have some sympathy; the study of the Bible is a highly complex endeavor today. The strongest attack I heard came at a Sunday Mass in the summer of 2008 when a priest declared in his homily that "higher criticism," by which he meant historical criticism—no one calls it higher criticism today—"is an evil which has infiltrated the church for the past forty years. It is not a Catholic method of interpretation." I sat in stunned silence wondering how we had gotten to this point.

Perhaps it is because biblical scholars have focused on the historical and literary aspects of the biblical text and have given less attention to the theological implications of what we do. Maybe we have been involved in too much speculation and reconstruction of the history behind the biblical text and too little concerned with the beauty and depth found in the biblical text. It might simply be due to the fact that biblical scholars are hard-pressed to find any argument against the ordination of women in the New Testament. Whatever the cause, Catholic biblical scholarship—that has been and is being done in conformity with the directives of Vatican II in *Dei verbum*—is increasingly being held suspect.

In the Apostolic Exhortation *Verbum Domini*, Pope Benedict XVI expresses gratitude for the work of biblical scholars, but the document shows a greater interest in the spiritual interpretation of the early church fathers than in anything that Catholic biblical scholars are saying today. This is underscored in the pope's *Jesus of Nazareth*. He declares, not once but twice in the foreword of the first volume, that historical criticism is "indispensable to the Church,"[23] but in the opening pages of volume two, he says that historical criticism has "already yielded its essential fruit" and calls for an interpretation based in a "faith-hermeneutics."[24] Yet the faith-hermeneutics that he applies to the New Testament in both volumes is a return to the spiritual interpretation of the early church fathers which renders the contributions of historical-critical scholarship null and void, and, thus, dispensable.

It is hard to predict where Catholic biblical scholarship will be in years to come, but I hope that we will remain faithful to the spirit of Vatican II. I hope that we will continue to come to understand the biblical text from within its historical and literary contexts and upon that basis articulate in a meaningful way what it means for us today. I am still enthused about studying the Bible, and I remain in awe at the simplicity and beauty of its message: the God who created us does not abandon us in our rebellion, but redeems us and is present with us even now effecting our sanctification.

DANIEL J. HARRINGTON, S.J.

My Hermeneutical Spiral

Daniel Harrington was born in Arlington, Massachusetts, on July 19, 1940. After graduating from Boston College High School, he entered the Society of Jesus in 1958. His academic degrees are from Boston College (B.A. 1964; M.A. 1965; B.D. 1971) and Harvard University (Ph.D. 1970). He was ordained a Roman Catholic priest in 1971. He is professor of New Testament at the Boston College School of Theology and Ministry, and has been editor of New Testament Abstracts *since 1972.*

His major academic interests have been Second Temple Judaism and the interpretation of the New Testament. He was the editor of the critical Latin text of Pseudo-Philo's Biblical Antiquities *for the* Sources chrétiennes *series (1976), and prepared* A Manual of Palestinian Aramaic Texts *with Joseph A. Fitzmyer (1978). He collaborated with John Strugnell in the official edition of 4QInstruction, an ancient Jewish wisdom text in Hebrew and discovered among the Dead Sea Scrolls (1999). He served as the editor of the Sacra Pagina series of eighteen major commentaries on the New Testament, and contributed the volumes on* Matthew *(1991),* Mark *(2002, with John R. Donahue), and* 2 Peter and Jude *(2003, with Donald Senior).*

He is past president of the Catholic Biblical Association of America (1985-1986) and is now chairman of its Board of Trustees. He is the author of more than fifty books. His recent publications include Jesus Ben Sira of Jerusalem *(2005);* How Do Catholics Read the Bible *(2005);* Jesus: A Historical Portrait *(2007);* The Synoptic Gospels Set Free: Preaching without Anti-Judaism *(2009);* Jesus and Prayer: What the New Testament Teaches Us *(2009);* Meeting St. John Today *(2011); and* Meeting St. Mark Today *(2011).*

Harrington has been a member of the New England Province of the Society of Jesus for over fifty years, and serves as a weekend pastoral associate at two parishes in the Boston area. He has received honorary doctoral degrees from the College of the Holy Cross (2005), Boston College (2009), and Fairfield University (2010). He regularly teaches courses on biblical languages, late Old Testament and early Jewish writings, the various books of the New Testament, and biblical theology.

I ENTERED THE JESUITS IN 1958 right out of high school. Early on I showed interest and proficiency in ancient languages and texts. The best advice anyone has ever given me came around 1962 from my academic dean, Patrick Sullivan, S.J., when he said, "You should go on in scripture; it's the coming field." I already had Greek and Latin, and set about learning Hebrew. My Hebrew studies coincided with the beginning of Vatican II. How thrilling it was for me and my fellow Jesuit scholastics in philosophy studies to follow the surprising and amazing events going on in Rome and being debated around the world. Most of us identified with the "new breed" of young Catholics described by Andrew Greeley in *America* magazine. While we loved the church of the 1950s, Vatican II seemed to be opening the door to an even brighter and better future.

When the documents of Vatican II were approved in 1965 and published in the version edited by Walter Abbott, S.J., I eagerly read those texts and prayed over them. In the meantime I was sharpening my scholarly interests in the Jewish world of the New Testament, and applying for doctoral studies in Harvard University's Department of Ancient Near Eastern Languages and Literatures. Over the years the two documents that have most shaped my life and ministry have been the section about the relationship between the Catholic Church and the Jewish people in *Nostra aetate* 4 and the "Dogmatic Constitution on Divine Revelation" (*Dei verbum*) 24. In my opinion these two documents have been among the most influential and successful literary products of the council. Through the years I have kept coming back to those statements, primarily when I have been asked to teach, lecture, or write something about the Jewish world of the New Testament and/or Catholic biblical scholarship.

In biblical studies the word "hermeneutics" refers to the process of interpreting texts. In its narrow sense it describes moving from the ancient text to life today. In its broad sense it embraces the whole process of reading an ancient text: textual criticism, philology, literary criticism, source criticism, redaction criticism, tradition history, historical criticism, and application to the present. Some scholars describe the interaction between the ancient text and the modern interpreter as the "hermeneutical circle." The problem with that term is that the circle analogy leaves one where one started. A better term is the "hermeneutical spiral." The spiral analogy captures the ongoing relationship between text and reader, and suggests that the interaction keeps changing and (one hopes) improving the reader by opening up new horizons and disclosing new truths. It captures nicely my relationship to Vatican II.

The part of *Nostra aetate* 4 that has been most important for me, and to which I keep returning in my hermeneutical spiral, is this: "Since Christians and Jews have such a common spiritual heritage, this sacred Council wishes to encourage and further mutual understanding and appreciation. This can be obtained, especially, by way of biblical and theological enquiry and through friendly discussions."

From the start of my interest in biblical studies I wanted to focus on the Jewish world of the New Testament in order to understand better the cultural and religious background of the Christian scriptures. My models were Raymond E. Brown, S.S., and Joseph A. Fitzmyer, S.J., who combined these two interests in creative and productive ways. My chief mentors at Harvard were Frank M. Cross and John Strugnell, two members of the international team of scholars charged with the publication of the Dead Sea Scrolls, especially those from Qumran Cave 4. There were also courses in archaeology and in various languages, not only various dialects of Hebrew and Aramaic but also Coptic and Arabic. My academic advisor was Rabbi Isidore Twersky, a specialist in medieval Jewish philosophy and a prominent figure in the local Jewish community, who initiated me into the field of rabbinics. On top of this was a year spent in Jerusalem (1968-1969) doing my doctoral dissertation with John Strugnell, and studying at the Hebrew University and the Dominicans' Ecole Biblique de Jérusalem. There I followed the lectures of Pierre Benoit and Roland de Vaux, as well as the young Jerome Murphy-O'Connor. What linked all these great scholars was their ability to study the ancient texts critically and religiously. That is, they showed me how to use the powers of critical reasoning along with a respect for the ancient people who produced these texts and a conviction that these texts might have meaningful things to say to us today.

In my forty years of teaching I have tried to convey to my students the common spiritual heritage that we share with the Jewish people, and to remind them about their responsibility to combat anti-Judaism in their preaching and teaching. In almost every course I find a way to work in *Nostra aetate* 4. In my most technical publications, especially the ones of which I am most proud—on Pseudo-Philo's *Biblical Antiquities,* Palestinian Aramaic texts, and the Qumran wisdom text known as *4QInstruction*—I have worked with other scholars in editing and interpreting ancient Jewish texts. I have often taught courses and written extensively on those books that are part of the Catholic and Orthodox Bibles, known in some circles as the Apocrypha or Deuterocanonical books, such as 1 and 2 Maccabees, 2 Esdras, the book of Wisdom, Sirach, and Tobit. From these often-neglected books one can learn much about the world of the New Testament and the common spiritual heritage that we share with the Jewish people.

The part of *Dei verbum* that has most shaped my life and ministry appears in paragraph 24: "Therefore, let the study of the sacred page be, as it were, the soul of Sacred Theology. Likewise the ministry of the Word—namely pastoral preaching, catechetics, and all forms of Christian instruction, among which the liturgical homily is to hold pride of place—takes a wholesome nourishment and thrives in holiness through this same Word of Scripture."

From the early 1960s I have been associated with *New Testament Abstracts,* a journal that appears three times a year, with summaries of over two thousand articles and eight hundred books in various languages. Thus I am in the position to see practically everything of value in my field. Our coverage includes not only the books of the New Testament and their interpretation but also the world of the New Testament. Many of the more than fifty books I have written have been intended for the general public. In writing these books I have been eager to share the fruits of first-line, technical scholarship with persons without a formal theological education. Likewise in the forty years since my ordination to the priesthood, I have preached in local churches every Sunday. I always focus on the assigned biblical texts and try to convey their significance for the people in the pews.

During this time I also edited and contributed to the Sacra Pagina commentary, initiated by my friend Michael Glazier and published by the Liturgical Press. The series title, of course, echoes the hope in *Dei verbum* 24 that the study of the sacred page should be the "soul of Sacred Theology." Involving scholars from various parts of the world, this is the first full-scale Catholic New Testament commentary series in English.

Like many Jesuits, I conceive my life as a "ministry of the word." I have had the particular good fortune of being able to teach, preach, and write about scripture, the Word of God. I love what I have done and still do, and am constantly grateful for the gift that was Vatican II.

JOHN DOMINIC CROSSAN

Bliss at Dawn, Darkness at Noon

John Dominic Crossan was born in Nenagh, Co. Tipperary, Ireland, on February 17, 1934, and received his primary education at the Christian Brothers School in Naas, Co. Kildare, followed by secondary education at St. Eunan's College in Letterkenny, Co. Donegal. Crossan received a doctorate of divinity from Maynooth College, Ireland, in 1959, and did postdoctoral research at the Pontifical Biblical Institute in Rome from 1959 to 1961 and at the Ecole Biblique in Jerusalem from 1965 to 1967.

He was a member of the Servites (a religious order founded in the thirteenth century) from 1950 to 1969, and was ordained a priest in 1957. Crossan taught for six years at his order's major seminary as it relocated from Stonebridge Priory, where he was a professor during the Second Vatican Council, to Mundelein Seminary and eventually to the Catholic Theological Union near the University of Chicago. In 1969 he was dispensed from his vows as monk and priest, married Margaret Dagenais, a professor at Loyola University, and taught at DePaul University in Chicago until his retirement as professor emeritus in its Department of Religious Studies (1969-1995). He was co-chair of the Jesus Seminar from 1985 to 1996 as it met in twice-annual meetings to debate the historicity of the life of Jesus in the Gospels. He was chair of the Parables Seminar in 1972-1976, editor of Semeia: An Experimental Journal for Biblical Criticism *from 1980 to 1986, and chair of the Historical Jesus Section in 1993-1998, within the Society of Biblical Literature, an international scholarly association for biblical study based in the United States. He was vice-president in 2010-2011 and president in 2011-2012 of the Society of Biblical Literature.*

Crossan has received awards for scholarly excellence from both the American Academy of Religion in 1989 and DePaul University in 1991 and 1995. Over the last forty-five years he has written twenty-seven books on the historical Jesus, the apostle Paul, and earliest Christianity. Four of his most recent books, The Historical Jesus: The Life of a Mediterranean Jewish Peasant *(1991),* Jesus: A Revolutionary Biography *(1994),* Who Killed Jesus: Exposing the Roots of Anti-Semitism in the

Gospel Story of the Death of Jesus *(1995), and* The Birth of Christianity *(1998) have been national religious bestsellers for a combined total of twenty-two months. His work has also been translated into thirteen foreign languages, including Polish, Hungarian, and Russian, as well as Korean, Chinese, and Japanese. He has lectured to lay and scholarly audiences across the United States as well as in Ireland and England, Scandinavia and Finland, Brazil and South Africa, Australia, New Zealand, and Japan.*

There is a Third Vatican Council. The Pope convenes all the bishops of the entire world. Then, in a solemn public ceremony in St. Peter's Basilica, they all implore God to take back the gift of infallibility and grant them instead the gift of accuracy. (From Crossan's *A Long Way from Tipperary,* p. 98)

I WAS ORDAINED WITHIN THE thirteenth-century Servite Order in 1957 and sent immediately for a doctorate in divinity at Ireland's Maynooth College and then for a postdoctoral licentiate at Rome's Biblical Institute. I returned to teach scripture from 1961 through 1965 at the Servite major seminary outside Chicago and after that went for a two-year sabbatical to Jerusalem's Ecole Biblique. Those dates meant that I had finished my postgraduate education just before the start of the Second Vatican Council and that my first four years of seminary teaching coincided with its proceedings from 1962 through 1965.

The amount of the Bible that I had covered in either undergraduate or postgraduate studies was unbelievably minuscule, and even if done well in depth, was certainly not covered at all in breadth. I never had a wide-sweeping survey course. And I had absolutely nothing on theory or method. At the Biblical Institute, for example, I had a course not on the New Testament, not on Paul, not on Romans, but on Romans 5:12b (actually, just on three Greek letters in that half a verse). There was also one about the Sermon on the Mount that never mentioned Q, and one about the Song of Songs that never mentioned sex. But, back in that Servite seminary, I was the entire Biblical Studies Department, and so, over a four-year curriculum, I had to teach the entire Bible, from Genesis to Apocalypse, slowly, steadily, unhurriedly, comprehensively. I had eight successive semesters for Pentateuch, Prophecy, History, Wisdom, Gospels, Acts, Epistles, and Apocalypse. It was a fantastic remedial education for whose necessity I am still most grateful. I had only two classes a week and usually distributed about ten footnoted pages every preceding weekend (remember mimeograph machines?). There were three results from that relentless concentration of time and focus.

One result was that my Father Prior became a little nervous about those handouts, as I was not using any tried-and-true textbooks filled with *sana doctrina* ["safe doctrine"], preferably in Latin. (Having defended my doctorate in Latin and taken classes in Latin at the Biblicum, I can witness that it totally concentrates the mind on what you can say rather than on what you might think.)

Another result was that, in those years of the Second Vatican Council, I was rather more involved in my biblical classes and ministerial students than on the council's ongoing deliberations and eventual documents. None of that meant indifference. Quite the opposite: it was bliss in that dawn to be alive. But more blissful still to be actually doing what it was announcing.

I was using critical history to understand the Bible, and the council was using critical history to understand the church. It intended *aggiornamento* ["updating"] of ecclesiastical community, and I was totally involved in *aggiornamento* of biblical tradition. I scarcely had time to read the council's proclamations (although I always had time for "Xavier Rynne") as I was so completely involved in typing and copying the next week's notes. But what was common between Bible and council was historicity, the presumption that nothing on earth escapes the historical conditioning of its time and its place. As I saw it then and now, the theological name for that was incarnation and the ecclesiastical result of that was sacrament. I found all of that to be, if I may borrow the phrase, a seamless garment. I emphasize one point. None of that made me presume any ascendancy of Bible over tradition or either over community. What I was finding in the Bible was exactly what was happening in the council. So the third result was my recognition that tradition was the living, ongoing, changing life of a community, and just as once it had created the Bible as its constitutive past, so now it had convoked the council as its determinative present. And, as far as I could discern, the Spirit of God had not changed procedures at any point along the way.

For me, however, the Second Vatican Council was finished up by Paul VI on December 8, 1965, and finished off by Paul VI on July 25, 1968. After *Humanae vitae* I asked and received dispensation from my vows as a monastic priest in order to get married, but in the sure conviction that I would still have left even if a married priesthood had been an option. I could no longer be both an obedient priest and an honest scholar. I was in research and development rather than either marketing and sales or publicity and public relations. All of those functions are necessary in any public institution, but it is equally necessary to know which is which, which you are, and never to confuse or collate one with the other.

Maybe this is a better or more biblical way to put it. In Israel's long march across the desert it needed a single leader, but also a band of scouts. The scouts went way up ahead of the march and found themselves in a very strange position, hidden under flax stalks on an alien rooftop, saved by a woman's courage. But, no matter what happened then or thereafter, they had been inside the promised land and had felt it beneath their feet. They had made it there even if only for an initial visit. The leader, however, never got there. He climbed only to the peak of Pisgah and was buried in the midst of Moab.

I epigraphed this reminiscence with lines from my fuller memoir. I conclude with another unsolicited suggestion, not this time for the next Vatican Council but for the next Holy Father. Listen to your scouts, but still, buy binoculars.

One final biographical note: During the years of the Second Vatican Council, I was a newly ordained priest and newly degreed professor teaching biblical studies at the Servite major seminary outside Chicago, in Lake Bluff, Illinois. I am no longer a priest, it is no longer a seminary, but biblical studies and the Servite Order are still doing well.

JOSEPH A. KOMONCHAK

Dei verbum *and Cardinal Bea*

Joseph Komonchak was born in Nyack, New York, on March 13, 1939, the son of Joseph Bernard and Hazel Meehan Komonchak. He attended Cathedral College and St. Joseph's Seminary at Dunwoodie, receiving a B.A. from the latter in 1960. For the next four years he studied theology at the Pontifical Gregorian University, from which he received an S.T.L. degree. Ordained to the priesthood on December 18, 1963, Komonchak returned to the archdiocese of New York and served as a curate at St. Bartholomew's Church, Yonkers. In 1967 he was assigned to teach dogmatic theology at St. Joseph's Seminary. He received a Ph.D. from Union Theological Seminary in 1976.

From 1977 to 2009 Komonchak taught theology at the Catholic University of America, Washington, DC, where for many years he held the John C. and Gertrude P. Hubbard Chair in Religious Studies. His areas of specialty were ecclesiology, modern Catholic theology, the thought of John Courtney Murray, and the history and theology of Vatican II. Komonchak was the chief editor of The New Dictionary of Theology *(1987), co-edited with Mary Collins and Dermot A. Lane, and is the editor of the English edition of the five-volume* History of Vatican II. *He was the recipient of a Woodrow Wilson fellowship at the Smithsonian Institute. He retired from Catholic University in 2009 and returned to the archdiocese of New York.*

Komonchak was a seminarian in Rome during the Second Vatican Council.

WHEN I WAS IN THE seminary, it was the custom that before our common meals a brief passage be read from the scriptures, the *Imitation of Christ*, or some other work of edification. This practice was also followed at the North American College, where I resided from 1960 to 1964. An exception was made, however, when the Second Vatican Council was in session: for those few months a summary of the day's discussions in the

152

council hall was read out to us before evening meals. The summary was drawn from the official releases of the conciliar press office. Particularly during the first session of the council, these releases were not terribly informative. Apparently feeling constrained by the promise of conciliar secrecy and perhaps out of fear of giving scandal if they were to report more fully the conciliar debates, the authors of the communications were sparse with details. The communiqué about the events of the day concerning the debate on the draft-text on the liturgy read: "Of the fathers who asked to speak, twenty intervened this morning, some to defend the schema, others to attack it." Nevertheless, those who had some interest in and knowledge of the issues at stake in the conciliar debates were often able to read between the lines and discern the drama of the unfolding discussions.

I just used the term "drama," and it is important to emphasize this character of the conciliar event, especially now that there are already generations of Catholics for whom the council is accessible only through the published final documents and through contemporary journalistic accounts or more critical histories. It is not rare that some who read the texts for the first time wonder what all the fuss was about. But for Catholics of the time, especially those resident in Rome, the council as it unfolded, particularly during its first session in 1962, was experienced as a tense drama. It was a drama we were living, with daily ups and downs depending on one's judgments of the issues at stake, and it was a drama whose outcome was by no means certain. We weren't watching a play whose plot we already knew; this was a story that we were involved in, had a stake in, and whose plot, course, and dénouement were quite undetermined.

I remember quite clearly the debate and the vote on the schema on the sources of revelation during the first session. The text would have settled prematurely the ecumenically delicate question of the relation between scripture and tradition, and it would have impeded the work of Catholic biblical scholars. Vigorous critiques of the draft were offered by many conciliar fathers, but they seemed to be counterbalanced by strong defenders of it. It was decided to ask the bishops if they wanted to table this text. A two-thirds vote was required, but only about 61 percent of the bishops voted to end the debate. The results of the vote were read out to us in the refectory that evening, and a good number of us were very disappointed that the debate on what we thought a very imperfect text would continue.

The next evening, however, we learned from the press release that Pope John had intervened. Judging that too large a percentage of the fathers were opposed to the prepared text, he ordered it withdrawn and assigned for revision to a mixed commission. Many of us regarded that moment as defining the conciliar identity. A good majority of the bishops had indicated what kind of documents they wished to produce (or at least what kind they did not want to issue), and the pope had backed them. There was a feeling among us of liberation. One fellow-student, not usually inclined to hyperbole, said that it did indeed feel like the "new Pentecost" that Pope John had asked the church to pray for.

Only later would I learn two anecdotes that expressed the contrasting moods of participants and observers of this dramatic moment in the council. People asked who had persuaded the pope to intervene. Rightly or wrongly (and the matter is still not clear), responsibility was assigned to Cardinal Augustin Bea, head of the Secretariat for Christian Unity. Those happy with what Bea was thought to have done were exultantly quoting a large billboard in Rome urging people to make use of British European Airlines. *Volate BEA*, it said. "*Fly BEA!*" Those displeased at Bea's alleged part went around muttering: *Bea culpa; Bea culpa; Bea maxima culpa!* ["Bea's fault; Bea's fault; Bea's most grievous fault!"]

DONALD SENIOR, C.P.

Vatican II and Biblical Renewal

Donald Senior, C.P., is president of Catholic Theological Union in Chicago, the largest Roman Catholic graduate school of ministry in the United States, where he is also a member of the faculty as professor of New Testament. Born in Philadelphia in 1940, he is a member of the Passionist Congregation and was ordained a priest in 1967. He received his doctorate in New Testament studies from the University of Louvain in Belgium in 1972. He is a frequent lecturer and speaker throughout the United States and abroad.

Father Senior has published extensively on biblical topics, with numerous books and articles for both scholarly and popular audiences. He is the general editor of the acclaimed Catholic Study Bible *(1990), editor-in-chief of* The Bible Today, *and co-editor of the twenty-two-volume international commentary series* New Testament Message. *Among his recent works is a four-volume series of studies of the passion narratives, a new and expanded edition of his widely read* Jesus: A Gospel Portrait *(1994),* What Are They Saying about Matthew? *(1996),* The Gospel of Matthew *(1997) in Abingdon Press's new Interpreting Biblical Text series, and most recently, a full-length commentary on the* Gospel of Matthew *in Abingdon's New Testament Commentary series (1998).*

Senior was the recipient of the National Catholic Library Association's 1994 Jerome Award for Outstanding Scholarship and was given the 1996 National Catholic Education Association's Bishop Loras Lane Award for outstanding service to Catholic education. He is past president of the Catholic Biblical Association of America (1997-1998) and is currently a member of the Executive Committee of the Association of Theological Schools of the United States and Canada. In fall of 2001 he was appointed a member of the Pontifical Biblical Commission by Pope John Paul II, which advises the pope on issues of biblical translation and interpretation. He was reappointed in 2006 and 2008 by Pope Benedict XVI.

GAUGING THE IMPACT OF VATICAN II on the field of biblical scholarship is something like calculating the impact on space travel of Neil Armstrong's first footstep on the moon. Nothing will ever be the same!

When Vatican II got under way, I had just completed three years of philosophy in Chicago as a Passionist seminarian and was preparing to go to our school of theology in Louisville, Kentucky. The election of John XXIII was a time of wonder for those of us who had grown up thinking that the lean and elegant Pius XII defined what a pope was supposed to look like. This new pope, rotund, lumpy, and smiling, was something entirely different. Little did I guess then what an impact he and his council would have on my life as priest.

I began to feel the impact of the council during my theology studies. I had the feeling of someone racing across an old bridge with the spans falling all around me. Old theology textbooks were shelved; English began working its way into the liturgy; for the first time we had Protestant theologians come and speak to us; our religious community began to discuss radical changes in our traditional way of life (including no longer rising to chant Matins at 2:00 A.M., a change not too many would lament). We Passionists had already been blessed with superb professors in scripture—Barnabas Ahern and Carroll Stuhlmueller—two giants who were in the forefront of the biblical renewal even before the council began, so the new emphasis on scripture that would emerge from the council was a seamless transition for most of us.

The council events reached right into our community when in 1964 Barnabas Ahern was selected by Cardinal Albert Meyer of Chicago to be his *peritus* at the beginning of the second session of the council. As things went in those days, my superiors "invited" me to begin preparation for a teaching assignment in scripture to eventually succeed Barnabas on our theology faculty. I loved my courses in scripture but had been looking forward to work as a Passionist missionary, the central focus of our corporate ministry. But I happily accepted this new assignment and during the summers began remote language preparation for my postordination graduate studies. I spent a memorable summer at Hebrew Union College in Cincinnati on a grueling crash course in Hebrew, one of three Gentiles in a large class of incoming rabbinical students. And I will never forget an intensive course at Harvard learning Arabic. Not only was the mystery of these Semitic languages a new discovery, but equally mysterious and wonderful for a young Catholic seminarian in those days was the exposure to the worlds of Reform Judaism and Harvard Square.

After ordination in 1967 I went to Louvain University in Belgium for my doctoral studies in New Testament. Several of the faculty were by then veterans of the council, great theologians who with many other European colleagues had helped shape the extraordinary theological perspectives reflected in the council declarations: Gustav Thils, Albert Descamps, Gerard Philips, Philippe Delhaye, Frans Neirynck. It was during my years at Louvain—glorious years, by the way—that I felt I truly awakened to the diversity and reality of the church. There one could see very different expressions of church, in the Netherlands (which was at the height of its turbulent experimental phase), in Germany and France, and in what one of my history professors referred to as the "sub-Alpine" church of Italy. Mirroring the growing agitation against the Vietnam War in America, this was also the time of the student revolts in Paris, and the rumblings were felt even in more staid Belgium. There were student strikes in Louvain and on more than one occasion the invasion of our medieval university town by riot police and water cannon. These were exciting and somewhat ominous revolutionary times hard to imagine now.

My doctoral work was on the Gospel of Matthew under the direction of Frans Neirynck, a brilliant and demanding mentor. I was able to pursue my work on this with complete freedom, and I realized more than ever that this supportive atmosphere had been purchased at a great price. It was clear that the council had affirmed a whole generation of patient and courageous Catholic scholars, mainly in Europe, who had pursued biblical studies for more than half a century, often under suspicion and sometimes with intense suffering. Loyal Catholics such as Marie-Joseph Lagrange, O.P., of the Ecole Biblique in Jerusalem, Stanislaus Lyonnet, S.J., and Maximillian Zerwick, S.J., of the Biblical Institute in Rome remain heroes for me. They suffered greatly but never gave up, and their integrity won the day, for all of us.

When I completed my doctoral work and returned in 1972 to teach New Testament at the recently formed Catholic Theological Union in Chicago, the implementation of the council had already entered a turbulent phase. In my own community, as in most others, a whole generation of religious and priests had decided to resign. Controversies were raging over difficult moral issues such as contraception and nuclear warfare. Some early advocates of the conciliar reforms began to have second thoughts about some of the directions and the pace that the liturgical and structural changes were taking. But strangely—and wonderfully—there seemed to be relatively little ambivalence about the now accelerated biblical renewal. No doubt some scholars and preachers played havoc by displaying seemingly cavalier attitudes to the historical roots of the biblical materials. But for most Catholics, the new biblical flavor of church teaching, preaching, and catechetics was a breath of fresh and livening air. It is something I would experience in every course and lecture and workshop that I would give over the next thirty years of ministry.

I think this biblical renewal is still going strong, even though there are countercurrents. Now and then I reread *Dei verbum*, the Vatican II dogmatic constitution that confirmed the biblical renewal and gave it its new charter. Its final chapter, titled "Sacred Scripture in the Life of the Church," recommended a series of initiatives for implementing the council's reforms: "wide open access" to the scriptures for all the faithful; new translations based on the original languages, including joint efforts with "separated brethren"; encouragement of more scholars to take up biblical studies; encouragement of theologians and catechists to use scripture in their materials; encouragement of priests, deacons, and catechists "to immerse themselves in the Scriptures by constant sacred reading and diligent study"; encouragement of bishops to provide the faithful with editions of the Bible that include explanatory notes. Coupled with these recommendations was the introduction of the three-year lectionary as part of the liturgical renewal that for the first time ever gave Catholic congregations the opportunity to hear wide expanses of the Old and New Testaments on a regular basis at their Sunday (and daily) Eucharist.

The list is breathtaking. Even more breathtaking is how many of these recommendations have been put into play and are still active in the church today. In 1943 Pius XII issued his groundbreaking encyclical on scripture, *Divino afflante spiritu*, which signaled a tidal change in the church's attitude to modern biblical scholarship. Fifty years later, with the council reforms concerning the use of scripture well on their way to implementation, the Pontifical Biblical Commission (over the signature of then Cardinal Joseph Ratzinger) published a remarkable document titled *The Interpretation of the Bible in the Church*. This official text is a stunning endorsement of the biblical movement, with its various methodologies and pastoral initiatives. It leads me to believe that, in fact, no decree of the council has been more faithfully implemented than the recommendations found in *Dei verbum*.

Where will the story of Vatican II ultimately lead? None of us now can see that future with any surety. In my most hopeful moments, I think the biblical renewal is ultimately the most potent change that Vatican II has unleashed on the church. We should never forget the power of the biblical word. Over time, routine exposure to the Bible's passionate language, its compelling stories, its epic vision of God's relationship to humanity, and its strong portrayal of Jesus and his teaching could profoundly change the church's consciousness.

BARBARA E. REID, O.P.

Vatican II Opened a Window for Biblical Scholars

Barbara E. Reid was born on May 26, 1953, in Detroit, Michigan. During the time of the Second Vatican Council she was a grade-school student at St. Kevin School in Inkster, Michigan.

Reid studied at Aquinas College in Grand Rapids, Michigan, where she received a B.A. (Spanish) in 1975 and an M.A. (religious studies) in 1981. In 1974 she joined the Dominican Sisters of Grand Rapids and made final profession in 1980. Her Ph.D. was awarded in 1988 from the Catholic University of America in biblical studies, with a specialization in New Testament.

Sister Reid has taught at the secondary and graduate levels of education. From 1976 to 1982, she taught and chaired the Spanish and Religion Departments at St. Mary Cathedral High School in Saginaw, Michigan. Since 1988 Sister Reid has taught at the Catholic Theological Union in Chicago, where she is professor of New Testament Studies. In 2009 she was named vice president and academic dean of CTU.

Sister Reid is an active member of many professional societies, including the Society of Biblical Literature; the Catholic Biblical Association of America, where she has served on the executive committee, the editorial board, and as New Testament book review editor for the Catholic Biblical Quarterly *and the Chicago Society of Biblical Research, which she served as president (2000-2001). In 2001 she was awarded the annual Sophia Award for theological excellence in service to ministry from Washington Theological Union, in 2010 the Elizabeth Seton Medal for Distinguished Women Theologians from the College of Mount St. Joseph, and in 2012 the Jerome Award from the Catholic Library Association.*

Sister Reid has published several hundred articles and book reviews. They have appeared in journals such as America, The Bible Today, Biblical Research, Catholic Biblical Quarterly, New Theology Review, Chicago Studies, Currents in Theology and Mission, St. Anthony

Messenger, *and* U.S. Catholic. *Her most recent books are* Abiding Word *(2011),* Taking Up the Cross: New Testament Interpretations through Latina and Feminist Eyes *(2007) [Spanish translation:* Reconsiderar La Cruz *(2009)], the* Parables for Preachers *series (1999),* A Retreat with St. Luke, *and* Choosing the Better Part? Women in the Gospel of Luke *(1996). In* 1996 The Collegeville Pastoral Dictionary of the Bible, *of which she was a co-editor, was awarded first place in the category of theology by the Catholic Press Association. Currently she is writing* Sophia's Table: An Introduction to Feminist Interpretation of the Scriptures *(forthcoming from Eerdmans Press) and is general editor for a new sixty-volume feminist commentary on the Bible,* Wisdom Commentary Series *(forthcoming from Liturgical Press).*

I WAS NINE YEARS OLD when the council opened in 1962. My third-grade teacher, a Dominican sister, a great history buff, was very excited about it and tried to instill in us a sense of the momentous changes that were about to occur. In our little corner of the world, in Inkster, Michigan, a suburb of Detroit, I was far too young to understand all that was about to change in our church and how that would impact my life choices and profession. Although I had attended Catholic school all my life, I had never been exposed to scripture study. As youngsters we memorized the *Baltimore Catechism.* We knew Bible stories, and we had a big leather-bound family Bible on the coffee table at home, but the only time we opened it was to record family events, never to read it. Like most Catholic families, our preferred prayer form outside of Mass was the rosary. My first course in the Old Testament, taken as an elective in my sophomore year of college, sparked in me a thirst for scripture study that would remain insatiable.

For six years (1976-1982) I taught Spanish and religion at St. Mary Cathedral High School in Saginaw, Michigan. During those summers I completed a master of arts in religious studies at Aquinas College, always drawn most to the scripture courses. I was also experiencing how, since Vatican II, scripture was becoming more central to our faith life, both in my religious community and in my place of ministry. Liturgical preaching was now based on the scripture readings. The pastoral team at the cathedral was intent on forming a parish community firmly founded on the vision of Vatican II. I saw a growing hunger among people in the parish for praying with scripture, and reading and studying the Bible. I could also see that the thirst for scripture, but lack of formal study of it, was leading some to a fundamentalistic approach, or sometimes to a dangerous game of "Bible roulette," in which someone seeking for a word from God would randomly open the Bible, and whatever passage fell open was supposedly a direct message from God for what they were to do. I could see the need at every level for good biblical scholarship in the church. And I kept wanting to study more, knowing that there was so much about the Bible I did not know or understand. My notion that it was a "Protestant thing" to study the Bible was dissolving. In the fall of 1982 I began six years of study at The Catholic University of America, where I completed a Ph.D. in biblical studies with a concentration in New Testament.

One of the highlights of that time was a semester of study in the Holy Lands, ten weeks of which were led by Leslie Hoppe, O.F.M., from Catholic Theological Union in Chicago, and the remainder of which was spent working on my dissertation with tutelage from Jerome Murphy-O'Connor and the Dominicans at the École Biblique et Archéologique Française in Jerusalem. Another whole aspect of scripture study was opened up to me in this experience, as these leading scholars introduced me to the world of archaeology and love of the land and its culture and peoples. I never dreamed at that time that I would be leading groups there myself almost every year.

After completing my dissertation under the direction of John Meier at The Catholic University of America, I began in the fall of 1988 to teach New Testament at Catholic Theological Union in Chicago (CTU), where I am now a tenured full professor. This graduate school of theology and ministry is a direct outgrowth of the vision of Vatican II. In 1967, on the heels of a visit of Cardinal Suenens to Chicago, three communities of men religious united to form CTU. Very shortly they would open their doors to women and lay students as well. Today the latter is the fastest-growing population of the thriving student body of over five hundred students. One of the most significant impacts of Vatican II is that the very notion of who ministers in the church and how that ministry is done has shifted dramatically. I don't know if I would have considered pursuing a doctorate in scripture in a pre-Vatican II church. And the possibility of my teaching scripture at the graduate level may have been slimmer yet.

The rise of feminist consciousness in the post-Vatican II church has resulted in a dramatic increase in the number of Catholic women biblical scholars. An increasing number of women have served in leadership, including president, of the Catholic Biblical Association of America. In addition, the ranks of Catholic biblical scholars now include a greater number of lay people, and people not from the dominant culture. There

has been an increased consciousness that the social location of the interpreter is a determinative factor in the way in which biblical studies are
done. There is an explosion of new methods since the time of the council,
including not only further developments in historical-critical methods,
but also a rise in various kinds of literary criticism, social science methods, liberation approaches, and postmodern hermeneutical perspectives.
The open window of Vatican II has enabled Catholic biblical scholars to
be fully immersed in these scholarly developments.

Another effect of Vatican II on scripture study is the encouragement
of ecumenical exchange. The "Constitution on Revelation" reaffirmed
for Catholic biblical scholars what had first been articulated in *Divino
afflante spiritu* in 1943: we were encouraged to use all the critical tools of
study already being developed by our Protestant colleagues. Shortly after
the council, new translations of the Bible were done by ecumenical teams
of scholars, based not on the Latin Vulgate but on the original Greek and
Hebrew texts. In Chicago, ecumenical collaboration is a given. Catholic
Theological Union chose to locate in the midst of the city, in a cluster
of twelve theological schools of differing Christian denominations. Not
only do students cross-register, but frequently the scripture faculty of the
various schools appear as guest lecturers in one another's classes. The
New Testament professors from the Association of Chicago Theological Schools meet four times a year to share a meal and a paper by one
of its members. In addition, the Chicago Society of Biblical Research, of
which I have been president, is one of the oldest ecumenical associations
of biblical scholars in the country. The Catholic Biblical Association of
America, for which I have been New Testament book review editor, likewise is intent on fostering ecumenism. I have also been part of the bilat-
eral dialogue between United Methodists and Roman Catholics. This
group also sees the need to ground the work toward unity in our common understanding of the scriptures.

Of the many ways in which Vatican II placed scripture at the heart of
the life of the church was the emphasis on preaching from the scriptures.
As a member of the Order of Preachers, I have been especially interested
in how biblical scholarship is placed at the service of preachers. There is
still a great need to form a biblically literate Catholic faithful. Seminaries
and schools of theology face an especially great challenge of forming students to place the scriptures at the center of their prayer life, study, and
ministry. A particular need is to teach them how to move from biblical
exegesis to interpretation of the scriptures for liturgical proclamation.[25]
My series of books, one for each liturgical cycle, *Parables for Preachers*
(1999, 2000, 2001), has attempted to put recent biblical scholarship into

an easily accessible format for preachers, teachers, and catechists. Like-wise, my book *Choosing the Better Part? Women in the Gospel of Luke* (1996) has aimed to bring feminist perspectives to bear on interpretation of the Third Gospel for all interested students of scripture.

The horizons opened by Vatican II for Catholic biblical scholarship are vast and exciting. My life's journey has been directly shaped by its vision and energy, and will, I hope, continue to bring new life to the church and the world.

JOSEPH A. FITZMYER, S.J.

The Word of God, Magisterium, and the Historical Character of the Gospels

Joseph Fitzmyer was born on November 4, 1920, in Philadelphia. After completing his education, he assumed a variety of teaching posts. At the time of the Second Vatican Council, he was teaching New Testament and biblical languages at the Jesuit theologate of the Maryland and New York provinces, Woodstock College in Maryland. He left there in 1969 and taught subsequently at the University of Chicago (1969-1971), Fordham University (1971-1974), Weston Jesuit School of Theology (1974-1976), and Catholic University of America (1976-1986).

Father Fitzmyer has published widely in the area of scriptural studies. He was the co-editor of The Jerome Biblical Commentary *(1968) and also of* The New Jerome Biblical Commentary *(1990). Some of his other important publications include* The Gospel according to Luke *(1981, 1985),* Acts of the Apostles *(1998), and* The Dead Sea Scrolls and Christian Origins *(2000).*

During the year 2000, Father Fitzmyer was the Royden B. Davis Visiting Professor at Georgetown University. Since 1990 he has held the position of professor emeritus and professorial lecturer in the Department of Biblical Studies at Catholic University of America.

I NOW RECALL HOW HAPPY I was when in November 1965 the dogmatic constitution *Dei verbum* was approved by the council fathers. Two of its assertions were and still are very important in my estimation. The first is the assertion in section 10:

> The task of authentically interpreting the Word of God, whether written or handed on, has been entrusted solely to the living teaching office of the Church (*soli vivo Ecclesiae magisterio*), whose authority is exercised in the name of Jesus Christ. This teaching office is not above the Word of God, but serves it, teach-

ing only what has been handed on, as it listens to it faithfully, guards it scrupulously, and explains it faithfully by divine commission and with the help of the Holy Spirit.[26]

For the first time one finds in an ecclesiastical document the admission that the magisterium is not above the word of God in scripture or tradition, but serves it. This admission thus undercuts the accusation sometimes heard that for Catholics the magisterium is the ultimate norm of faith (because of the encyclical *Humani generis*).[27] Rather one can admit with Lutherans that scripture is *norma normans non normata* ["the rule that measures, but itself is not measured"] and tradition is *norma normata* ["the rule that is measured—that is, measured by scripture"], as Karl Rahner rightly saw.[28]

The second assertion is found in *Dei verbum*, section 19, where once the "historical character" (*historicitatem*) of the four Gospels is affirmed, the text goes on to admit the stages of the Gospel tradition, which was commonly asserted by New Testament interpreters of that time:

> After the ascension of the Lord, the Apostles handed on to their hearers what he had said and done. (This they did) with that clearer understanding that they enjoyed after they had been instructed by the events of Christ's risen life (*eventibus gloriosis Christi*) and taught by the light of the Spirit of truth. The sacred authors composed the four Gospels, selecting some things from the many which had been handed on by word of mouth or in writing, reducing some of them to a synthesis, explicating (*explanantes*) some things in view of the situation in their churches, and preserving the form of proclamation, but always in such fashion that they told us the honest truth about Jesus (*Vera et sincera de Iesu*).[29]

Lest anyone fail to realize whence the substance of this double assertion was coming, the council fathers introduced section 19 with *Sancta Mater Ecclesia* ["Holy Mother Church"], using the very opening words of the Biblical Commission's Instruction of 1964, *De historica evangeliorum veritate* ["On the Historical Truth of the Gospels"].[30] For the double assertion was, in fact, a résumé of three paragraphs of that Instruction. In other words, *Dei verbum* distinguished in effect, as did the Biblical Commission before it, three stages of the gospel tradition: (1) What Jesus of Nazareth did and taught (A.D. 1-33); (2) what the apostles proclaimed with postresurrection faith and clarity about what he did and taught (A.D. 33-65); and (3) what the evangelists selected, synthesized, and explicated from stages one and two in their literary productions that we call the Gospels (A.D. 65-95).[31]

Thus the interpretation of the Gospels was liberated from earlier Catholic fundamentalism, which tended to equate stage three with stage one. Moreover, *vera et sincera de Iesu* was a carefully phrased expression that scarcely meant the same as "historical truth." Section 19 was, in fact, the product of much conservative and enlightened debate as *Dei verbum* took shape in the council, and the struggle between the two groups of council fathers can still be seen in the contrast between the "historical character" (*historicitatem*) of the Gospels asserted (in the first sentence) and the later nuanced double assertion (in the second and third sentences) of what the apostles and sacred authors have passed on to us, as the Biblical Commission had clarified.

PART FIVE

ECUMENISM AND INTERRELIGIOUS DIALOGUE

The Turn to the Other

WILLIAM MADGES

I CAN REMEMBER BEING TAUGHT in my early years in elementary school that if people wanted to be saved, they were "obliged" to belong to the Catholic Church, for it alone is the one true church established by Christ. When asked how I knew that no other church but the Catholic Church is the true church of Christ, the answer I had memorized through frequent recitation was because no other church has the four marks of Christ's church, that is, being one, holy, catholic, and apostolic. Although my *Baltimore Catechism* conceded that those who remained outside the Catholic Church "through no grave fault of their own and do not know it is the true Church" can be saved, the general impression with which I was left was that it was quite obvious that the Catholic Church was the true church. One would have to be blind or thick-headed not to see that.

From this perspective—as the Catholic Good Friday liturgy prior to Vatican II made clear—Orthodox Christians were "schismatics" and Protestants were "heretics." The Orthodox were called schismatics, even though they shared many beliefs and the sacraments in common with Catholics, because they did not recognize the pope as the legitimate head of the entire church of Christ. The Protestants were even further removed from the true church. They not only refused to recognize the pope as the rightful head of the church; they also deviated from the central, authentic doctrines of Christ's church. It is not surprising in this climate that Catholics were forbidden to visit the churches of other Christian denominations or to become too familiar with Protestant or Orthodox neighbors.

That situation changed in a dramatic way with the papacy of John XXIII. Prior to the Second Vatican Council, he established the Secretariat for Christian Unity (1960) and named five official observers to attend the third assembly of the World Council of Churches in New Delhi, India (1961). In addition, John XXIII declared that one of the principal purposes of the council was to contribute to the unity of the separated Christian churches.

The Second Vatican Council eventually produced two different documents that describe relationships with those who are not Catholic: the "Decree on Ecumenism" (Unitatis redintegratio) and the "Declaration on the Relationship of the Church to Non-Christian Religions" (Nostra aetate). The former document lays out Catholic principles of ecumenism and discusses how concern for restoring unity among Christians is to be put into practice. The latter document, which was originally a chapter in the "Decree on Ecumenism," addresses relations with non-Christians, with special emphasis placed on the relationship with Jews. Both documents owe much of their spirit and content to the special committees established to deal with other Christians and non-Christians: the Secretariat for Christian Unity, established by Pope John XXIII in 1960 and headed by Cardinal Augustin Bea, and the Secretariat for Non-Christian Religions, established by Pope Paul VI in 1964 and headed by Cardinal Paolo Marella.

Let us turn our attention first to the "Decree on Ecumenism."

The Decree on Ecumenism

From early in the twentieth century, Protestants had become increasingly involved in what came to be called "the ecumenical movement." This phenomenon exhibited growing joint cooperation among the Protestant churches, beginning with interdenominational cooperation in missionary work. The World Missionary Conference of 1910 in Edinburgh, Scotland, which was the eighth in a series of international meetings of Protestant Christians begun in 1854, gave decisive impetus to the desire for greater Christian unity. This conference differed from previous meetings in that most of those who attended came not only as deeply interested individuals, but also as official delegates of the various missionary societies. Out of collaboration fostered by this conference grew the International Missionary Council in 1921. Other areas of increasing ecumenical activity included youth work, Christian education, and united service to society. In 1908 the Federal Council of the Churches of Christ in America was founded, which merged in 1950 with a number of interdenominational agencies to form the National Council of the Churches of Christ in the U.S.A.

The Protestant ecumenical movement eventually broached even the more difficult issue of doctrinal differences, beginning with the first World Conference on Faith and Order in 1927. By 1938 a provisional structure for a world council of Christian churches had been worked out, but its implementation was interrupted by the Second World War. Finally in 1948, the World Council of Churches was established, initially including 145 churches from 44 countries.

The Roman Catholic Church officially remained aloof from these developments. Official Catholic sentiment in the early twentieth century continued to be guided by papal teaching of the previous century. Pope Pius IX, in his "Syllabus of Errors" (1864), had rejected the idea that it was no longer necessary that the Catholic Church be held as the only religion of the state and that there should be freedom of worship for all. In the twentieth century, Pope Pius XI, although supportive of greater understanding of the Eastern churches, maintained a negative attitude toward Protestants. In his encyclical *Mortalium animos* (1928), he declared that the only way in which the unity of Christianity could be fostered would be "by furthering the return to the one true church of Christ of those who are separated from it." This would involve their believing in "the infallibility of the Roman Pontiff in the sense of the Ecumenical Vatican Council [i.e., Vatican I] with the same faith as they believe in the Incarnation of Our Lord."[1]

In the light of this mindset, it is not surprising that, when Pope John strongly encouraged ecumenism, some members of the curia and others thought that he did not fully understand the doctrinal issues involved in the restoration of Christian unity. Others feared that his ecumenical openness would encourage those Catholic theologians who had been flirting with heterodoxy to minimize Catholic truth even further.[2] But Pope John persisted in his strong support of ecumenism. On October 19, 1962, he elevated the Secretariat for Christian Unity to the same level as the Preparatory Commissions, which had been charged with preparing the documents to be considered at the Second Vatican Council. He also invited Protestant and Orthodox communions to send observers to Vatican II, whose presence at the council was unprecedented in the history of Roman Catholicism.

During the council Pope John met personally with the non-Catholic observers. Departing from custom, he received the delegates in the Hall of the Consistory, and then sat down with them in a square, in much the same way as he was accustomed to sit with the cardinals in consistory. As Francis Murphy noted at the time, it was quite significant that the pope sat on the same kind of chair as the delegates, rather than on his throne. This symbolic gesture of equality made quite an impression on the non-Catholic observers, who were introduced as "our brethren in Christ." In his talk Pope John emphasized charity and mutual understanding as the keys to progress in ecumenism.[3]

Initially, three separate documents, each dealing with a different aspect of ecumenism, were prepared for the consideration of the council fathers. The Theological Commission had prepared a document dealing with the theme of unity, especially with Protestants. The Secretariat for Christian Unity wrote a draft on general ecumenical principles. And the Preparatory Commission for the Oriental Churches prepared a document, titled *Ut unum sint* ("That They May Be One"), which was the first of the documents to be considered by the council. This document concerned itself exclusively with the means of achieving reunion with the Eastern Orthodox.

One might wonder why it had not been decided to present a single schema to the council, or at least three coordinated drafts that could later be fused into one. One factor was apparently the reluctance of the Theological Commission to cooperate with other commissions or groups because of its conviction that doctrinal matters were within the exclusive competence of the Theological Commission.[4]

During the discussion of *Ut unum sint* (November 26-30, 1962), a number of sensitive issues were hotly debated. One such issue was whether both sides were equally to blame for the split between Roman Catholics and the Eastern Orthodox. Another was whether the Orthodox bodies were true "churches" or only "assemblies." On the final day of discussion, Cardinal Bea pointed out that many of the topics dealt with in *Ut unum sint* were the domain of his Secretariat for Christian Unity. He proposed that this document be fused together with the other two that had been prepared. The council fathers overwhelmingly endorsed this idea.

The new document that was prepared over the course of the next year was presented for discussion during the final two weeks of November 1963. It was radically different from the 1962 schema *Ut unum sint*. This revised schema now consisted of five chapters. The first dealt with the principles of Catholic ecumenism; the second, the practical aspects of ecumenism; the third, Christians separated from the Catholic Church. The third chapter was subdivided into two parts, one dealing with the

Eastern churches, the other with the Protestant churches. Chapter 4 was devoted to the Jews, and Chapter 5 to religious liberty.[5]

On the fourth day of discussion of the revised schema on ecumenism (November 21, 1963), the council moderators announced that the council would proceed to an immediate vote on the acceptance of Chapters 1-3 as a basis for discussion. Archbishop Felici, secretary general of the council, added that the voting on Chapters 4 and 5 would take place in a few days. A strong majority of 1,966 bishops voted in favor of accepting the text for discussion (with 86 opposed). Ultimately the decision was made to handle the subject matter of Chapters 4 and 5 in separate documents. The material of Chapter 4 grew into the "Declaration on the Relationship of the Church to Non-Christian Religions," which was approved on October 28, 1965, one year after the promulgation of the now shortened "Decree on Ecumenism." The material of Chapter 5 was developed into the "Declaration on Religious Freedom," which was also approved during the final session of the council (December 7, 1965).

During the debates about ecumenism at the council, two quite different perspectives came to light. On the one side were those bishops who defended wholeheartedly the mentality of the Counter-Reformation, according to which Christian unity meant nothing more than the return of other Christians to the Catholic Church.[6] On the other side were those who believed that the gospel and the contemporary situation both called for a common witness to the faith, which meant acknowledging that not all Catholic truths are on the same level.[7] The differences were quite sharp. A variety of proposals were made for revising the text. At the conclusion of the second session, Cardinal Bea said that these suggestions would all be carefully considered in working out a revised text of the "Decree on Ecumenism" to be voted on during the next session.

Pope Paul VI's pilgrimage to the Holy Land from January 4 to January 6, 1964, gave strong encouragement for advancing a positive statement on ecumenism. During this brief trip, the pope met with Orthodox and Armenian patriarchs and with representatives of other Christian communities. The most significant meeting was the pope's meeting with Athenagoras, patriarch of Constantinople. Not since the Council of Florence in 1439 had pope and patriarch met with the intent of resolving differences that had formally separated the two church bodies since 1054. The meeting between the two Christian leaders captured world attention and "presaged the declaration of mutual forgiveness they issued two years later at the conclusion of the council."[8]

In August of the same year, Paul VI issued his first encyclical, *Ecclesiam suam*, which had an important direct impact on the revision of the draft on ecumenism. The encyclical introduced the word "dialogue" into the conciliar vocabulary. Having appropriated the word from Jewish philosopher Martin Buber, the pope used the term seventy-seven times and devoted two-thirds of *Ecclesiam suam* to its meaning and application. In the original draft of the document on ecumenism, the word does not appear at all.

"In its revised version, presented after the publication of the encyclical, it becomes one of the text's most characteristic words. Thus it was that 'dialogue,' so typical of 'the spirit' of Vatican II, made its way into the council's vocabulary. . . ."[9]

During the first eight months of the year, the Secretariat for Christian Unity had to sort through over a thousand proposed changes to the text. A new, revised version of the "Decree on Ecumenism" was then presented for discussion during the third session of the council. The three chapters of the decree were voted on individually on November 10, 11, and 14, and each received overwhelming approval. But on the day before the final vote on the document as a whole (November 19, 1964), Archbishop Felici announced that the printing of the final text was not yet completed. This meant that the council fathers would not be able to examine it before casting their ballots on the next day. Felici explained that the reason for the delay was that some changes ("kind suggestions authoritatively expressed"), made on the authority of Pope Paul VI, had been introduced into the text to make it "clearer." The secretary general then read the nineteen last-minute changes, which had been submitted to and was hurriedly reviewed and accepted by Cardinal Bea and the Secretariat for Christian Unity.[10] It appears that a minority of prelates who were dissatisfied with the progressive ecumenical tone of the text had appealed directly to the pope to change portions of the text.[11] Although Paul VI did not forward the most destructive emendations to the Secretariat, he was adamant that he would not approve the schema without the changes that he put forward. The emendations that he passed along and that were incorporated into the final text changed the emphasis of some passages, but did not alter the fundamental sense of the decree.[12] Nonetheless, the pope's intervention seriously disturbed the mood at the council. A number of bishops and non-Catholic observers were irritated that the pope had proposed changes after it was too late for the council fathers to discuss them. The Protestant observers were particularly upset by the apparently arbitrary way in which the changes were imposed on the council at the last minute.[13] The next day, November 20, the council voted on the whole text, including the papal changes. The vote was 2,054 for, 64 against.

The decree goes beyond the traditional assertion that the Catholic Church is the true church to assert that Christ's Spirit is at work in the churches and communities beyond the visible boundaries of the Catholic Church. It acknowledges, moreover, that baptism establishes a communion among believers insofar as "all who have been justified by faith in baptism are incorporated into Christ" and therefore "have the right to be called Christians, and with good reason are accepted as sisters and brothers in the Lord by the children of the Catholic Church" (*Unitatis redintegratio*, sect. 3).[14] Dr. Oscar Cullmann, a Protestant observer at the council, rightly commented at the time: "This is more than the opening of a door; new ground has been broken. No Catholic document has ever spoken of non-Catholic Christians in this way."[15]

Declaration on Non-Christian Religions

For centuries it had been commonplace for Catholics to believe and to declare that "there is no salvation outside the church." And "church" meant the Roman Catholic Church. The Fourth Lateran Council (1215) had declared that there is "one universal church of the faithful, outside of which nobody at all is saved." The Council of Florence (1442) was more explicit in condemning those who remained outside the Catholic Church. In its Bull of Union with the Copts, also known as the Decree for the Jacobites, it explicitly declared that "all those who are outside the catholic church, not only pagans but also Jews or heretics and schismatics, cannot share in eternal life and will go *into the everlasting fire which was prepared for the devil and his angels* [Mt 25:41], unless they are joined to the catholic church before the end of their lives."[16]

It is no wonder, then, that the Jesuit Leonard Feeney (1897-1978) thought that the archbishop of Boston, Richard Cushing, was teaching heresy when he admitted that it was possible that non-Catholics might be saved.[17] Feeney was so convinced that church teaching was on his side that he persisted in his views and refused to leave Boston, although threatened with dismissal from the Jesuit order for refusing to do so. When he died, Feeney's ardent followers had the words *Extra ecclesiam nulla salus* ["Outside the church no salvation."] carved into the bottom of his gravestone.[18]

What Vatican II was prepared to say on this issue was clearly a matter of deep concern and divided opinion. As Robert Graham observed shortly after the conclusion of the council, the development of the "Declaration on the Relationship of the Church to Non-Christian Religions" (*Nostra aetate*) was one of the most dramatic stories of Vatican II.[19] As was noted above, this declaration began as Chapter 4 of the "Decree on

Ecumenism" and was focused exclusively on the Jews. The concern was not initially focused on making a statement about the possibility of salvation for those outside the Catholic Church, but rather on addressing the anti-Semitism that was rampant and so graphically embodied in the murder of Jews during World War II.

As the debate on the "Decree on Ecumenism" got under way during the second session of the council in 1963, a number of council fathers, such as Cardinal Tappouni, the Syrian patriarch of Antioch, argued for removing Chapters 4 and 5 from the document on ecumenism. Tappouni declared that ecumenism has to do with the unity of Christians, and, therefore, the church's relation to non-Christians ought not to be included in a document on ecumenism. Others, such as Patriarch Maximos IV Saigh, the Melkite patriarch of Antioch, insisted that if Jews were to be mentioned, then the church's relation to Muslims must also be included in the document. If only the Jews were named, the statement could be misunderstood as a political endorsement of the state of Israel or of Zionism. If so understood, the Christian minorities living in Arab countries might suffer reprisals.[20]

Cardinal Bea, president of the Secretariat for Promoting Christian Unity, had to address these concerns in his address to the council on November 19, 1963. He defended the existence of Chapter 4 by explaining that Pope John XXIII had personally directed Bea to formulate a statement on the Jews.[21] Five months before his death on June 3, 1963, Pope John had approved Bea's outline of the statement. Although the pope's approval did not necessarily settle the issue or bind his successor, Paul VI, Bea nonetheless was convinced that John's wishes resonated with a large number of council fathers and clearly reflected the spirit of Christ.[22] In response to the fear that the statement would be understood politically, Bea emphasized that the chapter on the Jews dealt only with the *religious* relation between Catholics and Jews. Bea proceeded to emphasize some of the most important aspects of the declaration's statement concerning Jews and Judaism. He stressed that Jews and Christians share a common spiritual heritage and he denied that the Jews, either today or at the time of Jesus, could be blamed indiscriminately for the suffering and death of Jesus. In attempting to account for the recent persecution of Jews, Bea did not identify Christian prejudice, rooted theologically in the charge of deicide ("killing of God," that is, Christ), as the cause of the Holocaust. Rather, he suggested that the Holocaust, and the anti-Semitism that made it possible, perhaps had had a negative influence on the attitude of contemporary Catholics toward Jews. Although the Gospel portrayal of Jewish responsibility for Jesus' death played a role in Christian attitudes toward Jews, it was not the principal cause of anti-Semitism. To find the principal cause, one would have to attend to social, political, and economic factors.[23]

During this second session of the council, the bishops in attendance decided to separate Chapter 4 (dealing with the Jews) and Chapter 5 (dealing with religious liberty) from the rest of the statement on ecumenism. Debate on the subject matter of those two chapters would be postponed. The official reason given for the postponement was a "lack of time." Many, however, suspected that this reason was merely a pretext. A variety of political and theological considerations were thought to be the real reasons for postponement.[24] Between the conclusion of the second session of the council (December 4, 1963) and February 1964, the Secretariat for Christian Unity had revised and strengthened the text on the Jews. Two months later, however, at a meeting of the Coordinating Commission, several changes were made in the revised text to make it more palatable to the theological minority, who opposed an overly conciliatory statement, and more acceptable to the Arab world. The text was broadened to include mention of Muslims, Hindus, and Buddhists. And the passage exonerating the Jewish people of deicide was watered down. When news of these changes were leaked in early May, Jewish communities, especially in the United States, became upset.

It was this text that the council fathers considered when they met during the third session to discuss the issue again (September 28-30, 1964). Although there was still some small opposition to the document, the majority supported it. A significant number—including Cardinals Liénart of Lille, France; Frings of Cologne, Germany; Lercaro of Bologna, Italy; Léger of Montreal, Canada; Koenig of Vienna, Austria; and the American Cardinals Cushing (Boston), Meyer (Chicago), and Ritter (St. Louis)—advocated the restoration of passages that had been removed, particularly the passage that absolved Jews of deicide.[25] It was even proposed that a request for forgiveness for Christian persecution of Jews be added to the text. Cardinal Ruffini of Palermo, Sicily, however, demurred. He proposed a linked process of exchange: the deicide charge could be dropped if certain anti-Christian statements in the Talmud were deleted.

In the final text that was approved on October 28, 1965, mutual understanding and respect were advocated. Although a Christian request for forgiveness was not added to the document, the declaration was unambiguous in its condemnation of anti-Semitism.

Indeed, the church reproves every form of persecution against whomsoever it may be directed. Remembering, then, its common heritage with the Jews and moved not by any political consideration, but solely by the religious motivation of Christian charity, it deplores all hatreds, persecutions, displays of anti-Semitism leveled at any time or from any source against the Jews.[26]

The declaration, however, went far beyond a statement concerning Catholic relations with Jews. It affirms the unity of the human community (no. 1). And it acknowledges that, although the fullness of religious life is to be found in Christ, there are elements of truth and goodness in other religions (no. 2). Although expected to continue to witness to their own faith, Christians are therefore exhorted to "acknowledge, preserve and encourage the spiritual and moral truths found among non-Christians, together with their social life and culture."[27] The statements dealing with Hinduism and Buddhism are very brief and descriptive, rather than evaluative. The statements dealing with Islam and Judaism are much fuller and appreciative. "High regard" for Muslims is expressed (no. 3) while gratitude for the "nourishment" Christianity draws from Judaism is acknowledged (no. 4).[28] The declaration concludes with an appeal to all Christians to be at peace with all people (no. 5).

When one reads section 2 of *Nostra aetate* together with section 16 of *Lumen gentium*, he or she might wonder whether Vatican II is proclaiming new doctrine about the possibility of salvation outside the Catholic Church. In the early centuries of Christianity, the slogan "no salvation outside the church" was first directed against those (former) Christians who were separated from the church through heresy or schism or those Christians who were in danger of being separated through excommunication. After Christianity became the official religion of the Roman Empire at the end of the fourth century, the slogan, however, began to be directed against non-Christians. The assumption was that the gospel had been proclaimed everywhere and that everyone had had sufficient opportunity to accept it. Those who had not accepted the gospel—pagans and Jews, for example—were believed to be guilty of refusing God's offer of salvation, for which refusal they would be justly condemned. Lateran Council IV and the Council of Florence reiterated this belief. After the division of the Western church into Catholic and Protestant communities, the statement "no salvation outside the church" was widely interpreted to mean "no salvation outside *my* church."

Although earlier theologians, such as Thomas Aquinas in the thirteenth century, had reflected upon possible exceptions to the principle that salvation could not be obtained outside the visible church, new impetus for thinking about this matter was given by the European voyages of discovery. Beginning with Columbus's "discovery" of the so-called

New World in 1492 and continuing with the voyages of the Spanish and the Portuguese explorers in the sixteenth century, European Christians encountered peoples who had never heard the gospel before. Was it possible for people living after the time of Jesus, who had never heard the Christian good news, to be saved? Or phrased differently, How could Christians continue to judge all pagans guilty of sinful unbelief, when they now knew that countless people had been living without the knowledge of the gospel, through no fault of their own?[29] Explicit faith in God, which could be interpreted to imply faith in Christ, and implicit desire for baptism might be sufficient to obtain the salvation of those who did not belong to the visible church.

Spanish theologians, such as Francisco de Vitoria (c. 1485-1546) broke new ground. Vitoria judged that Native Americans were not culpable for rejecting Christian faith, if the faith had not been presented to them in a convincing way. Vitoria was keenly aware of how the identification of the faith with the behavior of the conquistadors made it difficult for the natives to affirm and adopt Christianity.[30] Juan de Lugo (1583-1660) extended the thinking of Vitoria and other contemporaries. By paying careful attention to the ways in which people come to faith, Lugo concluded that even people who had been exposed to the Christian message over a long period of time might not be culpable for failing to embrace Christianity. From his perspective, pagans, Jews, or Muslims were obliged by the first preaching of the gospel to inquire further into its truth. If they make this inquiry, but are unable to find sufficient reasons to embrace the Christian faith, their ignorance of the truth of Christianity is invincible. Lugo's ideas were revolutionary in their historical context. He "dared to suggest that some who sincerely sought the truth might not recognize it in the Christian religion, and might still be saved by the faith in God which they found in their own religion."[31]

Ideas such as these were developed slowly over the course of several centuries until they were explicitly endorsed at Vatican II. Without repudiating the teaching of Lateran Council IV (that there "is one universal church of the faithful, outside of which no one is saved"), the bishops at Vatican II developed a broader understanding of the church. The "Dogmatic Constitution on the Church" (*Lumen gentium*) declared that all people are called to be "church," understood fundamentally as the assembly or People of God. And to the church, understood in this sense, "belong, or are related in different ways: the catholic faithful, others who believe in Christ, and finally all of humankind, called by God's grace to salvation."[32] The constitution proceeded to declare explicitly that Jews and Muslims are "related to the People of God in various ways" and are included in the plan of salvation. The essence of the constitution's teaching on the possibility of salvation outside of Christianity is summed up in section 16:

> Nor is God remote from those who in shadows and images seek the unknown God, since he gives to everyone life and breath and all things (see Acts 17:25-28) and since the Savior wills everyone to be saved (see 1 Tim 2:4). Those who, through no fault of their own, do not know the Gospel of Christ or his church, but who nevertheless seek God with a sincere heart, and, moved by grace, try in their actions to do his will as they know it through the dictates of their conscience—these too may attain eternal salvation.[33]

Nostra aetate's acknowledgment of elements of truth and goodness in other religions and its exhortation to dialogue and cooperation with followers of other religions, together with *Lumen gentium*'s affirmation of the possibility of salvation outside of Christianity, moved Catholics to embrace greater openness toward people of other faith traditions and ushered in a period of fruitful and sustained interreligious dialogue in the years immediately following the conclusion of the council.

ROGER OF TAIZÉ

Christ Is United to Every Human Being without Exception

Born on May 12, 1915, Brother Roger was the founder and prior of the Taizé Community in France. Founding that community in 1940, Brother Roger tried to open ways to heal the divisions between Christians and among human beings in general. The community is made up of Catholic brothers as well as brothers from different Protestant backgrounds; they come from over twenty-five different countries. The Taizé community works for reconciliation and peace. The brothers of Taizé make a life commitment to celibacy, living together, and a great simplicity. Some brothers live in small groups that share the life of the poor across the world. Week after week, thousands of young adults from every continent go to Taizé to pray and to prepare themselves to work for peace, reconciliation, and trust among human beings. At the end of each year, a meeting brings together 70,000 to 100,000 young adults in a large European city. Gatherings are also held on other continents.

Brother Roger wrote many books, including Struggle and Contemplation *(1974),* The Sources of Taizé *(1991),* Peace of Heart in All Things *(1996), and, together with Mother Teresa,* Seeking the Heart of God: Reflections on Prayer *(1993). Among the many awards Brother Roger received are the Templeton Prize, London 1974; the Peace Prize, Frankfurt 1974; the UNESCO Prize for Peace Education, Paris 1988; Karlspreis, Aachen 1989; the Robert Schuman Prize, Strasbourg 1992; the Award for International Humanitarian Service, Notre Dame University 1997. He died on August 16, 2005.*

IN THE MIDDLE OF THE twentieth century there appeared a man by the name of John, born in a humble peasant family in the north of Italy. The vast pastoral responsibility that was entrusted to him in his old age undoubtedly caused an exceptional intuition of reconciliation to come to fruition in him. That man, John XXIII, made that intuition part of the vocation of multitudes of Christians.

It was Cardinal Gerlier of Lyon who in 1958 took the initiative of introducing us to John XXIII shortly after his election as pope. Wishing to place in his heart the question of the reconciliation of Christians, the cardinal asked John XXIII to give his first audience to Taizé. Why so quickly? The pope was elderly, explained the cardinal, he would soon be hearing a great many words, and it was important that he remember well what we would say to him.

John XXIII agreed and received us just after his inauguration, the first morning on which private audiences were held. He showed himself to be very attentive to the question of reconciliation and ended the conversation by asking us to return. That first meeting with the pope communicated to us an unexpected impetus.

At the beginning of 1959, John XXIII announced the council. Brother Max and I were filled with gratefulness when we realized that he wished us to be present at the council as observers. I remember well the day when the letter arrived; to be invited to take part in that search made our hearts overflow.

Naturally, I had the impression that I was not made to participate in such an assembly. In the course of the four years of the council, however, I only missed two sessions. During the early days of the council, I used to read texts by Saint Teresa of Avila during the night. She gave me the courage to continue.

We rented a four-room apartment in the center of Rome. Our windows opened onto an inner courtyard, with no sun. Brothers took turns coming from Taizé to help with hospitality. Already early in the morning, we would meet for prayer. Then we left for the council. For the entire four years, as we went to Saint Peter's morning after morning, approaching the basilica awakened the same happiness when, as we came close to the Tiber, the sky opened up, a soft sky, filled with light.

As soon as we reached the basilica, before entering the section for the observers, we spent a moment of silent prayer with many bishops before the reserved Eucharist in a side chapel, long before the time of the daily assembly.

During the assembly, our attention was particularly awakened when we heard, under the dome of Saint Peter's, a bishop affirm what would open new ways forward for the future and corresponded to our own basic concerns: the presence of Christians in the contemporary world.

How often did we call to mind a face from the history of Christians, in particular, as soon as he died, the face of the beloved Pope John XXIII.

Still today, I cannot forget the moment in 1963 when I learned of his death. From the depths of my being this question rose up: what would become of Taizé without John XXIII?

At the end of the morning, leaving the basilica, we found the bishops with whom we had made an appointment, and we brought them to our apartment for the midday meal. We had set up a tiny chapel there, and we began with a sung prayer. Around the circular table for the meal, the topics of conversation were quite varied, depending on whether we were hosting Asians, Americans, or Africans. It was good to hear their concerns, to discover how they lived in faraway lands. The fourth year, women sometimes came to eat with us, when they were invited to the council as auditors. Around this table we also got to know Karol Wojtyla, the future Pope John Paul II, who was a young bishop at the time.

The meals were simple, sometimes overflowing with joy. We had so few resources that the food was frugal. We found out that some people used to say, "It's better to have something to eat before going to dine with the Taizé brothers!" There was usually rice and tomato sauce, a little wine, and we always found flowers to put on the table.

During the afternoon, people of the most varied sort came to visit us, particularly young people. At the end of the afternoon, often we replied to an invitation from a seminary to go and meet young people. Then we returned quickly through the crowded streets to come home for evening prayer and to welcome other bishops for a meal.

When there were letters to write, texts to compose, notes to prepare in order to express our viewpoint if it was asked for, it was only possible to spend time doing this at the end of the evening or late at night.

During those four years, we discovered multiple facets of that unique communion that is the church. We would perhaps have been unaware of them had we not had the opportunity of taking part in that event. Sometimes we wondered: why this vote, or that expression? Then the discovery of the mystery of the church returned again. And our hearts rejoiced once more.

At the beginning of the council, the ecumenical dynamism was such that it seemed as if a reconciliation would come to pass. John XXIII had called people "not to try and find out who had been wrong and who had been right." In his turn, as universal pastor, Paul VI had asked non-Catholics for forgiveness "if a wrong could be attributed to the Catholic Church regarding the causes of separation."

But were the denominations capable of seizing that historical moment? The weight of the past created irrational refusals, and after the council some people wondered whether an hour of ecumenism had been missed.

Great intuitions remain from the council. They are gospel treasures to respond to urgent needs at the beginning of the third millennium. For forty [sic] years now we have been welcoming a great many young adults to Taizé week after week, and we feel an unexpected hope: it is possible to discover in the spirit of the council responses to the longings of the younger generations.

There is one luminous gospel insight that the council brought to light; it had previously remained for a long time under the dust of the years: "Christ is united to every human being without exception." Later on, Pope John Paul II, in his first encyclical, quoted those words and added, "even if they are unaware of it." Multitudes of human beings are unfamiliar with even the name of God. But God is in communion with each person. This striking intuition can open up a new understanding of faith on earth. Yes, for every human being, the invisible God is a kind of influx of light, peace, and love.

PHILIP A. CUNNINGHAM

A Tectonic Shift in Relations
with Non-Catholics: Witnessing
a Transformation

Philip A. Cunningham was born in 1953 and attended the same Catholic grammar school in which he later taught as a young adult. After seven years of Catholic junior high school teaching, he became a parish director of religious education in southern New Jersey, and later the co-director of a regional adult religious education center that served thirteen Catholic parishes in southeastern New Hampshire.

Meanwhile he earned master's degrees in secondary school curriculum development from Fordham University in New York and in theology at LaSalle University in Philadelphia. Becoming increasingly focused on Catholic–Jewish relations, in 1992 he earned a Ph.D. from Boston College in religion and education. His dissertation, "A Content Analysis of the Presentation of Jews and Judaism in Current Roman Catholic Religion Textbooks," assessed the implementation of educational directives stemming from the Vatican II declaration Nostra aetate.

After earning his doctorate, Cunningham co-directed a Master of Arts in Theology program at Notre Dame College in Manchester, New Hampshire. He later became the founding executive director of the Center for Christian–Jewish Learning at Boston College. Since 2008 he has been a professor of theology at Saint Joseph's University in Philadelphia, where he also directs its Institute for Jewish-Catholic Relations.

He is the author or editor of numerous articles and twelve books; most recently he co-edited Christ Jesus and the Jewish People Today: New Explorations of Theological Interrelationships *(Grand Rapids, MI: Eerdmans, 2011). He serves as the founding secretary-treasurer of the Council of Centers on Jewish-Christian Relations, whose website he also manages (www.ccjr.us), and as second vice-president of the International Council of Christians and Jews. He has also been a*

*member of the U.S. Bishops Advisory Committee on Catholic–Jewish
relations and a Vatican delegate at three international conferences on
Catholic–Jewish relations.*

During the four sessions of the Second Vatican Council, I was a
student in the fourth through seventh grades at St. Teresa School in
Queens, New York City. The Sparkhill Dominican sisters who taught
us occasionally referred to the council during catechism lessons as having historical importance, but perhaps found it difficult to know how to
impart its emerging teachings to their young charges, especially without
the question-and-answer format in which "religion" was then taught.

In high school at Fordham Preparatory School (1966-1969) the impact
of the council was obvious. I recall writing an essay for a theology class
in which I suggested that the Second Coming of Christ and Jewish belief
in the coming of the messiah might be converging expectations. Such
ideas circulated in the postconciliar air, undoubtedly inspired by the
"Declaration on the Relationship of the Church to Non-Christian Religions," *Nostra aetate.*

Today as a professor whose life has been significantly shaped by that
document, I am often struck by how difficult it is to convey to my students the huge difference in the Catholic Church's stance toward non-
Catholics before and after the council. Sermons conveyed that public
schools were only for Protestants, Jews, atheists, and those Catholics
who didn't consider their faith important. Separate athletic and social
clubs segregated Catholic youth from their non-Catholic neighbors.
Since our parents were not supposed to attend weddings or funerals even
at other Christian churches, visiting a Jewish neighbor's synagogue was
almost unthinkable.

It was also in the 1960s that the appalling subject of the Shoah began
to be discussed in public. In my grammar school years when youngsters
asked how such horrific sufferings could have befallen European Jews
during World War II, some adults would reply that "they" must have
done something truly dreadful to meet such a fate. By my high school
years, more Catholics were becoming conscious of the centuries-old
Christian "teaching of contempt" for Jews, which helped me realize that
the reference to "something truly dreadful" was actually an appeal to the
hoary deicide charge, now serving as an explanation for the Holocaust.

On the other hand, in the early 1970s my home parish began sponsor-
ing Passover Seders during Lent. Their purpose was twofold: to make

tangible the Jewishness of Jesus and to acquaint parishioners with an important ritual of their Jewish neighbors. In looking back now, I cringe a bit at the realization that these ceremonies involved no Jews (except the caterers) and were really dramatizations of the Last Supper, anachronistically based on medieval Seder rituals. While today it has become more typical for Catholics to participate in interfaith educational Seders as guests of the local Jewish community, those early interreligious efforts vividly displayed something I have often encountered since: many if not most Christians have a latent but potent fascination with their Jewish roots, which once awakened can stimulate authentic dialogue with Jewish friends.

Nostra aetate after Fifty Years

Arguably, *Nostra aetate* was the most transformative of Vatican II's documents. Of course, other of the council's texts had huge effects on the church's self-understanding and worship, but *Nostra aetate* has resulted in a degree of positive Catholic engagement with other religions that is unprecedented in the church's history. Of all the conciliar documents, it is the only one whose anniversary is regularly and widely marked by official celebrations, reviews of current interfaith issues, or scholarly conferences on its theological legacy.

Although my brief remarks here focus on Catholic relations with Jews, it should be noted that *Nostra aetate* opens with a paradigm shift in perspective toward all religions. As Gregor Maria Hoff has recently pointed out, the declaration begins by asserting that the world's peoples share a common origin in God and are all drawn to seek the meaning of the human condition. Their search can lead to real encounters with the Transcendent that "penetrates their lives with a profound religious sense" (*Nostra aetate*, §2). By beginning with this universal human perspective and not by stating, for instance, that the church possesses revealed truths of which the rest of the world is ignorant, *Nostra aetate* "enables Christianity to have a new relationship with other religions."[34] Since 1965 new and positive interactions with the globe's great religions have indeed occurred, as, for example, in the previously scarcely imaginable multireligious gatherings at Assisi in 1986, 2002, and 2011.

However, *Nostra aetate* has most especially given birth to a new relationship with Jews, that people with whom Christians have had the longest history, much of it inimical. It is well known that the declaration decried anti-Semitism and definitively rejected the claim (that dates back to at least the second century) that Jews were cursed by God for the crucifixion of Jesus. These would seem to have been the minimal

preconditions merely for courteous relations with Jews. But in my opinion what enabled Catholic–Jewish dialogue to flourish as it has since
1965 were two subtle and interrelated theological steps taken by *Nostra
aetate.*

The first was the document's implicit but nonetheless undeniable portrayal of Jews as people living in covenant with God. Drawing heavily
on Paul's letter to the Romans, *Nostra aetate* §4 rendered an ambiguous
Greek sentence into the present tense: "theirs *is* the sonship and the glory
and the covenants and the law and the worship and the promises" (Rom
9:3-4; not "theirs *was* . . .").[35] It then cited Rom 11:28-29 to declare that
"God holds the Jews most dear for the sake of their Fathers; He does not
repent of the gifts He makes or of the calls He issues." Additionally, if
as *Nostra aetate* states, "the Jews should not be presented as rejected or
accursed by God, as if this followed from the Holy Scriptures," then log-
ically Jews must continue in special relationship with God even after the
coming of Christ. The declaration's implication here was later repeatedly
made explicit by Blessed John Paul II, who described Jews as the "people
of the covenant," most iconically at St. Peter's Basilica and the Western
Wall in Jerusalem.[36] The latter prayer has since been reiterated by Pope
Benedict XVI in formal remarks delivered on February 12, 2009, and
January 17, 2010.

The second key theological decision made during the council's deliberations over *Nostra aetate* §4 was to relegate any thought of a collective
Jewish "turn" to Christ into the indefinite eschatological future. This
had become a matter of public debate in the summer of 1964. A series
of interventions during the council session on September 28-29, 1964,
led to the declaration's final wording on this point: "the Church awaits
that day, known to God alone, on which all peoples will address the
Lord in a single voice and 'serve him shoulder to shoulder' (Zeph 3:9)."
Among other things, this sentence was intended to assure Jews that the
new Catholic interest in dialogue was not a veiled attempt at encouraging conversions.[37] As Archbishop Patrick O'Boyle of Washington, DC,
put it, "The destiny of the Jewish people depends totally on the ways of
Divine Providence and the grace of God. If we express our hope [for a
Jewish acceptance of Christ] in words [suggesting] we are guided by the
definite and conscious intention of working for their conversion, we set
up a new and high wall of division, which makes any fruitful dialogue
impossible. . . . [We should] remain within the limits of our knowledge
and respect the hidden ways of Divine Providence."[38]

It seems to me that it was these affirmations of Jews as a covenanted
people whose salvation rests "on the ways of Divine Providence" that have

made possible genuine Catholic dialogue with Jews. If left unchecked, the received traditions of contempt for Jews—which portrayed them as blind, stiff-necked, incomplete, or cursed—would have inhibited Catholics from seeing much value in Judaism. But viewing Jews as a people "dear to God" has opened Catholics to learning "by what essential traits Jews define themselves in the light of their own religious experience" (Preamble to the Pontifical Commission for Religious Relations with the Jews, "Guidelines for the Implementation of the Conciliar Declaration *Nostra aetate*, No. 4" [1974]).

Since *Nostra aetate* had a difficult gestation in the council, it is unsurprising that its subsequent reception in the Catholic community has also had bumpy moments. In the past few years, for instance, some prominent Catholic voices, fearful that a recognition of the dynamism of Jewish covenantal life would effectively deny that Christ is the universal savior, have tried to use the letter to the Hebrews to reassert that the Sinai covenant faded with the coming of Christ,[39] or have urged that "benign" missions to convert Jews should be undertaken,[40] or have argued that dialogue with Jews is an occasion for invitations to baptism.[41]

Fortunately, such efforts to constrict *Nostra aetate* have as yet had little impact on the growing Catholic–Jewish rapprochement. Significantly, at his address at the Great Synagogue of Rome on January 17, 2010, Pope Benedict XVI has taken up his predecessor's description of Jews as the "people of the Covenant" (and notably as "the people of the Covenant of Moses"). With regard to whether Catholics should seek to convert Jews, he has echoed the conciliar session described above by affirmatively quoting Hildegard Brem that "the Church must not concern herself with the conversion of the Jews, since she must wait for the time fixed for this by God, 'until the full number of the Gentiles come in' (Rom 11:25)."[42]

With fundamental perspectives of *Nostra aetate* thus buttressed, we can expect understanding and even mutual enrichment between Catholics and Jews to continue to deepen and bear fruit into the foreseeable future. There could be no better way to honor the declaration's fiftieth anniversary than for Catholics to embrace the attitude of that pope who directed the Second Vatican Council to issue a statement on the church's relationship to Judaism: when greeting Jewish visitors, Blessed John XXIII (Angelo Giuseppe Roncalli) declared, "I am Joseph, your brother" (Gen 45:4).

JEFFREY GROS, F.S.C.

A Marvelous Beginning of
a Pilgrimage toward Communion

*Jeffrey Gros is the Catholic Scholar in Residence at Lewis University,
Romeoville, Illinois. He was born in Memphis, Tennessee, on January
7, 1938. He completed his undergraduate education in Winona,
Minnesota. He earned a master's degree in theology from Marquette
University (1965) and a doctorate in theology from Fordham University
(1973).*

*Brother Gros has extensive experience in teaching and research at
the undergraduate and seminary level, including at Christian Brothers
University, St. Mary's University of Minnesota, Franciscan School of
Theology, Berkeley, St. Mary's College in Moraga, California, and
Memphis Theological Seminary. In addition, he has served as Director
of Faith and Order with the National Council of Churches and as
associate director in the Secretariat for Ecumenical and Interreligious
Affairs with the U.S. Conference of Catholic Bishops. He has participated
in numerous international meetings of the World Council of Churches.
Gros's recent responsibilities included dialogue staffing with the United
Methodist, Southern Baptist, Lutheran, Pentecostal, and Evangelical
churches, as well as the Faith and Order Committee of the National
Council of Churches. He is the dean of the Catholic Institute for
Ecumenical Leadership.*

*He has published widely in the area of ecumenism, with numerous
articles in a wide range of journals and anthologies. Among the books
he has written or edited are* Building Unity *(1989), co-edited with
Joseph Burgess;* Growing Consensus *(1995), co-edited with Joseph
Burgess;* Introduction to Ecumenism *(1998), with Ann Riggs and
Eamon McManus;* That All May Be One: Ecumenism *(2000);* Growth
in Agreement II *(2000), co-edited with William Rusch and Harding
Meyer; and* The Ecumenical Christian Dialogues and the Catechism of
the Catholic Church *(2006), with Daniel Mulhall.*

Among the special honors he has received are the James Fitzgerald

Award (1986) from the National Association of Diocesan Ecumenical Officers and honorary doctorates from Manhattan College (1995) and St. Mary's University (2011).

As a De La Salle Christian Brother, member of a lay religious community founded in 1680, with no clergy or theologically educated members since its foundation, my own calling has been to the ministry of education in the church. I graduated from college in 1959, with Pius XII dying in the fall, and John XXIII calling the council during the Week of Prayer that January. Studying in Minnesota and beginning teaching in Chicago, we were imbued with the liturgical movement and its hopes for reform, and the racial and social justice commitments of the church. My own teaching was in the field of biology.

In science, we were launching the post-Sputnik curricular reforms, moving from pedagogy based in memorization to more experimental and experiential forms of learning. In religion teaching, we were just beginning to incorporate the Bible-/liturgy-centered kerygmatic methods. Our brothers had moved from catechisms in high schools, to narrative texts in the 1940s.

I was teaching in St. Louis during the third session of the council, when *Time* magazine ran an article noting that the Catholic Church was moving ecumenical. I wandered across the street to Concordia Lutheran Seminary, into the offices of Arthur Carl Piepkorn—a providential happenstance. He was an author who knew the Council of Trent from its Latin text, as well as an interpreter of the Lutheran Confessions in their most catholic sense. Three years later he was in the "freshman class" of the new Lutheran-Catholic dialogue that has turned out to be so productive. Attending his Lutheran "Masses" on Wednesday evening, the prejudices I had learned about "Protestants not believing in the real presence" were dispelled, and subsequent reading of Luther and the Confessions showed me how misguided had been Catholic polemics before the council. Luther always affirmed the faith of the church that taught the change of the bread and wine into the true body and blood of Christ. The real presence of Christ in the Eucharist is what separated Calvinists and Lutherans in the sixteenth century, a division we have had the opportunity to see overcome in our own lifetime (1997).

However, in those days of 1963 and 1964, before the council was over and before the dialogues had begun, it was exciting to recite compline in the Lutheran dorm chapel with the seminarians. Gary Pence would take us to Luther Memorial for Wednesday night Eucharist and explain the Lutheran liturgical tradition over pizza afterward. We would take a car full of seminarians to the Easter Vigil, still celebrated in Latin, at Monsignor Martin Hellriegel's Holy Cross Church during Holy Week. We not only enjoyed learning about one another, but we also gained insights into our own worship tradition through these interchanges, long before there were books and articles available to explain our common heritage.

There are still a few Catholics who see fellow Christians in "us and them" categories. However, the position of the church, reinforced by the teachings of this Holy Father, the leadership of the U.S. bishops and their colleagues around the world, and the tireless work of the Pontifical Council for Promoting Christian Unity, demonstrate that, for the faithful Catholic, we have come to recognize that we share more than what separates us, and that zeal for the unity of the church is central to Catholic identity.

A Fascinating Journey

In 1963 a program of theology was opened for lay persons and religious at Marquette University. Before that there had been a few pioneers, like Brother Luke Salm, F.S.C. (1921-2009), who got a pontifical degree in theology at Catholic University, but there were few lay theologians in the world, even in religious communities.

In that year I was asked to enter doctoral studies, shifting from biology to theology. I graduated with a master's degree in 1965. With the council ending, we were able to get the documents, especially *Lumen gentium*, in time to incorporate them into our preparations for comprehensive exams.

Of course, day-by-day events brought the results of the council, and contemporary American Catholicism, into our lives: talks by Dorothy Day, Bernard Lonergan, Daniel Berrigan, Bernard Häring; a conference in Washington between the sessions, with John Courtney Murray and other *periti*; and the like. This experience, along with doctoral studies at Fordham while working in a black and Hispanic parish in the South Bronx, and professors of the stature of Bernard Cooke, Avery Dulles, Robert McNally, James Hennessey, Ewart Cousins, and Herbert Ryan began for me a pilgrimage of theological exploration that continues to open out to the richness of the tradition and the horizon of the church's future.

My own life, subsequent to the council, has been caught up in three dimensions of the reforms initiated there: (1) Catholic schools, (2) religious life, and (3) the church. In this brief essay I have been asked to reflect on reform of the church, and specifically the conversion of Catholicism to its ecumenical vocation, as I have experienced it. However, I am looking forward to reading a history of U.S. Catholic schools and their contribution to the reforms of Vatican II, including commitment to the visible unity of the churches.

I can sort out my own pilgrimage into three segments: (1) teaching in college and seminary, forming a new diocese; (2) working for the churches' ecumenical commitments in the National Council of Churches; and (3) serving the U.S. bishops in the Secretariat for Ecumenical and Interreligious Affairs. In my later years I have had the good fortune to be able to teach what I have learned in the ecumenical work, first as Distinguished Professor of Historical and Ecumenical Theology at Memphis Theological Seminary (2005-2011), and now as Catholic Scholar in Residence in the Chicagoland area at Lewis University, a De La Salle Christian Brothers' school. In all of these I have had an educational calling that has enriched my spiritual life, strengthened my vocation to "service of the poor through education," as our brotherhood is called to do, and hopefully had some service to offer to the church.

In 1970 the diocese of Memphis was erected, its first bishop taking as a pastoral theme "The Good Samaritan on the Banks of the Mississippi." Carroll T. Dozier was most known for his pastoral letters on peace and justice, his commitment to the council and its renewal of the roles of the laity and sacramental participation, and his advocacy of the place of women.

Among all of the things the diocese did was to implement the ecumenical commitment of the council. Those of us who were trained early on after the council were on deck for all of the renewal dimensions of the council. As "theological volunteers," who served diocesan concerns in our spare time after all of the teaching responsibilities, ecumenism seemed a rather minor, if central, dimension of all of the multiple reforms.

We had dialogues with Episcopalians, Southern Baptists, Presbyterians, and Lutherans—as well as close relations with Methodists and Disciples through the local interfaith agency. Relations with the black churches were strong (two national headquarters are in Memphis) because the bishop of Nashville had identified with Martin Luther King in the 1968 sanitation strike, and the 1973 pastoral letter on justice hit the press the same month that the public schools were integrated. We presumed this sort of ecumenical program was the standard of all Catholic dioceses responsive to the council, especially the larger ones with more theological, pastoral, and financial resources than were available in Memphis.

When agreements with the Anglicans came out in the 1970s, the dioceses of Memphis and Nashville and the Episcopal diocese of Tennessee would collaborate in providing study days for the priests on the Eucharist and on the ordained ministry. It was a great opportunity to meet old friends, now as colleagues building the unity of the church. My kindergarten teacher, Annabelle Payne Whitamore, from a prominent Episcopal family, was now on the committee with me to prepare for the priests' study day on the Eucharist. When we hosted the study day on ministry, led by Bishop Arthur Vogel and Father George Tavard, we had the opening service in Grace-St. Luke's Episcopal Church, in whose gym I had passed my years as a Boy Scout years before. (Actually, this was my first time in the church sanctuary, since in the 1940s as Catholics we were not allowed to attend Boy Scout Sunday in the church with the rest of our troop.) We began a journey to give theological grounding to human relationships and sharing of faith, which had been part of my experience since childhood.

Southern Baptists are generally not seen as very ecumenical. However, there are so many Baptists in Memphis that they say there are more churches than filling stations. Indeed, the phone book lists more than twenty "First Baptist Church" of some part of town or another. We grew up with Baptists; we argued with them about their differences from us; and we learned from them. My father, a successful businessman and frequent leader in fund drives for parishes and schools, always complained about the stinginess of Catholics as compared with Baptists, who were frequently expected to tithe for their churches. We had African American "help" in our home, and I always used to enjoy joining folks for their Sunday worship in their Baptist congregation. There seemed to be so much more vitality and faith there in these black congregations than in our staid and Latin Mass.

Today we still walk together, in many ways, even though—sadly—the present Southern Baptist dialogue ended in 2002. Thanks to Glenmary Home Missioners and dozens of other ecumenically oriented Catholics in local situations, there is a vast network of Southern Baptist and Catholic parishes that have close collaboration and deep spiritual relationships. In my years of service in the National Council of Churches, I have had the good fortune to host two conferences, which published results, bringing together black churches, including Catholics and Baptists, to deepen the communion we share in Christ. In 2011, as president of the Society for Pentecostal Studies, we hosted in Memphis the annual meeting with a focus on the African American Church of God in Christ, headquartered there. This conference focused not only on the participation of Pentecostals ecumenically in the civil rights movement, but also provided reflection on Catholic Latino Pentecostal relations and the impact of Pentecostal eschatology on thinking about peace in the Middle East.

From Volunteer to Ecclesial Ministry

In 1981, after ten years of teaching at Christian Brothers University and Memphis Theological Seminary (Presbyterian), I took a position in New York at the Faith and Order Commission of the National Council of Churches. This was a great time of reception of the results of the (then) fifteen years of theological dialogue in which Catholics had been involved. In 1982 the Anglican–Roman Catholic International Commission submitted its *Final Report* to these two churches, and the World Council of Churches finished its fifty-year-project *Baptism, Eucharist and Ministry* convergence text for the churches' evaluation.

Among other things, I had a rich ten years of theological ministry and administration helping the churches with their study of these and other ecumenical texts, like those emerging from the most productive Lutheran-Catholic dialogue and the variety of concerns brought by Orthodox members.

My "southern exposure" was a great resource, since it was during this decade that the Pentecostal, Holiness, and some Evangelical churches came into full participation in these dialogues and the international dialogues. It was also a decade of linking the African American church concerns and the emerging feminist theological developments into the sixty-year tradition of Faith and Order theological discussions. In 1991 I was called to serve the U.S. bishops in their ecumenical office, where I served until 2005. During this time the Holy See has provided the 1993 ecumenical *Directory*, the 1995 encyclical *Ut unum sint*, *The Ecumenical Dimension in the Formation of Pastoral Workers* (1998), the rich celebration of the 2000 Jubilee, which the Holy Father attempted to move from a papalist triumphal celebration to a time of ecumenical, social, and spiritual renewal.

Today, the Catholic Church has the task of harvesting the results of fifty years of relationships, receiving the fruits of the dialogues and building educational models to deepen religious literacy and ecumenical commitment among our people. I have now the good fortune of working to turn these fruitful years of learning into a "common heritage," as the late Pope John Paul II has challenged us to do. The Lord has blessed the churches with a vision of visible unity unimagined by those of us formed in the 1950s, and with a rich harvest of dialogue and relationships that are a stimulus to even greater zeal on this pilgrimage toward full communion.

GEORGE H. TAVARD, A.A.

The Secretariat for Christian Unity and Ecumenism

George H. Tavard, an Augustinian of the Assumption, was born in France on February 6, 1922, and ordained in 1947. Two years later he received his S.T.D. degree from the Facultés Catholiques de Lyon. Father Tavard came to the United States in 1959. He was chairperson of the Department of Theology at Mount Mercy (today, Carlow) College in Pittsburgh, Pennsylvania, when Pope John called the council.

Father Tavard was a prominent figure in ecumenical activities for more than forty-five years. Since his first books in 1952 and 1954, he pursued a teaching and writing career. After the council he served in some of the official ecumenical dialogues (internationally: the Anglican-Roman Catholic dialogue, ARCIC-I, and with the World Methodist Council; in the United States: with Lutherans and with the Episcopal Church). He also served on some of the task forces that prepared the Joint Statement on Justification, signed by the World Lutheran Federation and the Catholic Church in 1999.

After teaching in Pittsburgh, he taught at Pennsylvania State University and Methodist Theological School in Ohio. He was a visiting professor at Wesleyan University, Princeton Theological Seminary, St. Thomas Seminary in Denver, the Josephinum School of Theology, Hekima Theological College in Nairobi, the Catholic University of America, and Regis College at the University of Toronto, and was Distinguished Professor at Marquette University.

Some of Father Tavard's honors include the John Courtney Murray Award from the Catholic Theological Society of America in 1974; the Medal of St. Augustine of Canterbury granted by the archbishop of Canterbury in 1981; a Catholic Press Association Book Award, for The Spiritual Way of St. Jeanne d'Arc *in 1999; and an honorary doctorate in humane letters from Duquense University, Pittsburgh, in 2002.*

He has published over fifty books, including The Pilgrim Church *(1967) shortly after the conclusion of Vatican II. His more recent publi-*

cations include Vatican II and the Ecumenical Way *(2007);* The Starting-Point of Calvin's Theology *(2000);* The Thousand Faces of the Virgin Mary *(1996); and* The Church, Community of Salvation: An Ecumenical Ecclesiology *(1992).*

A Festschrift has been published in Father Tavard's honor: Kenneth Hagen, ed., The Quadrilog: Essays in Honor of George H. Tavard *(Collegeville, MN: Liturgical Press, 1994).*

Father Tavard died on August 13, 2007.

IN SEPTEMBER 1960, AFTER JOHN XXIII had created the Pontifical Secretariat for the Unity of the Christians, I was named among the consultants. In September 1962 I was included in the first list of conciliar theologians (*periti*). As a consultant I attended the meetings of the Secretariat during the preparatory phase of the council. As a *peritus* I was involved in the writing of the decrees on ecumenism, on Judaism and other religions, and on religious liberty. In this double function I took part in the work of the Secretariat before, during, and between the sessions. Several brothers in my religious congregation were on the preparatory commissions, but I was the only one among the theologians of the council. The council's participants being classified according to their place of work, I figured among the Americans. Joseph Fenton wrote in his diary: "Tavard is here as an American (God help us)." Made by virtue of the pope's immediate jurisdiction, these nominations bypassed the usual channels of authority. The Secretariat for Unity met about eight times before the opening of the council, in the vicinity of Rome (once also in a convent in Bühl, Germany), for periods of four to six days.

When the council opened in October 1962, there was no talk yet of a decree on ecumenism. The Secretariat had prepared a few statements (*vota*) relating to ecumenism and partial drafts on prayer for unity, the Word of God, and religious liberty. None of them referred to common prayer or *communicatio in sacris*. The concern of the Secretariat, at that moment, was more basic: it was to attempt to insert an ecumenical note into the work of the council. There was as yet no way of foreseeing how far the bishops would be willing to go along this line. The task done by the preliminary Theological Commission scarcely permitted any optimism in regard to the ecumenical dimension of the council. But the picture changed dramatically as soon as it became clear that there was widespread dissatisfaction with the work of the Theological Commission, especially with its schema "On the Church." On December 1,

1962, the council decided, by a vote of 2,083 to 36, that the Secretariat for Unity should prepare a document that would incorporate elements from the schema on "the Unity of the Church" (*Ut unum sint*) prepared by the Commission for the Oriental Churches, elements from the last chapter, "On Ecumenism," of the rejected schema on the church, and an expanded version of the *vota* already prepared by the Secretariat.

In keeping with this resolution, the Secretariat formed several sub-commissions, made up of theological experts and bishops, to work along the proposed lines. During the four sessions of the council, the full Secretariat met about once a week, in different locations. The language was a mixture of French and English, with an occasional intervention in Latin, German, or Italian. Every Friday the Secretariat met with the Orthodox and Protestant observers. Outside of this I had no regular contact with the observers, though I got to know the delegates of the French Reformed Church and Oscar Cullmann, Paul VI's special invitee, the Taizé brothers, and some of the Americans, especially the Quaker Douglas Steere.

The first version of the "Decree on Ecumenism" was distributed to the council fathers in May 1963. When the bishops turned their attention to the second chapter of this first version (November 25-27, 1963), a number of them asked for a positive statement on the possibility of some shared liturgical participation among separated Christians, especially, but not exclusively, in relation to the Orthodox. In keeping with these debates and the recommendations made in writing to the Secretariat, Chapter 2 was rewritten. In February 1964, meeting at the residence of Bishop Willebrands on Monte Mario, five *periti* were given the task of rewriting section 7 (now become section 8). Besides Pierre Michalon as the original author of section 7, there were Gregory Baum, Jérôme Hamer, Emmanuel Lanne, and myself. Hamer chaired the meeting. At some point in our discussion of the issue, prior to writing anything on *communicatio in sacris*, Hamer stated, approximately: "The idea is simple; the problem is how to express it properly. There are two principles involved. The liturgy is an expression of unity. But it is also a means of grace. As an expression of unity, it presupposes oneness. As a means of grace, it brings it about." Just then, word came that he had a telephone call. While he was gone, I wrote a couple of Latin sentences formulating what he had said in French, the most common language of this small group. When Hamer returned from the telephone, I read my sentences aloud. A few words were changed. And this became the statement of the "Decree on Ecumenism" concerning *communicatio in sacris*. This new version was approved by the entire Secretariat for Unity at its session from February 25 to March 7, 1964.

When Bishop Helmsing of Kansas City was given by Cardinal Bea the task of formally presenting Chapter 2 of the "Decree on Ecumenism" to the council on October 6, 1964, William Baum conveyed to me Helmsing's request that I compose a suitable text for this *relatio* [report]. I spent the following Saturday writing a draft. On Sunday afternoon I brought it to the hotel where Helmsing and Baum were staying. On Monday afternoon I read it to the whole Secretariat for Unity. One word was changed, and Bishop Helmsing read it to the council a few days later.

In the daily sessions of the council, I took a seat in the tribune next to that of the superiors general. Fred McManus, Godfrey Diekmann, Joseph Baker, adviser to Cardinal Ritter, William Baum from Kansas City, William Keeler from Harrisburg (these last two, future cardinals) were usually in the same area. The view was good. Occasionally I looked for bishops I knew. Cardinal Cody of Chicago never stayed long at his place. As Charles Helmsing, bishop of Kansas City-St. Joseph, once told me, most bishops found the sessions painful, for if they are used to sitting at their desk all morning long, in more comfortable chairs, they tend to deal with one question after another and they seldom stay on the same point for long. The council sessions, however, called for a different kind of attention, and the seats were far from comfortable! Looking over the assembly I once caught Fulton Sheen distributing chocolate to his neighbors. From time to time I left the tribune to walk in the side aisles, talk with a bishop or two, or get a cup of something in one of the bars.

Personal reminiscences are of small value when compared with the achievements of Vatican Council II. They can nevertheless illustrate little-known aspects of the work that was done, especially by the mostly unrecognized conciliar *periti*. They should encourage younger scholars to delve deeper into the history of the most important religious event of the twentieth century.

ROBERT F. DRINAN, S.J.

The Declaration on Religious Freedom
(Dignitatis humanae)

Robert F. Drinan was professor of law at Georgetown University from 1981 to 2007. After completing elementary education, he earned both the B.A. (1942) and the M.A. degree (1947) from Boston College. He entered the Society of Jesus in the same year that he completed his undergraduate education, and he was ordained a Jesuit priest in 1953.

Father Drinan served as guest lecturer and visiting professor at numerous universities in the United States, England, and Africa, including Oxford University (1988), the University of Michigan (1984), and Swarthmore College (1984). From 1956 to 1970, he served as dean and professor of law at the Boston College Law School, where he specialized in criminal law, constitutional law, and the philosophy of law and church-state relations. In 1971 he was elected to the U.S. House of Representatives, where he served for the next ten years. During his time in Congress, he was a member of several important committees, including the House Committee on the Judiciary (1971-1981). In addition, he was part of official congressional delegations to Vietnam, China, South Africa, Israel, and the Soviet Union. After leaving Congress, Father Drinan was a professor of law at Georgetown University, specializing in international human rights, constitutional law, civil liberties, and arms control. Because of his expertise and concern for human rights, he served on human rights missions to Chile, the Philippines, and El Salvador, among others.

Drinan was a regular contributor to several journals and newspapers, including the Christian Century *and the* London Tablet. *He published over fifteen books. Among them are* God & Caesar on the Potomac: A Pilgrimage of Conscience *(1985),* Cry of the Oppressed: The History and Hope of the Human Rights Revolution *(1987),* Stories from the American Soul *(1990),* The Fractured Dream: America's Divisive Moral Choices *(1991), and* Can God & Caesar Coexist: Balancing Religious Freedom and International Law *(2005).*

Father Drinan served on the board of numerous legal and human rights organizations, including Common Cause (1981-1987, 1996-2007), People for the American Way (1986-2007), and the Lawyers Committee for Human Rights (1981-2007). For his distinguished work on behalf of human rights and civil liberties, Father Drinan was awarded over twenty honorary degrees.

He died on January 28, 2007.

I RECALL VIVIDLY THE DAY, December 7, 1965, when Vatican II finally published its decree on religious freedom. I and countless others had followed that topic for many years. During my studies in the seminary I read diligently the articles of Father John Courtney Murray, S.J., in *Theological Studies* and the response to them by Father Fenton, a professor at Catholic University, in the *Ecclesiastical Review.*

By instinct I agreed with Father Murray's plea for religious freedom, but I recognized that the traditional view that the Catholic Church should disadvantage non-Catholic groups was ancient and firmly held in some quarters.

I almost thought that Father Murray's views would never get a hearing when Rome told Father Murray not to publish anything on the question of the church's view of proper church-state relations.

The views opposed by Father Murray seem incredibly wrong now. Catholic theologians actually held that "error has no rights." And that in nations where Catholics constituted the majority, the church also had the right to penalize and even to suppress Protestant churches.

For eight years before Vatican II issued its final declaration vindicating religious freedom, I was dean of Boston College Law School and an active participant in ecumenical activities. Beginning in 1962 it appeared possible, but apparently unlikely, that Vatican II would change the church's narrow view on its attitude toward a pluralistic society.

Everyone followed the five versions of the text on religious freedom. Three public debates were held at the council with a total of 120 speeches. Accurate text and reliable predictions were hard to come by in the days before e-mail and fax.

But the people—at least in Boston—knew that Cardinal Richard Cushing was going to speak at the council on what we used to say was the "side of the angels." He did speak—in Latin—and echoed the opinions of Father Murray—by then a *peritus* at the council.

When the final text of the "Declaration on Religious Freedom" was issued, it was clear that something monumental had happened in the church. The change took away the embarrassment and the humiliation of having to live with a tradition that contradicted the principle of religious freedom, which had long been recognized in the constitutional law of the West. The declaration brought a credibility to the church, which I had never before experienced. It was a joy to go to interreligious events. I saw in the declaration the ideas and even the words that Father Murray used in his many explanations of why religious freedom, and not merely tolerance, should be given to non-Catholic denominations.

For many years I have gloried in the thrust of Vatican II's defense of religious freedom. When I re-read some of it, I discover new implications. Father Murray, in his comments on the declaration in *The Documents of Vatican II* (edited by Walter Abbott, S.J.), asserts that the church was "late" in acknowledging the validity of the principles of religious freedom.[43] But the document has more depth and is more thoughtful than some of the legal and philosophical explications of the free exercise of religion.

There are many passages in the document on religious freedom that I quote regularly in my talks, writings, and class on international human rights at Georgetown University Law Center.

When I criticize the religious right movement in America, I like to cite these words of Vatican II: "However, in spreading religious belief and in introducing religious practices everybody must, at all times, avoid any action which seems to suggest coercion or dishonest or unworthy persuasion."[44]

I always love to quote the language that comes directly from the writings of Father Murray. They express sound jurisprudential principles: "For the rest, the principle of the integrity of freedom in society should continue to be upheld. According to this principle, people's freedom should be given the fullest possible recognition and should not be curtailed except when and in so far as is necessary."[45]

WALTER J. BURGHARDT, S.J.

Vatican II and Religious Freedom: The Role of John Courtney Murray, S.J.

Walter J. Burghardt was born in New York City on July 10, 1914. He earned the M.A. (1937), Ph.L. (1938), and S.T.L. (1942) degrees from Woodstock College in Maryland. In 1941 he was ordained a priest in the Society of Jesus. Father Burghardt received his doctorate in theology (S.T.D.) in 1957 from the Catholic University of America. He then embarked upon a distinguished career of teaching and writing. He taught historical theology for thirty-two years at Woodstock College and the Catholic University of America. He was also visiting lecturer or professor at Princeton Theological Seminary and Union Theological Seminary and, at the time of his death, a senior fellow at the Woodstock Theological Center in Washington, DC, directing its "Preaching the Just Word" project. Editor-in-chief of the journal Theological Studies *for twenty-three years, Father Burghardt also co-edited the ecumenical publication* The Living Pulpit *and the Ancient Christian Writers series of translations.*

Father Burghardt published over twenty-five books and about three hundred articles in over seventy journals during his distinguished career. Among his most recent titles are Justice: A Global Adventure *(2004);* Hear the Just Word and Live It *(2000); and* Christ in Ten Thousand Places: Homilies toward a New Millennium *(1999). In 2000 Burghardt published his memoirs,* Long Have I Loved You: A Theologian Reflects on His Church, *which was awarded a first prize by the Catholic Press Association.*

Twenty-one colleges and universities awarded him honorary degrees. In addition, he received the William Toohey, C.S.C., Award for Distinguished Catholic Preaching from the University of Notre Dame (1984), the Warren Distinguished Catholic Service Award from the University of Tulsa (1991), and the Jerome Award from the Catholic Library Association for Outstanding Contribution and Commitment to Excellence in Scholarship (1999), among others. In 1996 a two-year

Baylor University survey included him as one of the twelve "most effective preachers" in the English-speaking world.
   He died on February 16, 2007.

When Vatican II opened, J. C. Murray was not there. In his own ironic word, he had been "disinvited." A decade before, he had incurred Roman displeasure by his writings on church-state issues and religious freedom. He had been informed through his Jesuit superiors that anything he wrote henceforth in those areas would require a prior critique—in Rome. With his love for the church and the Society of Jesus, Murray felt he could not disobey. But with his love for truth and the human person, he did not see how he could operate honestly in such chains.

So he cleared the bookshelves in his room at old Woodstock College of those books that dealt with religious freedom, with church and state, with Catholicism and the American proposition. He saw no further use for them. Unable to present his position to his peers for challenge and criticism, Murray decided to forgo publication on these subjects until a more favorable climate was created.

Before Vatican II opened, New York's Cardinal Francis Spellman requested of Rome that Murray be named a *peritus*. According to the cardinal's secretary at the time, Patrick V. Ahern, the request was politely but firmly turned down by Cardinal Alfredo Ottaviani, who headed the screening committee involved. Spellman replied sharply, "I would not certify Father Murray if I were not sure of his credentials and his orthodoxy." Ottaviani responded, "Thank you very much; the matter has been brought again before the screening committee." Unfortunately Cardinal Spellman's response to this letter has vanished from the archdiocesan files, as has the other correspondence in the matter—victims, Bishop Ahern believes, of the cardinal's determination to expunge the record of unpleasantness that might "give scandal." But the bishop has no difficulty recalling the nature of the letter. "It came down to something like, 'Father Murray is going as my personal *peritus*,' he said. And if he doesn't go, I don't go." Then, of course, the final reply came back to the effect that Father Murray would be most welcome. I don't think there's any doubt that Cardinal Spellman singlehandedly got Father Murray into the council.[46]

Murray himself was convinced that he owed his participation to Spellman. "Between us," he wrote to Notre Dame's Leo Ward, "it was my Eminent friend of New York who pried me in. He said (and meant it, I think) that the Jesuits had got too slim a deal about *periti*, and that it was 'no more than right' that I in particular should be there. Which was nice of him."[47] The full story of Murray's influence on *Dignitatis humanae* has still to be written. Early on he addressed a significant commission, decisive for the fate of the religious freedom issue. He was commissioned by the Secretariat for Promoting Christian Unity to analyze the comments sent in by the bishops on religious freedom. He fashioned preliminary drafts of the document, addressed American and other national groups of bishops, shaped interventions for many a U.S. bishop, and eloquently interpreted the issues for reporters at the daily press panels. The Casa Villanova, where Murray lodged, "became the Council's intellectual crossroads. Cardinal and bishop, priest and layman, European and American, liberal and conservative were all part of the cast which lived, worked, prayed, and talked there. 'To be anything in Rome was to be at the Villanova,' [John] Cogley wrote in *Commonweal*."[48]

Still, even during the council, Roman hostility threatened Murray's full participation. The courageous moral theologian Bernard Häring recently revealed a discussion within a subcommission of the council's Doctrinal Commission, on a draft of the projected "Declaration on Religious Freedom" prior to its submission for public discussion. He reports that the task of co-ordinating secretary fell to him and that "the subcommission did not water down the text, but rather strengthened it." Haring writes:

In view of this situation, Cardinal Ottaviani, the President of the Doctrinal Commission, tried delaying tactics. Since the admonitions from our side accomplished nothing, we had to request a decisive action by Pope Paul VI that forced Cardinal Ottaviani to place the text on the table for discussion in the full Commission as soon as possible. For this the bishops brought Father Murray along. Nevertheless Ottaviani refused to let him speak, despite loud protests from bishops. Since I had been chosen as speaker for this draft, I could not be refused the opportunity to speak. Ottaviani responded angrily that one did not need this whole text since there was already too much freedom in the Church. Now my patience was tested to the limit. I said: The fact that the head of the Holy Office answers thus is sufficient proof of the pressing need of this declaration and the necessity to allow the theologian whom he had so long condemned to silence the opportunity finally to speak. Ottaviani grimly relented. It was a pleasure to experience how magnificently Murray presented his viewpoint in beautifully fluent Latin and with sovereign dignity. The subsequent vote resulted in the overwhelming majority approving the strengthened text and passing it on to the Council.[49]

Dignitatis humanae has often been styled the council's "American document." Here I counsel caution. (1) The declaration, approved 2,308 to 70, was an act of the universal church. (2) It was not the product of U.S. participants alone. Such an interpretation would overlook the crucial contributions of men like Jan Willebrands and Charles Moeller, Carlo Colombo and Yves Congar, Jérôme Hamer and Pietro Pavan, Augustin Bea and Emile Joseph De Smedt. (3) The most significant drafts set before the council emerged officially from the Secretariat for Promoting Christian Unity—a group whose competence to present texts with a theological content was disputed until October 22, 1962, when Pope John XXIII put that Secretariat on the same level as the other commissions and authorized it to lay drafts and schemata before the council. Still, we must recognize the startling truth expressed by Pietro Pavan, one of the document's architects:

> I took part in the Second Vatican Council from beginning to end. At the preparatory stage I was a member of two pontifical commissions, the Theological Commission and the Commission on the Lay Apostolate. In the four sessions . . . I was a *peritus*. I am therefore in a position to say with full assurance that the impact of the American episcopate—above all, all the bishops of the United States—was decisive (1) in bringing about the "Declaration on Religious Freedom" and (2) in assuring that its main line of argument should be the one which it now exhibits.[50]

An important observation indeed. Still, another observation by the same Pavan is perhaps equally important:

> In the drafting [of the third schema—separate from the schema on ecumenism] as well as in subsequent redraftings down to the time when the declaration *Dignitatis Humanae* took its final shape, an outstanding part was played by John Courtney Murray, S.J. He was distinguished at all times for his unique grasp of the subject, for his wisdom, his nobility of mind, his loyalty to the Church, and his love of truth.[51]

What was so important about the declaration? In Murray's summation, three doctrinal tenets: (1) the ethical doctrine—religious freedom as a human right; (2) the political doctrine—the functions and limits of government in matters religious; (3) the theological doctrine—the freedom of the church as the fundamental principle in the relations between the church and the sociopolitical order.

FRANCIS CARDINAL ARINZE

Vatican II Encourages
Interreligious Dialogue

Francis Arinze was born on November 1, 1932, at Eziowelle in Anambra State of Nigeria. After secondary school studies in All Hallows Seminary, Nnewi and Enugu, he studied philosophy in Bigard Memorial Seminary, Enugu, Nigeria (1953-1955), and theology in Urban University Rome (1955-1960). He received the bachelor's in divinity degree in 1957 from the Urban University, and earned the master's (1959) and doctorate in divinity (1969) from the same institution.

After his ordination as a Catholic priest on November 23, 1958, he became a lecturer in liturgy and philosophy at the Bigard Memorial Seminary, Enugu (1961-1962), and then became Catholic Education Secretary for the Enugu Diocese (1962-1965). He was in Rome as a young priest when Pope John XXIII announced the Second Vatican Council in January 1959. As Catholic Education Secretary, he followed the first three sessions of the council from afar. During this time, he engaged in further study (1963-1964), earning a diploma in education from the University of London Institute of Education.

On August 29, 1965, Arinze was ordained auxiliary bishop of Onitsha, Nigeria. Two weeks later, he joined other council fathers in St. Peter's Basilica, Rome, in the entire fourth session of the Second Vatican Council, from September 11 to December 8, 1965. Bishop Arinze, thirty-two years old at that time, was the youngest bishop in the church and at the council. Arinze was made archbishop of Onitsha in 1967 and held that post until 1984, when Pope John Paul II transferred him to Rome and made him president of the Secretariat for Non-Christians. In 1985 he was made a cardinal. In 2002 he was made prefect of the Congregation for Divine Worship. He retired from this position in 2008.

In addition to many articles, Cardinal Arinze has published a number of books, including Sacrifice in Ibo Religion *(1970),* Answering God's Call *(1982),* Alone with God *(1986),* Church in Dialogue *(1990),* Living

Our Faith *(1990),* Meeting Other Believers *(1997), and* God's Invisible Hand *(2006).*

THE ATTITUDE OF THE SECOND Vatican Council toward the people of other religions and its directives on dialogue with them are best understood if they are seen in the context of the open-arms approach that Pope (now Blessed) John XXIII gave to the council. The council wanted the church to meet every human being, whether that person be a Christian in a church or community not in full union with the Roman See, or a follower of another religion, or indeed a person of no declared religious conviction.

The council declaration *Nostra aetate,* approved on October 28, 1965, spells out the attitude of the Catholic Church toward people of other religions. It is the first ever major document of a general council on the subject. In its earlier draft, the declaration was only on relations with the Jews. But over the years 1964 to 1965 it was expanded to cover relations with all other religions, with express mention of Islam, Hinduism, and Buddhism.

The underlying doctrine is also available in other Vatican II documents, especially the "Dogmatic Constitution on the Church" (*Lumen gentium,* nos. 13, 16, 17); the "Decree on the Church's Missionary Activity" (*Ad gentes,* nos. 7, 9); and the "Pastoral Constitution on the Church in the Modern World" (*Gaudium et spes,* no. 92).

Nostra aetate exhorts Catholics to meet the people of other religions and, through dialogue and collaboration with them and in witness to Christian faith and life, to "acknowledge, preserve, and encourage the spiritual and moral truths found among non-Christians, together with their social life and culture" (*Nostra aetate,* no. 2).[52]

On Pentecost Day 1964, between the second and third sessions of Vatican II, Pope Paul VI had instituted the Secretariat for Non-Christians as an autonomous dicastery of the Roman curia, the central offices of the church, for the promotion of interreligious dialogue. In 1988 the name was changed to the more positive one of Pontifical Council for Interreligious Dialogue.

Not everyone in the church immediately absorbed the spirit of the council as articulated in *Nostra aetate.* Some people feared that an attitude of dialogue and friendship with other religions would discourage missionaries from preaching Jesus Christ and proposing faith and baptism to people. It has to be admitted that this risk exists, but only when dialogue is not properly understood or where it is conducted on erroneous theology.

Some of the encouraging developments following on the attitude of the Second Vatican Council toward other religions are the following. In 1974 Pope Paul VI instituted a Commission for Religious Relations with the Jews and a parallel Commission for Religious Relations with the Muslims. In 1986 Pope John Paul II took the unprecedented step of inviting representatives of the major world religions to come to Assisi (Italy) to fast and pray for peace, each religion according to its own tradition. It was the International Year for Peace. The Assisi event improved the general world climate for interreligious dialogue tremendously. The following year, the religions of Japan—especially Buddhists, Shintoists, Catholics, and Protestants—invited the major religions of the world to come to Kyoto, Hiroshima, and Nagasaki to pray for peace.

A yearly commemoration has been done in Japan ever since. And the Community of Sant'Egidio, a Catholic lay association based in Rome, has, since 1987, held a yearly commemoration of the Assisi celebration, from one city to another. In October 1999, in preparation for the Jubilee Year 2000, two hundred representatives of twenty world religions held a four-day meeting in Vatican City to reflect on their collaboration in the forthcoming third millennium.

A development of great importance in the church is in the area of a Christian theology of religions. In the face of a world increasingly pluralistic from the religious point of view, theology cannot be done today without attention to the fact of the existence of other religions. What is their place in God's plan of salvation? What is the relationship between dialogue and proclamation? What does inculturation of the gospel gain from the religious and cultural backgrounds of the people who receive the gospel?

For me, who has been able to follow these developments for over sixteen [sic] years, it has been enriching indeed. To observe and take part in joint reflections between the World Council of Churches and the Catholic Church on aspects of interreligious dialogue, to meet Catholic seminary and university faculties over the question, and to visit and discuss with Muslims, Hindus, Buddhists, and followers of traditional religions: all these have been great graces indeed.

Thanks to Vatican II, the Catholic Church is irrevocably committed to meeting other believers.

EUGENE J. FISHER

The Council and the Invention of Catholic–Jewish Relations

Eugene Fisher was born on September 10, 1943, in Detroit, Michigan. He received his B.A. from Detroit's archdiocesan seminary, Sacred Heart, in 1965, just as the council was coming to a close. In 1968 he completed his M.A. in Catholic theology from what was then the University of Detroit (now Detroit-Mercy). He was awarded a Ph.D. from New York University in 1976, in the area of Hebrew culture and education.

Prior to 1977, Dr. Fisher was director of catechist formation for the archdiocese of Detroit, as well as adjunct professor of sacred scripture at St. John's Seminary in Plymouth, Michigan, and for the Religious Studies Department of the University of Detroit. From 1977 to 2007 Dr. Fisher served as associate director of the Secretariat for Ecumenical and Interreligious Affairs of the U.S. Conference of Catholic Bishops, in charge of Catholic–Jewish relations. He succeeded Father Edward H. Flannery, who held the post since its establishment in 1967 following the Second Vatican Council. Dr. Fisher was the first layperson to hold the post.

Dr. Fisher is an active member of numerous learned and professional societies and associations, such as the Catholic Biblical Association, the National Association of Professors of Hebrew, and the Society of Biblical Literature (SBL). He has lectured widely throughout the United States, Canada, Europe, Latin America, and Australia. He has published twenty books and monographs, and over 250 articles in major religious journals, many of which have been translated into French, Spanish, Italian, Portuguese, Polish, and German for publication in Latin America and Europe.

Most recently his writings, all of which seek to foster religious dialogue and appreciation, include Catholics Remember the Holocaust *(1988),* In Our Time: The Flowering of Jewish-Catholic Dialogue *(co-edited with Rabbi Leon Klenicki) (1991), and* Interwoven Destinies *(1992).*

In April 1981, Dr. Fisher was appointed by Pope John Paul II to be consultor to the Vatican Commission for Religious Relations with the Jews. In 1985, he was named a member of the International Vatican–Jewish Liaison Committee, representing the Holy See. In 1999, he was appointed by the Holy See as Catholic coordinator of the International Catholic–Jewish Historical Team, and in 2000 as Catholic coordinator of the International Catholic–Jewish Liaison Committee for its meeting in New York in June of that year. He represented the Holy See on several occasions: at the International Conference on Holocaust Education (January 2000) and as Vatican observer at the meeting of the Lutheran World Federation (September 2001).

On the eve of his retirement in 2007, Dr. Fisher received the Anti-Defamation League's Dr. Joseph L. Lichten Award, which recognized his pioneering role in helping to promote and further dialogue between Catholic and Jews.

THE SECOND VATICAN COUNCIL HAPPENED while I was in college. It could not have come at a better time for me. The council's documents, which we read and studied and debated as they came out in stately procession from Rome, blew away my childhood impression of what Catholicism was all about and replaced it with a more dynamic sense of a community chosen by God to change history itself and to improve the lot of all humankind (I would have said "mankind" then).

Salvation was not just a spiritual, personal thing. It was a challenge to humanity to overcome its own evil. College is a crucial time in one's life. For during it, one chooses who one will be and the basic values one will uphold for the rest of one's life. The council thus permeated my being thoroughly and permanently. One could say that the way I experienced the council and its remarkable teaching was not simply existential but ontological as well. The council's statements on ecumenism and interreligious understanding (*Nostra aetate*) became, along with the rest, part of the fiber of my being.

After college, I attended St. John's Seminary for two years. There, I took some optional scripture and biblical Hebrew courses from John J. Castelot, S.S., who had written a popular series of introductions to the Bible. There were only two or three of us in these classes, which he held informally in his room in the evening. His evident love of scripture and his joy at probing its depth infused me. But what astonished me was the fact that the Hebrew Bible, read in its original, had a whole lot more in it than any translation can really convey. Genesis, for example, even its elegant and poetic creation accounts, is filled with puns and delightful and provocative word plays that satirize elements of the common worldview of the ancient Near East and give the reader a sense of the ironies of life. In scripture, tragedy and comedy constantly intertwine. The Bible is a far more sophisticated (and funny) set of books than our rather straight-laced approach to it as Christians allows us to see. It's no wonder that Jews are over-represented in American comedy. They've got a three-millennia-long tradition going for them!

Then I wanted to go on for a doctorate in theology. I had applied to, and been accepted by, both the Chicago and Princeton divinity schools, but would have had to take out major loans to pay for them. Dr. Marinoff suggested I write to his good friend David Rudavsky, at New York University's Institute for Hebrew Studies. I found the idea of studying the Hebrew Bible with the people who wrote them quite appealing, so I dashed off a résumé. He responded with a generous scholarship covering not only tuition but modest living expenses as well. On a warm day in early September 1968, I walked out of New York's Grand Central Station with the address of the school in my pocket and two large suitcases. I did not know where I would spend the night, but I did know that my relatively sheltered midwestern life was about to change. I set the bags down for a moment to take it all in. A young man promptly picked one up and began to walk off with it, mumbling something about carrying my luggage for me. I chased after him, carrying the other bag and would have lost the race if a policeman had not intervened. Welcome to New York!

I didn't know it then, but I had stepped into a career in a field that did not even exist before the Second Vatican Council, Catholic–Jewish relations. The changes and challenges in lifestyle, intellectual environment, and religious perspective I experienced in New York were dramatic. This was the period of massive antiwar demonstrations, in which I took part with enthusiasm, thanks to the great vision of peace of John XXIII (*Pacem in terris*), the council itself (*Gaudium et spes*), and Paul VI at the United Nations: "War no more! War never again!" as I recall the phrase from my seminary days.

I had been in the seminary just at the right moment to go through the council as it was happening, and been fortunate to be quite actively involved in the civil rights movement in Detroit during the same period. The winds of change promised a new and more equal American society, as the open windows of theological *aggiornamento* ["updating"] promised a reformed and more open Roman Catholic Church. For us, change represented hope, not something to be feared. One could acknowledge freely the shortcomings of the past, whether in society or the church, because both were actively engaged in rectifying what had gone wrong. Admitting American racism and Christian anti-Semitism, then, was not to risk becoming mired down in the guilt of the past (as it continued to be for some time in Europe). It was simply to open oneself to hope for a better future.

When I saw Pope John Paul II visit Yad Vashem in Jerusalem and place a prayer of repentance in the name of the church in the Kotel (Western Wall), I thanked God that I have lived in a time in which the future has become a reality. Along with hundreds, perhaps thousands of veterans of the Jewish-Christian dialogue on all levels from parishes to the Holy See itself, I cried tears of joy. *Gaudium et spes*, indeed.

JOHN T. PAWLIKOWSKI, O.S.M.

Christian–Jewish Relations and Vatican II

John T. Pawlikowski, a priest of the Servite Order, was born in Chicago on November 2, 1940. Educated at Loyola University in Chicago (A.B., 1963) and the University of Chicago (Ph.D., 1970), he did specialized study at the University of Wisconsin and at Mansfield College, Oxford University. He has also served as a Fellow at St. Edmund's College, University of Cambridge, and the Catholic University of Leuven (Belgium).

Since 1968 he has been a member of the faculty at the Catholic Theological Union in Chicago (CTU), where he currently holds the position of professor of social ethics and director of the Catholic–Jewish Studies Program in CTU's Cardinal Bernardin Center for Theology and Ministry. He has been active in Christian–Jewish relations locally, nationally, and internationally for more than four decades. He has served on the Christian–Jewish Relations Committee of the National Council of Churches and the National Advisory Committee of the U.S. Catholic Bishop's Office for Catholic–Jewish Relations.

In 1980 he was appointed to the United States Holocaust Memorial Council by President Jimmy Carter. He was subsequently reappointed to three additional terms by Presidents Bush and Clinton. He currently serves on the Council's Academic Committee and its Committee on Conscience and chairs its Church Relations Committee. In 2000 he was elected as vice-president of the International Council of Christians and Jews, and in 2002 he was elected the ICCJ's president, a position he held for six years. He remains a member of the ICCJ board. He has also served twice as co-chair of the National Polish American-Jewish American Council. In 2011, Governor Pat Quinn of Illinois appointed him to the state's Holocaust & Genocide Commission. He has edited or written some twenty volumes, including Christ in the Light of the Christian–Jewish Dialogue *(1982),* Jesus and the Theology of Israel

(1989), Reinterpreting Revelation and Tradition: Jews and Christians in Conversation *(2000)*, *and* Ethics in the Shadow of the Holocaust *(2004)*.

MY OWN ACADEMIC AND MINISTERIAL development was very much part of the Vatican II scene. I was in the final years of my preparation for the Catholic priesthood during the time of the council, with my ordination taking place in 1967. The "Vatican II" spirit was very much alive at the Servite theologate in Lake Bluff, Illinois. A number of the professors there, including John Dominic Crossan (then a Servite priest), became involved in an ecumenical association of theologians in the Chicago area as a result of Cardinal Suenens's visit to the University of Chicago campus during the council. The visit and subsequent association led to the development of the Catholic Theological Union, where I now teach, and the move of McCormick Theological Seminary (Presbyterian) and the Lutheran School to the University of Chicago area, where they joined Chicago Theological Seminary, Meadville-Lombard Theological School, and the Divinity School of the University of Chicago in the Hyde Park Cluster of Theological Schools.

In 1967, a year prior to the opening of Catholic Theological Union, I enrolled in a doctoral program at the University of Chicago, at a time when Catholic students were entering the university in droves in response to the ecumenical atmosphere created by the council. This was a significant reversal for Catholics. When I was a senior in a Catholic high school in the late 1950s and considering a choice of college, I was warned not to consider the University of Chicago for fear that I would lose my faith there. While at the University of Chicago, I came under the influence of Dr. J. Coert Rylaarsdam, a pioneer scholar in the rethinking of Christian–Jewish relations, and Professor Martin Marty, who had considerable interest in the present-day relations between Christians and Jews.

My more than three decades of interest in the Christian–Jewish relationship were in many ways the result of the influence of Professors Crossan, Rylaarsdam, and Marty. Without their encouragement and insights, I doubt that I would have walked the road of Christian–Jewish encounter for so long a time.

My initial interest in Christian–Jewish relations must be laid at the feet of John Dominic Crossan. In his courses at the Servite theologate, Crossan instilled in me a tremendous respect and an appreciation for sacred scripture and an interest in the long history of Christian anti-Semitism, which he saw as rooted in New Testament interpretation. Crossan delivered one of the earliest lectures on anti-Semitism and the New Testament in light of *Nostra aetate* at a public series on the Second Vatican Council held at Chicago's Loyola University, a lecture eventually published in *Theological Studies* (June 1965). I was in the audience that evening as a proud student. It was only later on that I would recognize that, despite his deep commitment to the elimination of anti-Semitism, his approach to the interpretation of Jesus' parables, rooted in the views of Rudolf Bultmann and his disciples such as Norman Perrin, contained the seeds of theological anti-Judaism with an emphasis on the displacement of "those who first heard the word" from the sacred table. Scholars such as Clemens Thoma have shown how destructive such parabolic interpretation can be for our image of Jews and Judaism.

Reflecting later on this dual experience of Crossan as both profound critic of anti-Semitism and at the same time purveyor of theological anti-Judaism, it became apparent to me how deep-seated and yet subtle anti-Semitism remains in Christian self-understanding so that even those who staunchly oppose its outer manifestations sometimes remain unaware of its subtle dimensions. Despite this lapse, I shall always be grateful to him for instilling in me a profound concern for anti-Semitism and a deep commitment to develop a new, constructive theology of the Jewish-Christian relationship. Without his encouragement in the midst of the new spirit of the Vatican Council, I doubt I would have ever made Christian–Jewish relations such a central part of my academic and ministerial career.

When I entered the University of Chicago in autumn 1967, I had no intention of pursuing Christian–Jewish relations as the focal point of my doctoral work. But under the influence of J. Coert Rylaarsdam, I began to see the importance of a new look at the Old Testament and to recognize how significantly Jesus and the early church were influenced by the progressive Jewish forces of their day. I began to see a rethinking of the Christian–Jewish relationship as critical to the overall reform of the Catholic Church that had been mandated by the council. I remain convinced that a renewed, constructive understanding of this relationship remains central to the full implementation of Vatican II's call for liturgical renewal, enhancement of the role of the laity, and an openness to all other religious traditions. My one, ongoing criticism is that Christian theology has not taken seriously enough the fundamental restatement of the church's self-identity that occurred in section 4 of *Nostra aetate*, where the council repudiated the centuries-old Christology and ecclesiology rooted in the notion of Jewish covenantal displacement.

My encounter with Martin Marty at the University of Chicago introduced me to the debate about continuing anti-Semitism in the churches. I became acquainted with the early pioneers in this area, such as Franklin Littell, Alice and Roy Eckardt, John Oesterreicher, and Edward Flannery. My world, incidentally, had now become ecumenically Christian, not just Catholic (although my "Catholic" identity was in fact strengthened in an institution where, as I said above, my high school teachers feared for my faith). This was the prevailing spirit at the University of Chicago Divinity School and was very much in keeping with the orientation of the council. This experience solidified my life-long interest in combating anti-Semitism, starting with the decision to use the St. Louis University studies on prejudice in Catholic teaching materials (which had directly impacted support for the passage of *Nostra aetate* at the council) as the basis of my doctoral dissertation.

The era of the council, which coincided with my ordination and pursuit of doctoral studies, has set the basic framework for my life. Vatican II taught me how destructive it is to try to confine God's redemptive presence.

In my subsequent academic career I have made the promotion of a new theology of the Christian–Jewish relationship a central focus. This has been intensified during the past several years as efforts to minimize the theological breakthrough that was *Nostra aetate* have emerged, led by certain theologians such as the late Cardinal Avery Dulles. My response has been to join some fifteen colleagues in Europe and North America in an ongoing consultation, in part sponsored by Catholic Theological Union, to reflect on the metaquestion, how can Christians affirm the ongoing validity of the Jewish covenant while still affirming a certain universalism for the Christ event? Cardinal Walter Kasper in his capacity as president of the Holy See's Commission for Religious Relations with the Jews gave strong endorsement to this consultation. He took part in the opening session and subsequently wrote an extensive, in-depth reflection for the first collection of essays to emerge as a book (*Christ Jesus and the Jewish People Today* [Grand Rapids, MI: Eerdmans, 2011]). I will continue this effort in the future.

PART SIX

WORLD ISSUES AND SOCIAL JUSTICE

The Church and the World: Reading the Signs of the Times

MICHAEL J. DALEY

THOUGH SHE ALWAYS SHAKES HER head whenever I say something like this, I could not resist telling my wife that the movie we were watching, *Chocolat*, would make a great introduction to an article I was writing.

The movie opens in a small French village gathered together for Mass on a windswept Sunday morning on the eve of Lent. The year is 1959. The opening lines and images convey to the viewer that this village is a place of tranquility, guided by tradition. Whether it be religious, political, economic, or social—things had remained pretty much the same since the late sixteenth century. It was then that the villagers threw the Huguenots, French Calvinists, from their homes and land. This world would soon be turned on its head, though, with the unplanned and unannounced arrival of three things: an unmarried woman, her daughter, and a chocolate shop.

Viewed from afar, the woman is immediately considered an occasion of sin. Her marital status, good looks, and vocational choice are enough to make her almost demonic. Representing the town's conscience, the mayor, a Jansenist if there ever was one, is offended at what seems to be her lack of discretion—opening up a confection store during Lent. Over the course of several weeks, any and all means are attempted to shut the store and see to it that this woman and her daughter leave town.

In a last-ditch effort on the eve of Easter (no midnight vigils yet!), the mayor breaks into the store and begins destroying all of the shop's delicious offerings only to fall victim to its seductive smells. Unable to refrain any longer, in a fit of uncontrolled passion, he consumes as much chocolate as he possibly can fit into his stomach. At which point the mayor passes out in the store's front window. By chance, on his way to church Easter morning, the village's young curate comes upon the mayor and rescues him from imminent personal and professional embarrassment. Additionally, by the grace of a strong wind, the priest finally gets the chance to deliver his own sermon, which was prepared by the mayor but had blown away.

With great determination in his voice, the curate looks out over the congregation and, encapsulating the preceding days and events of the village, says: "Here's what I think. I think we can't go round measuring our goodness by what we don't do, by what we deny ourselves, what we resist, and who we exclude. I think we've got to measure goodness by what we embrace, what we create, and who we include."

Knowing that I still had an introduction to write, the words *gaudium et spes* ("joy and hope") echoed in my ears.

And the Walls Came Tumbling Down

Rather than avoid the world as a den of iniquity, the Catholic Church at the Second Vatican Council embraced it as a graced community, placing itself at the service of all of humanity whom it sought to make more whole through Christ. This conciliar sentiment is found most expressly in "The Pastoral Constitution on the Church in the Modern World" (*Gaudium et spes*), which was issued during the council's last session and approved on December 7, 1965. Its introduction, though written decades ago, still reads with the freshness of wet ink:

> The joys and the hopes, the grief and the anguish of the people of our time, especially of those who are poor or afflicted, are the joys and hopes, the grief and anguish of the followers of Christ as well. Nothing that is genuinely human fails to find an echo in their hearts. For theirs is a community of people united in Christ and guided by the holy Spirit in their pilgrimage towards the Father's kingdom, bearers of a message of salvation for all of humanity. That is why they cherish a feeling of deep solidarity with the human race and its history.[1]

Considering the church's recent history up to that point, the content and tone of the document caught many Catholics off guard.

From the end of the eighteenth century up to the very eve of the council, says University of Notre Dame historian Jay P. Dolan, a general mood existed within the Catholic Church that cast "an attitude toward the world or secular society that was quite negative. Church leaders frequently spoke as if Armageddon was just around the corner. The power of darkness seemed to be in control, and religious error, like 'a sheep in wolf's clothing,' prowls about the earth seeking whom it may devour. Though European Catholics were more extreme in this regard, Americans also evidenced a hostile attitude toward the world."[2]

The culprits were easily seen. In France, with the Revolution (ca. 1789), the prerogatives of the church seemed at risk everywhere you turned. Religious life, for all practical purposes, was disbanded; thousands were forced to flee in exile. The grand cathedral of Notre Dame became a temple of reason. A nonreligious calendar, with a new communion of saints (voices of reason rather than faith) was created. The Constantinian age of the church was falling, and a new one characterized by separation of church and state was emerging. This was the case not only in France but throughout Europe and included what would be the countries of Italy, Austria, and Germany.

The person of Pope Pius IX (pope, 1846-1878) and his Syllabus of Errors (appended to the encyclical *Quanta cura*, December 8, 1864) perhaps best illustrate the church's siege or fortress mentality with regard to the movements besetting it. In the syllabus Pius IX condemned eighty propositions, including pantheism, religious freedom, religious indifferentism, rationalism, socialism, the denial of temporal power to the pope, freedom of the press, and separation of church and state. In the conclusion to the syllabus, Pius refuted the notion that "the Roman Pontiff can and should be reconciled with, and agree to, progress, liberalism and modern civilization."[3] As was long presumed, now declared, the church and the modern world were at odds with each other.

Yet alongside this "ghetto" attitude on the part of the church, exemplified by the pope becoming a "prisoner of the Vatican," a world-engaging tradition of Catholic social teaching was developing.[4] It has even been termed by some to be Catholicism's "best-kept secret."[5] Most people see its beginning in Pope Leo XIII's encyclical *Rerum novarum* (also referred to as "On the Condition of Labor"), in 1891. Responding to the excesses of the Industrial Revolution, Leo XIII stated that workers had rights—to work, to private property, to a just wage, and to form and join unions. This was followed by Pius XI's encyclical *Quadragesimo anno* ("The Reconstruction of the Social Order"), which commemorated *Rerum novarum*'s fortieth anniversary. This encyclical, written during the height of the Great Depression, with its devastating economic and social effects and the emergence of European fascism, challenged

both capitalism and socialism as economic systems. It also introduced
the concept of subsidiarity, which states that problems should be solved,
as much as possible, at the local level.

In 1961, on the eve of Vatican II, following the example of his predecessors, Pope John XXIII issued an encyclical, *Mater et magistra*
("Christianity and Social Progress"), which, in light of increasing inter-
nationalization and interdependence of economies, sought to bring
attention to the gap between the rich (first-world) nations and poor
(third-world) nations. During the council itself, just prior to his death,
John issued another encyclical related to social justice, *Pacem in terris*
("Peace on Earth"). Addressed to "all people of good will," in the aftermath of World War II and in the shadow of the Cold War, John called for
an end to the arms race and stressed the common good of all humanity.

Thus, both on the eve of and during the council itself, it was hard to
deny the presence and concerns of the wider world, whether they were
economic, social, cultural, or political. Yet, as Father Donald Campion, S.J., relates, "despite the existence of such a body of authoritative
pronouncements in the Church, the several commissions charged with
drafting tentative texts for consideration by the council had not felt it
necessary or desirable to prepare a document dealing with the theme of
the Church in the modern world."[6]

The Origins of a New Church

Though *Gaudium et spes* was the last document to be approved (December 7, 1965) by the council, its origin actually predates the council by
almost six months. In March 1962, Archbishop (soon to be cardinal)
Leon Joseph Suenens of Malines (Belgium) had an audience with Pope
John, in which they discussed the council's direction and overall plan. In
the course of the conversation, Pope John asked him, "Who is attending
to the making of an overall plan for the council?"[7] At this seeming invitation from John XXIII to express his feelings on the state of the council's
preparations, Suenens took "exception to the number of draft texts that
had been prepared and were intended for discussion at the upcoming
council. There were . . . far too many, in my opinion. Their quality varied greatly, and in any case, their sheer bulk would have precluded *a
priori* any possibility of useful and fruitful work within the council."[8]

Taking advantage of Suenens's observations, Pope John asked him,
"Would you then like to make a plan?"[9] After carefully studying the proposed schemata, Suenens states that he "drafted a preliminary note for
Pope John. Its intent was to pare down the texts, and to give the council
a truly pastoral perspective. My note," he stressed, "was both negative

and positive; the *idem nolle* [what I didn't want] was as essential as the *idem velle* [what I did want] and together they provided the groundwork for a more detailed plan."[10] This plan was finished by the end of April 1962 and met with the approval of Pope John and several other influential cardinals, with whom Suenens shared it, including Montini, the cardinal archbishop of Milan and soon-to-be successor to Pope John XXIII.

Suenens's plan was basically divided into two parts: the church *ad intra* (inner life) and the church *ad extra* (outside world). Related to the church *ad extra*, Suenens wrote that "the Church must bring Christ to the world. The world has its own problems, and seeks with anguish for solutions; some of these problems are obstacles to the spread of truth and grace. Some of the major problems can be grouped as follows: What do men and women seek? They seek love in their homes; daily bread for themselves and their families; peace both within each nation and among nations. These are basic aspirations. Does the Church have anything to contribute at these levels?"[11]

On September 11, 1962, during a rather memorable radio address to announce and introduce the council, Pope John shared with others his vision. During his address it is clear that he had adopted Suenens's plan: "Considered in the relations of her vitality *ad extra*, that is, the Church facing the needs and demands of peoples—those human situations which turn them instead to appreciate and enjoy the things of earth—the Church considers it her duty to do justice to her responsibilities by her teaching."[12]

Not to be forgotten in all of this development is a group whom some claim "gave the impulse which led to the decision to produce a schema on the Church in the world."[13] Led by Dom Helder Camara, who at the beginning of the council was an auxiliary bishop of Rio de Janeiro but in 1964 was appointed archbishop of Olinda y Recife, they were known as "the Church of the Poor."[14] Canon Charles Moeller, a *peritus* at the council, relates that Camara "constantly discussed with visitors the problems of the Third World" and quotes Camara asking others: "What ought we to do now? . . . Are we to spend our whole time discussing internal Church problems while two-thirds of mankind is dying of hunger? What have we to say on the problem of underdevelopment? Will the Council express its concern about the great problems of mankind?"[15]

The first few weeks of the council were a whirlwind of activity and chaos. The assembled fathers were looking for direction in the midst of confusion. To make matters worse, Pope John's health was failing. In an attempt to give the council greater structure and order, Cardinal

Montini wrote Pope John a letter, alluding at the end to Suenens's plan. Eventually, Suenens himself got into the act and was faced with the difficult decision: "Should I take the initiative and present my plan, or should I wait, since Pope John had wanted to be the one to choose the appropriate moment for making it public?"[16] On December 4, 1962, in the *aula* of St. Peter's, with the approval of Pope John, Suenens proposed his plan of the church *ad intra* and the church *ad extra* to the council fathers. "The unanimous endorsement of the Council," Suenens shared, "was further reinforced on the following day, when Cardinal Montini . . . spoke with enthusiasm in favor of my proposal, as also did Cardinal Lercaro."[17] For there to have been "The Pastoral Constitution on the Church in the Modern World" then, there first had to be the vision. By no means, however, did the existence of this vision make it any easier for the document to come to life.

Better Late than Never

As stated by numerous commentators on the council, no other document went through as laborious or precarious a process of birth as did "The Pastoral Constitution on the Church in the Modern World."[18] Jan Grootaers notes that this is indicated by the very name it was first given—Schema XVII. He goes on to say that "this odd bestowal of a purely numerical title is by itself enough to show the anonymity that marked a draft text that one group refused to study for a long time. It would be put on the agenda of the full assembly of Vatican II only in the fall of 1964 and then only after lengthy hesitation on the part of Paul VI."[19] The constitution would eventually take the "unlucky" working title of Schema XIII.

The two commissions given the task of developing the schema were the Doctrinal Commission and the Commission for the Lay Apostolate. Cardinal Suenens was named *relator* ["reporter"] of the schema by his fellow bishops. In the beginning this now-mixed commission drew on previously prepared material. Speaking of the constitution's first draft, Father Joseph Ratzinger, then professor of theology at Tübingen and conciliar *peritus*, later cardinal prefect of the Congregation for the Doctrine of the Faith, and now Pope Benedict XVI, said:

> The prepared text did definitely broach topical contemporary questions. One of the texts treated Christian ethics in general; another dealt with marriage and family. But their solutions were too pat to be convincing. They were marked by an assurance which had no basis in revelation, and by an authoritarian

decisiveness which is simply no longer suited to the complexity of reality. They were put in categories that came more from classical antiquity than from Christianity. Marriage was discussed in terms of the basic category of "end"; its morality was deduced abstractly from the concept of nature. Here social utility was viewed as overriding the reality of the human person. The whole emphasis was on asserting and reiterating the rights of the Church. The Church's ministerial function was virtually forgotten.[20]

There was still much work to be done. The newly elected Pope Paul VI gave a needed boost to the schema's efforts when, in his address reconvening the council, he spoke of one of its aims being to dialogue with the modern world. Meeting in Rome, Malines, Zurich, and Ariccia, the work of the mixed commission would last three years and produce several texts for consideration and amendment. Not surprisingly, the schema "followed the course of development of all the conciliar texts, which moved from a more abstract, conceptual, and timeless perspective toward a biblical, patristic, liturgical, and conciliar outlook."[21] Furthermore, three papal actions would directly affect the document and would lead some to ask whether work on the schema was redundant—the publication of the encyclicals *Mater et magistra* and *Pacem in terris*, and the removal of any discussion of artificial birth control from the council with the establishment of a papal committee on birth regulation.[22] On December 7, 1965, before its public promulgation, the final vote was taken. Out of the 2,391 votes cast, 2,309 were in favor of the constitution.

The Document Itself

The longest of the council's sixteen documents, "The Pastoral Constitution on the Church in the Modern World" is divided into two main parts. The first part, "The Church and the Human Vocation" (nos. 11-45), articulates what can best be called a Christian anthropology or, in other words, what it means to be human in light of Christ. The second part, "Some More Urgent Problems" (nos. 46-90), speaks to issues related to marriage and family, culture, economics, politics, and war and peace.

Moving beyond the oft-quoted opening paragraph, the constitution seeks to enlarge the church's "audience" and "addresses not only the daughters and sons of the church and all who call upon the name of Christ, but the whole of humanity" (no. 2). The means through which this will be done is conversation rather than diatribe (no. 3). This will enable the church not only to offer to the world the fruits of its "reading the signs of the times and of interpreting them in the light of the Gospel" (no. 4), but create the possibility and likelihood of the reception of these insights on the part of the world. As Bernard Häring, C.Ss.R., one of the twentieth century's greatest moral theologians and a council *peritus*, was quick to point out, "Christians never will mold the world if they do not pay attention to the signs of the times. Christian presence in the world is only possible if Christians are at the same time imbued with the spirit of the gospel and are men of their time."[23]

In looking at these "signs" the most easily recognized one is change. The council fathers recognized "the accelerated pace of history is such that one can scarcely keep abreast of it. . . . And so humankind substitutes a dynamic and more evolutionary concept of nature for a static one" (no. 5). These areas of change included the social, psychological, moral, and religious. Usually, whether it's slow or fast, change brings imbalance and, "[i]n the midst of it all stands humanity, at once the author and the victim of mutual distrust, animosity, conflict and woe" (no. 8).

With this as the backdrop, the constitution spoke of the world in an almost paradoxical way, saying that "[i]n the light of the foregoing factors there appears the dichotomy of a world that is at once powerful and weak, capable of doing what is noble and what is base, disposed to freedom and slavery, progress and decline, amity and hatred. People are becoming conscious that the forces they have unleashed are in their own hands and that it is up to themselves to control them or be enslaved by them. Here lies the modern dilemma" (no. 9). The church's solution to the questions of the age is to be found in conveying to humanity that it is made in the image and likeness of God—as both persons (nos. 12-22) and community (nos. 23-32). Yet, the reality of sin blocks this recognition from taking place (nos. 13, 37).

Though tempted at times and having the opportunity to do so, "the Council refused to hurl anathemas."[24] Instead the church envisioned its role "to be a leaven and, as it were, the soul of human society in its renewal by Christ and transformation into the family of God. . . . In pursuing its own salvific purpose not only does the church communicate divine life to humanity but in a certain sense it casts the reflected light of that divine life over all the earth, notably in the way it heals and elevates the dignity of the human person, in the way it consolidates society, and endows people's daily activity with a deeper sense and meaning" (no. 40).

This leads the church to address what it considers "some more urgent problems." The second part begins by speaking to the challenges faced by those seeking to make and maintain marital commitments and support their families (nos. 47-52). One of the ways in which the council did this was by emphasizing conjugal love in marriage (no. 50). No longer was procreation said to be the sole objective of marriage. Unfortunately, though the need for "responsible parenthood" was admitted, the council was not allowed to discuss the issue of artificial birth control. Enda McDonagh makes the interesting observation that if the organizational and time pressures could have been overcome, and even if the council would have decided to maintain the traditional teaching, "it would probably have received much more widespread support than *Humanae vitae* did subsequently."[25]

The next chapter looks at the church and culture (nos. 53-62). The council defines "culture" very broadly as "all those things which go to the refining and developing of humanity's diverse mental and physical endowments" (no. 53). It admits of new forms of culture and the anxiety that comes from that process of change or, for some, disruption. From this would come the challenge to be open to communicating the gospel in new ways. As Pope John often said, "The substance of the faith is one thing, the way in which it is presented is another."

With respect to economics (nos. 63-72), the constitution basically represents the themes of the emerging Catholic social tradition beginning with Leo XIII up to John XXIII. Echoing the first part, this chapter demands that "the dignity and vocation of the human person as well as the welfare of society as a whole have to be respected and fostered; for people are the source, the focus and the aim of all economic and social life" (no. 63). It highlights the growing international economic inequalities and advocates reform not just on the practical level, but in ideas and attitudes as well. This situation is well summarized in a quote used by the council fathers: "Feed the people dying of hunger, because if you do not feed them you are killing them" (no. 69).

Chapter 4 concerns politics (nos. 73-76) and takes as its starting point the common good. With long-entrenched political structures falling and new ones emerging throughout the world, the constitution urges that any political order must "provide all citizens with effective opportunities to play a free, active part in the establishment of the juridical foundations of the political community, in determining the aims and the terms of reference of public bodies, and in the election of political leaders" (no. 75). All the while the church remains ready "to preach the faith, to proclaim its teachings about society, to carry out its task among people without hindrance, and to pass moral judgments even in matters relating to politics, whenever the fundamental human rights or the salvation of souls requires it" (no. 76).

Finally, written during the heart of the Cold War, the last chapter deals with the promotion of peace and the building up of the international community as opposed to simply avoiding war (nos. 77-90). Here it calls special attention to the arms race, saying it "is one of the greatest curses on the human race and the harm it inflicts on the poor is more than can be endured" (no. 81). The second section of the chapter promotes greater cooperation between international institutions as a means to increase global progress and prevent war (no. 84). It states that "Christians should willingly and wholeheartedly support the establishment of an international order that includes a genuine respect for legitimate freedom and amity towards all" (no. 88).

The constitution ends with what could be termed a call to social action: "Christians can yearn for nothing more ardently than to serve the people of this age successfully with increasing generosity. Holding loyally to the gospel, enriched by its resources, and joining forces with all who love and practice justice, they have shouldered a weighty task here on earth and they must render an account of it to him who will judge all people on the last day" (no. 93).

Looking back now, some like to diminish the constitution's weight and vision by referring to it as a pastoral constitution rather than a dogmatic one like "The Dogmatic Constitution on the Church" (*Lumen gentium*). Quoting the words of Archbishop Garrone, though, Bishop Mark G. McGrath, C.S.C., who was present at the council as a representative from Latin America (Panama), says that "The Pastoral Constitution on the Church in the Modern World" is "at the very heart of the Council. One could say that it is the only schema formally willed by John XXIII."[26] Seen in this light, as representative of the central purpose for the council, it could be argued that this document possesses the most authority.[27]

MARY LUKE TOBIN, S.L.

Women Are Also "Church"

Ruth Tobin, daughter of William and Mary McGovern Tobin, was born May 16, 1908, in Denver, Colorado. She was educated in Denver public elementary and high schools. After two years at Loretto Heights College (Denver), Tobin entered the novitiate of the Sisters of Loretto, in Nerinx, Kentucky. At her reception into the congregation, she received the name Sister Mary Luke.

Sister Mary Luke received her B.A. degree at Loretto Heights College (1934) and her M.A. (1942) in history at Notre Dame University. After serving as principal in several Loretto high schools, Sister was elected in 1952 to the General Council of the Sisters of Loretto. In 1958 she was elected superior general, in which position she served two six-year terms. From 1964 to 1967 Sister Mary Luke was president of the Conference of Major Superiors of Women. As leader of women religious in the United States at the time of Vatican II, Sister Mary Luke was invited to the last two sessions of the council. She was one of fifteen women auditors.

Since that time Sister was active in issues of peace and justice, as well as in women's issues and ecumenism. After 1970 she served on the staff of Church Women United in New York. Later, drawing on her early friendship with Thomas Merton during her years at the Motherhouse, she directed the Thomas Merton Center in Denver until 1995. Her book, Hope Is an Open Door: Journeys in Faith, *was published in 1981. Over the course of her life she was awarded seven honorary degrees.*

Until her death on August 24, 2006, Sister Mary Luke championed issues of peace and justice, including the dismantling of racism, women's rights, and abolition of the death penalty.

WHEN THE SECOND VATICAN COUNCIL opened in 1962, I was superior general of the Sisters of Loretto. Religious communities were aware that a new era was upon us and were studying proposed changes suggested by such authors as Archbishop Philippe, secretary of the Sacred

Congregation of Religious, the Belgian Cardinal Suenens, and many others. The liturgical movement in the United States, spearheaded by Godfrey Diekmann, O.S.B., was well under way.

In August 1964, I was elected president of the Conference of Major Superiors of Women in the United States. This group had been working since 1950 to effect the renewal and adaptation called for by some far-sighted members of the Sacred Congregation. It was at their suggestion and encouragement, as well as that of my own congregation, that I proceeded to Rome during the third session of the council to learn from the periphery the developments occurring daily at the Vatican. On September 23, 1964, while watching the moon on the waters, I was summoned to the radio tower on the S.S. *Constitution* for three messages. The operator remarked that in his twenty years on this ship, this was the first time he had three messages for one person. The media had just been informed that fifteen women auditors had been invited to the council and that I was the one from the United States. The Associated Press was calling from New York wanting to be the first to offer congratulations. The other two were calls from Loretto superiors in Kentucky and St. Louis.

When interviewed, the layman in charge of the "auditors" indicated that women had been invited to participate in those sessions "which would be of interest to them." I made a mental note that I would never miss a session—a decision I later learned was shared by all the women. We were eight women religious and seven laywomen.

Early in the council, the bishops, in the "Dogmatic Constitution on the Church" (*Lumen gentium*), insisted that the church should be titled "The People of God." The people *are* the church, with the result that as such the doors would be open for wider participation of all. From this understanding would flow the ideal of collegiality and the formation of parish councils.

The importance and dignity of the individual were becoming recognized, as well as the responsibilities of that person for participation and decision making within the total community. An outgrowth was the extension of the boundaries of the church to include all Christians and those of other world faiths. For the first time, Protestant Christian churches were acknowledged as churches.

The presence of women in and around the council hall called to consciousness the issues that women were facing. Although council documents spoke out clearly against discrimination, women were still looked upon (perhaps unconsciously) as second-class citizens. I recall an incident when Rosemary Goldie, an auditor who held a curial position in

Rome, and I were attending a meeting in preparation for documents to be presented to the bishops. Father Yves Congar, after giving his position paper asked, "What do you think of my presentation?" Rosemary replied, "Père Congar, you can leave out all the pretty phrases about women and omit the flowers. Just make it clear that men *and women* constitute the church."

Related to the above incident, at the great outdoor Mass at the conclusion of the council, part of the program involved the presentation of certificates of honor to distinguished persons in various categories. Four philosophers, for example, were so honored; they walked across the platform and received from the hands of the pope some special insignia of recognition. Then four *literati*, four musicians, and so on, were singled out for praise. Finally, four women walked across the stage. And the announcer proclaimed that "women would be honored for their contribution to the church." I turned to Father Godfrey Diekmann and said: "But women are not a *category* in the church. They should not be honored as women more than men should be honored as men. Men *and women* are the church, aren't they?" Father Godfrey looked at me and said, "You're right, Sister; you women need to help us see this."

Two statements within the council documents speak out clearly against discrimination. In "The Pastoral Constitution on the Church in the Modern World" we see: "But any kind of social or cultural discrimination in basic personal rights on the grounds of sex . . . must be curbed and eradicated as incompatible with God's design."[28]

Also, in "The Dogmatic Constitution on the Church," we read that "the chosen People of God is, therefore, one: 'one Lord, one faith, one baptism' (Eph 4:5); there is a common dignity of members deriving from their rebirth in Christ. . . . In Christ and in the church there is, then, no inequality arising from race or nationality, social condition or sex, for 'there is neither Jew nor Greek; there is neither slave nor free man; there is neither male nor female. For you are all one in Christ Jesus' (Gal 3:28 Greek; see Col 3:11)."[29]

Unfortunately, an insensitive state of affairs regarding women in the church still remains. The open door that revealed to me the enormous discrepancy between Christian faith and practice, in the area of women in church and society, has only opened wider as I have become more conscious of the need to work ceaselessly for the goal of the equality of all persons.

However, the greater freedom, flexibility, experimentation, and new apostolic ventures were exciting to me. But I was perplexed and disappointed to discover later that the authorities at the Vatican were not equally enthusiastic about our plans for "the renewal and adaptation in the religious life" that had been called for.

In formal meetings of religious women as a follow-up to the council, these women were expressing their desire to have a part in the decision making that affected their lives, either by a deliberative vote or in a consultative manner.

In assessing the developments of the council, those which I consider healthy and hopeful include (1) a more flexible liturgy; (2) wider participation of both men and women in pastoral ministry; (3) religious education, which has incorporated the teachings of Vatican II; (4) the establishment of parish councils (which now include women); (5) peace and justice commissions instituted at diocesan and local levels; (6) ecumenical involvement through participation in these commissions.

Although in many places it appears that the promises of Vatican II have not occurred, to me it seems that the event of Vatican II was a special epiphany of hope for the church in our time. The council was a door opened wide—too wide to be closed.

PETER C. PHAN

Vatican II and
the Asian Catholic Church

Peter C. Phan is the inaugural holder of the Ignacio Ellacuría Chair of Catholic Social Thought at Georgetown University and is the founding director of the Graduate Studies Program in Theology and Religious Studies. Holding multiple doctorates in theology, he has taught at many universities, including the Catholic University of America, Washington, DC, where he held the Warren-Blanding Chair of Religion and Culture and at Union Theological Seminary in New York City. Phan has received two honorary degrees: Doctor of Theology from Catholic Theological Union and Doctor of Humane Letters from Elms College. He is the first non-Anglo to be elected president of the Catholic Theological Society of America. In 2010 he was awarded the John Courtney Murray Award, the highest honor given by the Catholic Theological Society of America for outstanding achievements in theology.

His publications in theology are wide ranging, have been translated into numerous languages, and cover topics such as the theology of icon in Orthodox theology, patristic theology, and eschatology. Concerning the history of mission in Asia, he has published Mission and Catechesis: Alexandre de Rhodes and Inculturation in Seventeenth-Century Vietnam *(2006); concerning liberation, inculturation, and interreligious dialogue, he has published* Christianity with an Asian Face *(2003);* In Our Own Tongues *(2003); and* Being Religious Interreligiously *(2004). In addition, Phan has edited some twenty volumes. He is the general editor of a multivolume series titled* Theology in Global Perspective *for Orbis Books and a multivolume series titled* Ethnic American Pastoral Spirituality *for Paulist Press. His writings have received many awards from learned societies.*

IF THE VATICAN COUNCIL WERE an earthquake, I was too young and too far away to be at its epicenter, and yet too old and near enough not to have felt its immediate aftershocks. The first time I heard of the council was in 1963. I was studying philosophy at Don Bosco College in Cheung Chau, Hong Kong. The bishop of Hong Kong, Lorenzo Bianchi (1899-1983), who had attended the council, was invited by the college to give a talk on it. Of this eyewitness account I remember nothing except that the Italian missionary bishop seemed to have been deeply shaken by the changes wrought by the council thus far. To a seventeen-year-old boy, still innocent in matters of theology and church, that was enough proof that Vatican II was something momentous.

Where I was, the late 1960s was not yet the age of television, and of course not Facebook and Twitter. What we knew of the council was through black-and-white, occasionally color, print. I remember having seen the photos of some of the key players at the council, all of whom bore European names, mostly German, French, and Italian: Ottaviani, Bea, Döpfner, Léger, Liénart, Suenens. In their sartorial accouterments they exuded omniscience and power. Of theologians I recall having read the names of Congar, Chenu, de Lubac, Küng, and Rahner (strangely, not Ratzinger). Soon, wide-ranging changes mandated by Vatican II were introduced, especially in the liturgy, without fuss and fanfare, perhaps because they responded to our deepest spiritual needs.

My first personal encounter with Vatican II occurred in my first year as a student of theology in Rome in 1968. Change was in the air. A new theology was taught. But this time, change was not always smooth. Three of our professors were dismissed for allegedly heterodox ideas. Our class, of which I was the president, went on a hunger strike in protest. Eventually, religious authorities won out; some students were dismissed, and life went on. But never the same. Freedom was tasted, and there was no going back. And for this I have Vatican II to thank. The council had a profound effect on me and on the Asian Catholic Church.

The Council

The presence of the bishops from Asia at Vatican II was insignificant—some 300 out of about 2,500 participants—most of them expatriate missionaries. The council was dominated by the bishops of central Europe, notably Germany and France. Rahner's assessment of Vatican II as marking the end of the Eurocentric church and the beginning of a world church is true—up to a point. It was still essentially a European affair.

In spite of their tiny presence, Asian bishops did have a voice at the

council. A survey of their interventions shows that consistent with their pragmatic outlook, their main concern was not with doctrinal issues but with practical church reforms. The first area to which they contributed significantly is liturgy. Cardinal Valerian Gracias of Bombay, India, asked that local episcopal conferences be given sufficient authority to implement liturgical reform. A Chinese bishop requested the inclusion of St. Joseph in the eucharistic prayer. Bishop Nguyen Van Hien of Saigon (now Ho Chi Minh City, Vietnam) asked on behalf of the Vietnamese bishops that episcopal conferences be permitted to introduce liturgical feasts on certain civil feast days in order to give them a Christian dimension and to show non-Christians that Christians respect ancestral traditions. He also requested permission to honor Asian martyrs with a liturgical feast in order to hold them up as models of Christian life appropriate to the Asian context. Bishop Yoshigoro Taguchi of Osaka (Japan) pointed out that the splendor of the liturgical vessels gave offense in Japan because the Japanese love simplicity. He added that his people had trouble understanding certain Western rituals such as putting on and taking off the miter, kneeling to kiss the bishop's ring, and so on. He also proposed that liturgical vestments conform to local tastes and customs. Along the same line, Bishop Paul Seitz of Kontum (Vietnam) said that sacred art should be marked by simplicity, integrity, and poverty.

The second area on which the Asian bishops focused their attention is inculturation. Bishop Stanislaus Lokuang of Tainan (Taiwan) emphasized that every people has its own culture and that the church must respect all of them and use them as means for evangelization. Immediately after the promulgation of the constitution on the liturgy (*Sacrosanctum concilium*) at the end of the second session (December 4, 1963), the Asian bishops energetically initiated this process of inculturation in liturgical matters.

The third area of interest was interreligious dialogue. Given the fact that Asian Catholics live in the midst of other religions, the Asian bishops were deeply concerned about dialogue with people of other faiths. The goal was to create conditions leading to mutual collaboration, religious harmony, and freedom.

Fourth, since the Asian churches were in mission lands, the Asian bishops showed a marked interest in mission. Here the greatest contribution was made by Bishop Stanislaus Lokuang, vice-president of the Commission for the Missions. After the schema on mission prepared by the Congregation for the Propagation of the Faith was rejected by the council fathers, a five-member editorial team was selected to do the revisions, and Archbishop Lokuang received the greatest number of votes. With Lokuang's shepherding, the revised document on mission, *Ad gentes* ("Decree on the Missionary Activity of the Church"), was eventually approved by the council.

Fifth, another practical matter that drew the attention of the Asian bishops was priestly training and mandatory celibacy. During the fourth session of the council, the Indonesian bishops challenged the statement that "major seminaries are necessary for priestly formation" (*Ad gentes*, 4) and suggested that new organizations, more suitable to contemporary needs, be adopted. In addition, they urged a reconsideration of the requirement of priestly celibacy. The council, however, ultimately reaffirmed the appropriateness of priestly celibacy (see *Ad gentes*, 10).

In sum, the contributions of the Asian bishops to Vatican II, while not as extensive as that of other bishops, were not insignificant. They focused less on doctrinal formulations than on how the Christian faith can be effectively practiced in their socio-political and religious locations. It is in this pastoral direction that their reception of the council must be evaluated. Among the many challenges facing the Asian churches in the immediate aftermath of Vatican II was the translation of the council's sixteen documents as well as the numerous postconciliar texts into various languages. This undertaking in itself was an immense achievement. In addition, various liturgical innovations were made to inculturate the liturgy, including the use of indigenous vestments, music and songs, gestures, rituals, sacred objects, architecture and art, and even the sacred texts of other religions. Contextualized theologies, which take into account Asian philosophies, socio-political conditions, monastic and spiritual traditions, and cultural practices, began to be elaborated.

Reception of the Council

Two events marked a full reception of Vatican II and the maturity of the Asian churches. The first is the founding in 1972 of the Federation of the Asian Bishops' Conferences (FABC). The FABC's supreme body is the plenary assembly that meets every four years. The FABC also has a central secretariat with seven offices, each responsible for a particular area of Christian life. The overall task of the FABC's plenary assembly and its various offices includes

> to work for and to intensify the dynamic presence of the church
> in the total developments of the peoples of Asia; to help in the
> study of problems of common interest to the church in Asia, and
> to investigate possibilities of solutions and coordinate actions;
> to promote inter-communion and cooperation among local

churches and bishops of Asia; to render service to episcopal conferences of Asia in order to help them to meet better the needs of the People of God; to foster a more ordered development of organizations and movements in the church at the international level; to foster ecumenical and interreligious communication and collaboration.[30]

The second event is the Special Assembly of the Synod of Bishops for Asia that was convoked by Pope John Paul II and met in Rome April 19 to May 14, 1998. In contrast to Vatican II, where their voice was small, the Asian bishops came to the Asian Synod with an agenda of their own. As the Filipino bishops put it, "Ensure that the Synod is truly Asian, with an Asian reflection, with an Asian output, reflecting the Asian perspective of evangelization."[31]

Following the by now well-established theological orientations of the FABC, Asian bishops emphasized the necessity of the threefold dialogue that constitutes the mission of the church in Asia: dialogue with the Asian peoples, especially their poor and marginalized (liberation); dialogue with their cultures (inculturation); and dialogue with their religions (interreligious dialogue). They urged a radical decentralization of the church, real and effective collegiality between the pope and the other bishops, and genuine autonomy-within-communion of the local churches. They proposed the establishment of new "patriarchates" in Asia, similar to those of the first millennium of Christianity, with catholicity, collegiality, and subsidiarity (and not papal primacy) as the basic ecclesiological principles and the triadic structure of local (the bishop), regional (the patriarch), and universal (the pope) churches as the appropriate organizational model.

Without Vatican II the Asian Catholic Church would not be what it is today. By the same token, without the process of reception of the council—both receiving and giving back (at times subverting) what is given—the Asian Catholic Church would not be what it is today, either. What the future holds for the Asian Catholic Church is of course unknown. What is known, however, is what the Asian Colloquium on Ministries (held in Hong Kong on March 5, 1977) asserted: "If the Asian Churches do not discover their own identity, they will have no future."

ELIZABETH A. JOHNSON, C.S.J.

Worth a Life—A Vatican II Story

Currently the Distinguished Professor of Theology at Fordham University in New York City, Elizabeth Johnson is a teacher, writer, editor, and public lecturer in theology. She began her professional life by teaching science and religion in Catholic elementary and high schools before moving on to teaching theology at college (St. Joseph's College, Brooklyn, New York) and university levels (Catholic University of America, 1980-1991). Her formal education includes a B.S. from Brentwood College (1964), an M.A. in theology from Manhattan College (1970), and a Ph.D. in theology from Catholic University of America (1981).

Former president of the Catholic Theological Society of America (CTSA), the oldest and largest society of theologians in the world, and former president of the ecumenical American Theological Society, Elizabeth Johnson has written books that include Consider Jesus: Waves of Renewal in Christology *(1990);* She Who Is: The Mystery of God in Feminist Theological Discourse *(1992);* Women, Earth, and Creator Spirit *(1993);* Friends of God and Prophets: A Feminist Theological Reading of the Communion of Saints *(1998);* The Church Women Want: Catholic Women in Dialogue *(editor, 2002);* Truly Our Sister: A Theology of Mary in the Communion of Saints *(2003);* Dangerous Memories: A Mosaic of Mary in Scripture *(2004); and* Quest for the Living God: Mapping Frontiers in the Theology of God *(2007). Her books, numerous scholarly essays, chapters in books, and popular articles have been translated into German, Spanish, Portuguese, Italian, French, Dutch, Lithuanian, Romanian, Indonesian, Korean, and Thai. She serves on the editorial boards of the journals* Theological Studies, Horizons: Journal of the College Theology Society, *and* Theoforum.

The recipient of fourteen honorary degrees, Elizabeth Johnson loves to teach. She was awarded Fordham University's Teaching Award in 1998, and was voted Professor of the Year by the students of the Graduate School of Arts and Sciences in 2011. By now she has lectured on every continent, making presentations to church and academic groups both at home and abroad.

Johnson's books have garnered major awards: She Who Is *(the Grawemeyer Award in Religion);* Friends of God and Prophets *(the American Academy of Religion's Excellence in the Study of Religion Award);* Truly Our Sister *(the College Theology Society's Book of the Year Award); four of her books received awards from the Catholic Press Association. In addition to the John Courtney Murray Award from the CTSA for excellence in theology, and the Monika Hellwig Award from the Association of Catholic Colleges and Universities for promoting the intellectual life of Catholics, she has received the gift of numerous other awards from colleges, universities, associations, and journals.*

Deeply involved in the life of the church, she is a religious sister in the Congregation of St. Joseph, Brentwood, New York. Her public service in the church has included being a theologian on the national Lutheran-Catholic Dialogue; a consultant to the Catholic Bishops' Committee on Women in Church and Society; a theologian on the Vatican-sponsored dialogue between science and religion, and on the Vatican-sponsored study of Christ and world religions; and an initial member of the core committee of the Common Ground Initiative, started by Cardinal Joseph Bernardin to reconcile polarized groups in the Catholic Church.

At the time of the council, she was a young sister in temporary vows engaged in teaching in Catholic elementary school.

IT WAS THE SUMMER OF 1965. The Watts riots were roiling Los Angeles. Thousands of young people were gathering in Washington to protest the Vietnam War. Congress was debating the historic Voting Rights Act, spurred by the march in Selma, Alabama, its indelible images of violence, and its third successful attempt (in which two Sisters of my congregation participated). All of this was on my mind when I gathered with sixty other young Sisters to prepare for making our final vows at the end of August. We were to spend two months of prayer and reflection at our rolling, green, cloistered motherhouse on Long Island, far from riots, protests, and the struggle for civil rights.

Truth be told, my heart was very conflicted about whether to make this life-committing decision. The reason was a fundamental tension. On the one hand was the spirituality of world-denying asceticism, which as novices we had been taught was the ideal of religious life. On the other hand was my own growing spiritual desire to engage with this fascinating world. On the one hand our congregation was living religious life in a way typical of the preconciliar era: strong top-down authority, strict daily horarium, full religious garb, restricted human relationships, emphasis on distance from the world and saving one's soul and the souls of others. On the other hand the 1960s were in mid-swing: John F. Kennedy newly dead, Joan Baez and Bob Dylan singing changing-times tunes, Martin Luther King dreaming his dream, LBJ's war on poverty, my own peers in "the outside world" beginning to rebel against society's strictures. My deepest sympathies lay with the latter. In contrast to the teachings of our vow preparation, I kept thinking that if God created and loved this world, then shouldn't those of us radically seeking to serve God in religious life be in the forefront of engagement with this world? Wouldn't making final vows box me into a narrow life of perfection when the struggling world needed us to get our hands dirty for the love of God? Wouldn't I be denying the divine call that I felt in my own spirit? And so I struggled.

One day we were handed, among other materials for personal reading, a poorly printed pamphlet. It was the draft of a conciliar document then under discussion and not yet voted on. Out of curiosity, I took it on my daily walk. Coming to a favorite pine tree, I settled in its shade and began to read. The opening words riveted me: "The joys and the hopes, the grief and the anguish of the people of our time, especially of those who are poor or afflicted, are the joys and hopes, the grief and anguish of the followers of Christ as well." Stunned, I read that sentence over and over again. Amen to that! And weren't nuns supposed to be followers of Christ? Here was the highest authority in the church challenging the spiritual tradition in which I felt imprisoned, endorsing rather than warning against involvement with the world. But more than that. This document painted a theological vision of humanity created in the image of God, defaced by the evil of sin, but redeemed by Christ and now led in history by the Spirit through the witness of the church. This was a vision I had never before encountered, and it was so beautiful.

All afternoon long I slowly read *Gaudium et spes*, drinking it in like water in the desert. The sun began to slide down the sky but in a very real way the light was rising. I loved the way the council aimed its message at the "whole of humanity" in a spirit of respect and love. I admired the way it admitted that atheism often arose as a critical reaction to deficiencies in the way believers themselves acted. I thrilled to the idea that the church and the world should be in mutual relationship, each learning from the specific wisdom of the other—the gospel on the one hand, and science, humanities, and technology on the other. I resonated with its analysis of changed conditions in the modern world—new technologies, the desire for freedom even on the part of women, enormous inequity of material wealth resulting in poverty and hunger, the danger of nuclear weapons—and the impact all of these conditions had on religion. The document spoke of marriage and family, culture, socioeconomic justice, political participation, war and peace, international cooperation: I stirred to the way these issues were addressed in the spirit of the gospel.

Most of all, I reveled in *Gaudium et spes*'s emphasis on the dignity of the human person. Every human being is created in the image of God. This anthropology grounds the essential equality of all persons and the need for an ethic that serves their well-being within the common good. Indeed, "with respect to the fundamental rights of the person, every type of discrimination, whether social or cultural, whether based on sex, race, color, social condition, language, or religion, is to be overcome and eradicated as contrary to God's intent" (§29). What ringing words! Just as attractive was the way Jesus Christ gets connected to struggling humanity, first as the incarnate Word who is truly one of us: "he worked with human hands, he thought with a human mind, acted by human choice, and loved with a human heart" (§22); and then through his dying and rising as the savior who transforms the world with hope. And wonder of wonders: "All this holds true not only for Christians, but for all persons of good will in whose hearts grace works in an unseen way. For since Christ died for all people, and since the ultimate vocation of human beings is in fact one, we ought to believe that the Holy Spirit in a manner known only to God offers to every person the possibility of being associated with this paschal mystery" (§22). The universal scope of this vision took my breath away. By the time *Gaudium et spes* concluded with a ringing call for harmony within the church "through the full recognition of lawful diversity," so Christians can then serve the modern world ever more generously and effectively—by this time I was possessed with an overriding conviction: This is worth my life.

And so it has proved to be.

On that hot summer day, my young, questing spirit intersected with this council document and found its life-long direction. In the decades since then much has changed in myself, the church, and the world. But the power of *Gaudium et spes* to inspire and challenge me has not waned. Many of my decisions in ministry and the direction of my theological scholarship have been made in its light. Rather than reacting fearfully to conflicts between faith and culture, I imbibed its confidence that these "do not necessarily harm the life of faith; rather they can stimulate the mind to a deeper and more accurate understanding of the faith. The recent studies and findings of science, history and philosophy raise new questions which affect life and which demand new theological investigations" (§62). In particular, *Gaudium et spes*'s teachings have become ever more telling as I have read them through the lens of feminism, which focuses the desire of women for equal human dignity in church and society.

Given this personal history, I meet current official ecclesiastical efforts to reverse Vatican II's direction with dismay. After a half century of living in the spirit of *Gaudium et spes*, it is spiritually and intellectually impossible for me to return to that narrow-minded attitude, hostile to the world, in which I was originally formed. Weaned into my life's commitment by this profoundly Christ-centered, humanistic, generous pastoral constitution on the church in the modern world, I continue to join with others who walk by its light, regardless. At the same time, the respectful, loving intent of *Gaudium et spes* stands as prophetic witness against any and all current official dicta that are mean-spirited, arrogant, and reactionary. While its wisdom is not always followed, its teaching remains cogent: "let there be unity in what is necessary, freedom in what is unsettled, and charity in any case" (§92).

DAVID HOLLENBACH, S.J.

A World Church

David Hollenbach, S.J., holds the University Chair in Human Rights and International Justice at Boston College, where he teaches theological ethics in the theology department and directs the Center for Human Rights and International Justice.

Hollenbach was born in Philadelphia in 1942 and attended Saint Joseph's University, receiving his B.S. in physics in 1964 as Vatican II was approaching its conclusion. A charismatic Jesuit inspired him to reconsider his interest in the sciences and to enter the Society of Jesus. As a young Jesuit, under the influence of both the council and the ferment in American life, he pursued the links between his studies and work of justice and peace. On completing his M.Div. at Woodstock College, Hollenbach was ordained a priest in 1971. He then studied religious ethics at Yale University, writing his Ph.D. dissertation on the development of Catholic thought on human rights. He has taught at Georgetown University, Weston Jesuit School of Theology, Boston College, and regularly as a visiting professor at Hekima College in Nairobi, Kenya.

Hollenbach's books include Claims in Conflict *(1979),* The Common Good and Christian Ethics *(2002), and* The Global Face of Public Faith *(2003). He helped the U.S. Catholic bishops draft their 1986 pastoral letter,* Economic Justice for All.

His honors and awards include being president of the Society of Christian Ethics (1995-1996), and receiving the John Courtney Murray Award for distinguished scholarship and service to the academy and church from the Catholic Theological Society of America in 1998, as well as the Marianist Award for major contribution to the intellectual life from the University of Dayton in 2009.

Vatican II continues to inspire all his work.

FOR AN EVENT CELEBRATING HIS seventieth birthday, the eminent theologian Karl Rahner was invited to address the faculty and students of Weston Jesuit School of Theology where I was then teaching. As I listened to his lecture, I found myself quietly saying to myself: Yes! Yes! That's it! This is truly where God is moving the church today! Rahner's talk was an extraordinarily insightful analysis of one of the deeper implications of the Second Vatican Council for the life of the church in the late twentieth century and beyond. It was published in *Theological Studies* in 1979 under the title "Toward a Fundamental Theological Interpretation of Vatican II."[32]

Rahner proposed that perhaps the most basic influence of the council would prove to be the way it transformed the church's self-understanding from that of a European community with missionary outposts in other parts of the world to that of a truly global body with members from all the cultures of the world. In Rahner's view, a transformation of this magnitude occurred only once previously in the church's history: the shift during the church's first centuries when it moved from being a movement within Palestinian Judaism to the genuinely new religious community that became European Christendom. At Vatican II the church again changed dramatically, coming for the first time to understand itself as a truly "world church." This dramatic shift was due, at least in part, to the fact that the bishops at the council came from almost all of the countries around the world and from cultures where the church was forced to interact with all of the great world religions and ideologies. The experience the bishops themselves brought to the council showed them that the church needed to take global economic differences and cultural diversity with great seriousness. Thus Rahner argued that Vatican II was "in a rudimentary form still groping for identity, the Church's first official self-actualization as a world Church."[33]

The council itself expressed the importance of this global reach for the church's mission in the "Pastoral Constitution of the Church in the Modern World" (*Gaudium et spes*). Among the "signs of the times" to which the church is called to bring the light of the gospel is the deep division of the world into societies enjoying "abundance of wealth, resources, and economic power" on the one side, and those "tormented by hunger and poverty" and even suffering from total illiteracy on the other. Further, the council saw the world torn into opposing camps by political, social, economic, racial, and ideological disputes (*Gaudium et spes*, no. 4). Anticipating the phenomenon that has since come to be called globalization, the council noted the "growing interdependence" that links people together in numerous new ways (*Gaudium et spes*, no. 23). This interdependence challenges the human community both to discover new ways of protecting the dignity of every person as created in the image of God and at the same time to create new forms of global interaction and new global institutions that embody true fraternity and solidarity.

During the council, Pope John XXIII had formulated this global challenge in very blunt language. He argued that the political institutions governing worldwide interaction were simply inadequate to the task of securing the common good of the people of the world (*Pacem in terris*, no. 135). The nation-state system that divides the world into self-determining, independent nation-states lacks that capacity to grapple with the economic inequalities, technological interconnections, and human movement that are so characteristic of the emerging world. With John XXIII, therefore, the council called the church to a ministry that will help create the solidarity and new institutions required to protect the dignity of all. It called the church to become more effectively a sacrament, that is, a sign and instrument, of both "communion with God and of the unity of the entire human race" (*Lumen gentium*, no. 1; *Gaudium et spes*, no. 42).

There have been numerous efforts to respond to this challenge of global mission since the council. Let me highlight a few that have been personally significant in my own ministry as a theologian working in the domain of social morality. As I began my teaching, the doctoral dissertation I had written on the development of Catholic thought concerning human rights became more relevant than I ever anticipated it might. The role human rights should play in foreign policy became a central point of contention in the United States in the 1970s and '80s. At the same time, the church came to play an increasingly important role working for human rights in countries ranging from Spain and Portugal in the 1970s to many Latin American counties as well as the Philippines and South Korea in the early 1980s, to Poland and eastern Europe in the late 1980s and early 1990s. One noted political scientist has argued that the Catholic community played a determining role in the transition of most of the countries that moved from authoritarian to democratic governance in the last third of the twentieth century.[34] Having worked on human rights in a Catholic perspective gave me a privileged position from which to observe and to some extent to participate in the council's notable contribution to global justice in the human rights domain. It has also been the source of my present-day concern that very recently church leaders have been notably less engaged in the continuing global struggles for human rights.

The council's challenge to become a truly world church has also affected the lives of many religious men and women by calling them to a solidarity that has led them to see their ministry as genuinely transnational. The Jesuit community I am a member of, like other religious orders, sees international mission as the vocation of all its members, not just of those who leave home for good to work in the "missions." The boundaries between home and abroad are much less sharp than they were before the council. So my frequent movement between work in a U.S. Jesuit institution like Boston College and one in the developing world like Hekima College in Nairobi, Kenya, has been a direct outcome of being part of the world church to which Vatican II made such an important contribution.

One of the most negative global phenomena of our time—the forcible displacement of people from their homes as refugees by war, oppression, and disasters—has also become one of the important ministries of the Jesuit community. Both Pope John XXIII and the council had noted that the global system of nation-states is not capable of an adequate response to some of today's global challenges. This is surely true of the challenge of refugees, for these are people who fall through the cracks of the nation-state system. A refugee is a person whose home country is either unable or unwilling to provide the social protection all persons require if they are to live in dignity. Seeking to respond to the council's call that the church should be a sacrament or sign of the unity of humankind, the Jesuit order founded the Jesuit Refugee Service (JRS) to provide ministries of accompaniment, service, and advocacy to refugees. Working today in fifty-five countries, JRS has become a path to engagement in the mission of a world church for some Jesuits and for the laity and other religious who work with them. The privilege of collaborating with JRS has given my own work in theology and ethics an orientation it would never have had otherwise.

I think this new orientation to the struggle for global justice and human rights has been a profound effect of Vatican II. It is well known, of course, that in very recent years there have been some efforts to pull back from some of the initiatives launched by the council, and this has been true in some aspects of the work for global justice. It is my hope, however, that the irreversible contributions of the council will sustain and even intensify this work in the years ahead. The fact that the global interconnections among peoples continue to grow, both for good and for ill, surely calls for nothing less.

MARY JO WEAVER

Lower-Case Catholic

Mary Jo Weaver is the oldest of six children, born to Bob and Ann Weaver on December 16, 1942 (missing the feast of St. John of the Cross by two days, but landing on Beethoven's birthday). She received her undergraduate education at St. Mary of the Springs College (now Ohio Dominican), graduating in 1964 with a B.A. in chemistry. After graduation, she worked on birth control research for Parke-Davis & Co., in Ann Arbor, Michigan, until she began her doctoral work at Notre Dame in 1967. Weaver has two versions of her diploma: one in traditional masculine language, dated June 1972, and (after her complaints) one in feminine language, dated January 1973.

Weaver describes her academic "trajectory" as quirky: she wrote her dissertation on Philo, but published her first two books on the modernist controversy (late nineteenth-century England), her next two books on American Catholic women and the church, and the next two on rifts in contemporary Catholicism. The book dear to her heart but not on that list is her textbook, Introduction to Christianity, *now in its fourth edition (2009). Her most recent book is* Cloister and Community: Life within a Carmelite Monastery *(2002).*

Weaver worked for three years at the Pontifical College Josephinum and was at Indiana University since 1975 until she retired there in 2006. Much of her research was funded by Indiana University and by outside grants (such as the National Endowment for the Humanities and the Indiana Council for the Humanities). But she reserves most of her thanks for the Lilly Endowment, whose generous support led to two edited volumes: Being Right: Conservative Catholics in America, *with Scott Appleby (1995), and* What's Left: Liberal American Catholics *(1999). In the 1990s Weaver was often interviewed on NPR programs like* Talk of the Nation, All Things Considered, *and* Fresh Air.

At the time of the council, Weaver was in college welcoming the chance to escape from predigested Aquinas. Those chances to study scripture and contemporary issues eventually led to her decision to abandon chemistry for theology.

PARADOXICALLY, BY OPENING AN AVENUE for me toward a Ph.D. in theology, the Second Vatican Council paved the way to life in a secular university. Put another way, although the council tapped into a carefully nurtured desire to understand the faith in order to become one of its apologists, I have spent my professional life not defending Catholicism but learning to understand it as a lower-case word. The council allowed me to train myself for more effective service within the tradition but gave me the desire to move beyond it, into the very territory I was taught to avoid.

I grew up defending myself for being a Catholic. In my little backwater town in Ohio, residual Klan embers were alive in bullies and bigots. I was sometimes beaten up for attending Catholic school, and my parents were not permitted to join the local country club lest the smell of incense distract the duffers. We had been in that town for generations, knew the game (factories that would not hire us, people who would not associate with us), and played our part. That is to say, we were as public and outrageous in our faith as we dared to be (parading around the block during May aided by a loudspeaker as we recited the rosary, for example), thereby reinforcing the worst fears of our neighbors.

When I got bored with the Catholic school students (I graduated in a class of twelve) and wanted to be part of the more glamorous life of the public school kids, I boned up on a little book called (I think) *Forty Questions Most Asked by Protestants*. It did not really help: they were much more interested in French kissing (why a mortal sin) and birth control (why not permitted) than in the questions in the book ("Is it true that Catholics chained up Bibles in the Middle Ages?"). But it was a start, and I spent many a slumber party engaged in these issues, while some of my friends were happily making out under blankets in finished basements.

But, if I were somehow part of this world, I was clearly different as well. When everyone else tucked into sleeping bags at dawn, I got on my bike to ride in to church where for several years I was our only organist. Because I was in church constantly, bright, and apparently interested in religion (what else was there?), I was an obvious target for convent hustlers. But my wise old mother told me that going to the convent before I finished college would mean that I wouldn't get my B.A. degree until I was forty. "Forget it," she said, "until you're old enough."

Of course, when I was old enough, I was no longer interested. I had survived sixteen years of Catholic education, had a degree in chemistry, and landed, by some perverse providence, in a pharmaceutical company to work on birth control research. Since it was the only job offer I had, whatever moral scruples I may have entertained were trumped by the desire to get out on my own. Besides, when I had argued in an ethics paper that the "population explosion" was real and that birth control might be a moral alternative, I received a C– and a lecture on obedience to church teaching. Making birth control pills was a declaration of independence.

Distressingly, the world of science turned out to be almost as bigoted as my hometown. So, I spent some time defending the church while deconstructing the company prejudice that girls from good Catholic colleges were naturally pliable. My job was interesting but repetitive, rather like being a short-order cook with a limited menu. Since it was the mid-'60s and the council was in gear, I read some of the new theology books for fun. Louis Bouyer's *Liturgical Piety* changed my life in my senior year of college; Peter Ellis's *The Men and Message of the Old Testament* drew me into the Bible for the first time in my life, and Teilhard de Chardin was magical for me. At the same time, I was reading Betty Friedan and finding that I could not defend the Catholic Church where women were concerned. Into this mix of professional boredom, theological turn-on, and early feminism came news of a new doctoral program in theology at Notre Dame. I applied saying that I had no real idea what theology was, but knew I would love it. When I accepted a fellowship, I thought I would learn how to demolish all those lunks I grew up with. I just assumed I would end up in a Catholic college somewhere.

I will pass quietly over my years under the Golden Dome, saying only that I was not very well trained by today's standards (no theory), but I knew the basics. I loved church history (which they did not offer) and was bewildered by theological discourse. Halfway through my dissertation, I was a finalist for a postdoctoral fellowship at Oxford. I was flown over for an interview and, believe it or not, was greeted with a question about being a "Roman Catholic" (didn't I find it depressing?). I remember (or have invented) a couple of snappy answers to that question (which came up several times). When I did not get the fellowship, I ended up teaching in a seminary where I was hired by the apostolic delegate as M. J. Weaver with a degree in history (not Mary Jo Weaver with a degree in theology). They wanted a Catholic, not a woman, and my three years there taught me about patriarchy and the validity of Weberian leadership types. I pass over this time, too, though often think it might make a good novel.

At Indiana University, where I was from 1975 to 2006, I learned to be catholic. I uncoupled myself from the "we-language" that marked my religious conversation and abandoned theology for the academic study of religion. In many ways, it was a baptism by fire. A ghetto Catholic from a small town, a small Catholic college, and Notre Dame was now teaching an introduction to Judaism, Christianity, and Islam. I had never met a Jewish person, knew nothing about Islam, and was teaching more students in one classroom than had comprised the entire student body in my last institution. Most embarrassing for me was my total ignorance of non-Catholic Christianity, something I worked hard to remedy as I taught that course every semester for the next decade.

I was reared in a Catholic ghetto but shaped in the secular intellectual environment of a state university department, a department that accepts the face value of all religious traditions, fosters cross-cultural dialogue, and demands that we pay attention to the ecumenical complexities of historical context. An old music hall song chides a runaway woman saying, "you'd be out of place in your own home town." That is true for me geographically and intellectually, and I thank the council every day for that escape route. It has given me an angle of vision on myself, my tradition, and American Catholicism that I cannot imagine getting anywhere else.

MARY CATHERINE HILKERT, O.P.

The Impact of Vatican II

Mary Catherine Hilkert, professor of theology at the University of Notre Dame, received her B.A. degree from the University of Dayton in 1971, with a major in English and a minor in theology. From 1971 to 1977 she taught religious studies and co-chaired that department at St. Vincent–St. Mary High School in Akron. She subsequently earned an M.A. (1979) and a Ph.D. (1984) in theology from the Catholic University of America, and taught systematic theology at Aquinas Institute of Theology in St. Louis, Missouri, before joining the theology faculty at Notre Dame in 1995.

Hilkert is the author of Speaking with Authority: Catherine of Siena and the Voices of Women Today *(2001, rev. ed., 2008);* Naming Grace: Preaching and the Sacramental Imagination *(1997); and numerous articles on contemporary theology, spirituality, and preaching. She edited William Hill's* Search for the Absent God *(1992), and with Robert Schreiter coedited* The Praxis of the Reign of God: An Introduction to the Theology of Edward Schillebeeckx *(1989, rev. ed., 2002). Hilkert has lectured and preached throughout the United States, as well as in Canada, Ireland, the Netherlands, Australia, and South Africa.*

A past president of the Catholic Theological Society of America, Hilkert was awarded an honorary doctorate from Providence College in 2002. She was the first recipient of Washington Theological Union's Sophia Award for Theological Excellence in Service to Ministry (1997), the Madeleva Lecturer in Spirituality at St. Mary's College (2001), and the recipient of Barry University's Yves Congar Award for Theological Excellence (2011).

At the time of the opening of the Second Vatican Council, Hilkert was a high school student. In 1966, just after the close of the council, she joined the Sisters of St. Dominic of Akron, Ohio (Order of Preachers).

As I began what I thought would be an easy assignment—to reflect retrospectively on the repercussions or meaning of the council for my work or ministry—I realized that my memories of the council, like all memories, have shifted and taken on new significance at various points over the past half century.

In 1962 I was more concerned about the opening of my high school years than about the new moment unfolding in the history of the church. November 1963 was etched in my mind not because I realized then how profoundly the first conciliar document to be approved, the "Constitution on the Sacred Liturgy," would impact the life and thinking of the church, but because of John F. Kennedy's assassination. That same year I mourned the death of Pope John XXIII with the rest of the world, but with little awareness of how his surprising call for a council to open the windows of the Catholic Church would affect the future of the church as well as my own future.

In religion class during my junior year of high school, we were required to keep a scrapbook of newspaper articles chronicling the developments at the council. I was intrigued by all of the interest in the surprising new document, "Schema XIII" ("Pastoral Constitution on the Church in the Modern World") and mystified as to why a priest would find it necessary to report on the council under the pseudonym "Xavier Rynne." As I graduated from high school, the war in Vietnam was of far greater concern to me than the council in Rome that closed that year.

Several months later I joined a religious congregation—the Akron Dominicans—to explore what was becoming the increasingly murky area of "discerning one's vocation in life." Neither I nor the majority of Dominican sisters throughout the world had any idea at that time that the call of the "Decree on the Appropriate Renewal of the Religious Life" to return to "the spirit of the founder" of the order would involve in many ways a profound shift in our consciousness, lifestyle, and ministry.

Fifty years later, I find myself re-embracing that vocation as a member of the Dominican Sisters of Peace formed from seven previous Dominican congregations. Numbering almost a thousand sisters and lay associates and serving on four continents, we are committed to "Preaching the Gospel with a New Fire" in a world that longs for peace and suffers from the effects of violence, poverty, dehumanization, and ecological destruction. Beyond my imagination at the time of the council, the seeds of this new initiative, along with the seeds of my vocation as preacher and theologian as well as teacher, were planted at the time of the council.

My novice director in the late 1960s decided that, in addition to scripture and the history of the Order, the most appropriate theological formation we could pursue would be a careful study of the documents of Vatican II. Since the commentaries were not yet written, we were guided in our studies by tapes of talks by Karl Rahner, Edward Schillebeeckx, Yves Congar, Jean Daniélou, and other major theologians who helped to shape the vision and documents of the council. With little theological background, we struggled to listen as the major theologians who had helped bishops to formulate contemporary doctrine explained the significance of a turn of a phrase, a debated omission, the placement of a chapter, or the introduction of a whole new document.

Almost fifty years later, as I teach graduate and undergraduate students who were not born at the time of Vatican II, they look incredulous as yellowed pages fall from my original paperback copy of Abbott's *Documents of Vatican II* while they read the parallel texts on Kindles and iPads. The sense I try to convey to them of the major significance of that ecclesiastical event is one that I learned during my graduate studies in the Department of Theology at Catholic University of America in the late 1970s. It wasn't until my systematic study of those documents for our dreaded master's comprehensive examinations that I realized the historic significance of the decrees on religious liberty, or ecumenism, or the relationship of the church to Judaism and "non-Christian religions." In those days the names Karl Rahner, Edward Schillebeeckx, Yves Congar, Hans Küng, Henri de Lubac, Joseph Ratzinger, and Jean Daniélou all fit together in my mind as theologians with differing perspectives, all of whom were fostering and interpreting the vision of Vatican II.

From my present vantage point, my memories of the impact of the council on my life and ministry over the last fifty years are poignant ones. I can see how my own identity as a baptized woman, a professed member of the Order of Preachers, and a Catholic theologian has been profoundly shaped by the vision of the council. Texts written fifty years ago take on new significance and power. At the same time, the stories I studied of the silencing of theologians and the censuring of their writings before the council are now being relived in the lives of colleagues, teachers, and friends with whom I studied. Reflecting on the way that both my contemporaries and those who helped to shape the council in spite of the earlier rejection of their insights have responded to these challenges, I continue to be inspired by their commitment to handing on a living tradition of faith, their fidelity to their vocation as theologians, and their love of the church.

Likewise, I have been encouraged by a renewed evangelical awakening sparked at the time of the council which has continued to take root in multiple ways around the world as communities of believers gather around the Word of God and reflect on the "signs of the times." At the same time, the diminishment of canonical and episcopal initiatives that supported the liturgical preaching of the gospel by trained lay ecclesial ministers in the decade after the council is a loss for the church as a whole. Neither the academic community where I first preached in trepidation to a community that included my theological professors and colleagues, nor the theological school where I preached regularly as one of the many theologically trained preachers on the faculty, nor the academic campus where I now teach as a full professor of theology now invite women or lay persons to preach during eucharistic celebrations on any regular basis. I also realize, with sadness, that many of the women with whom I studied or whom I later taught no longer can find a home in the Roman Catholic Church.

Nevertheless, my deepest memory of the Second Vatican Council is that of a window that was opened quite unexpectedly and can never be closed. The Spirit does indeed breathe freely, forming reluctant prophets like Oscar Romero, drawing women and men into lives of ministry that recent Vatican documents question, developing common ground in some of the most unlikely places, calling all of us to a deeper awareness of our social responsibilities and the vast suffering in our world, and working wonders in communities of believers. In the late 1960s, just years after the council, Cardinal Suenens detected pessimism and a sense of defeat within the church and the broader society and confessed to his own "dark night of hope" during what he called the "winter of the post-Council era." But he also reminded Christians that it is precisely in situations that appear hopeless that genuine hope—a sheer gift of the Spirit—is born. The memory of words from a letter he wrote on Pentecost in 1974 continues to inspire and challenge me: "Who would dare to say that the love and imagination of God were exhausted?"

ROBERT BLAIR KAISER

The Story of Archbishop Thomas Roberts*

Robert Blair Kaiser went through ten years in the Society of Jesus, then, three years shy of ordination, left the Jesuits to pursue a career in journalism. He covered Vatican II for Time, *worked on the religion beat for the* New York Times, *and served as journalism chairman at the University of Nevada Reno. Three of his eleven published books deal with Vatican II:* Pope, Council and World *(1963) is a report on the council's first session.* The Politics of Sex and Religion *(1985) is a narrative history of the papal birth control commission, and his recent* Clerical Error *(2002) is a lights-and-shadows memoir about Vatican II.*

*Kaiser won the Overseas Press Club Award in 1963 for the "best magazine reporting of foreign affairs"—for his reporting on the Vatican Council. Editors at three newspapers have nominated him for Pulitzer Prizes, and the book publisher E. P. Dutton nominated him for another Pulitzer for his exhaustive 634-page book (*R.F.K. Must Die!*) on the assassination of Robert F. Kennedy, a work that was republished in 2008.*

Kaiser's home town is Phoenix, Arizona, where he co-authored a musical comedy, Jubilee 2000, *which celebrates two thousand years of Christian history in ninety minutes of song and dance. This play was produced all over the United States and Canada in the Jubilee Year 2000, and has been seen by at least a half million persons.*

During the papal conclave of 2005, Kaiser reported for Newsweek *as well as a number of television networks. Kaiser currently covers Rome for* The Tablet. *Two of his most recent books are* Cardinal Mahony: A Novel *(2007), and* A Church in Search of Itself: Benedict XVI and the Battle for the Future *(2007).*

---

* This story is excerpted from Kaiser's book *Clerical Error* (New York: Continuum Books, 2002).

EARLY IN THE FIRST SESSION of Vatican II, I walked into a dim, oversized kind of library room at the Foyer Unitas near the Piazza Navona, and found a slight figure with great bushy eyebrows sitting under a small lamp reading his breviary. Thomas D'Esterre Roberts was wearing a black cassock speckled with a thin layer of fine cigarette ash; it gave him a slightly raffish look, like Alec Guinness playing Gulley Jimson. He lowered a pair of black horn-rimmed spectacles, looked over the top of them at me, *Time*'s correspondent in Rome, with a twinkle in his eye and a wrinkle of his nose, and said, "Are you a Papist?" I burst out laughing.

"Not only am I a Papist," I said, "I was a Jesuit for ten years. Sometimes, I think I am still a Jesuit." His bushy eyebrows worked a bit over that news, but I could tell that this created an instant understanding between us. I only enhanced the good feelings by telling him that I loved his seminal treatise on authority, *Black Popes*.

He wrinkled his nose again. I would soon learn that he always wrinkled his nose, like a rabbit, whenever he was pleased, or about to deliver a zinger. He told me he wasn't even sure he was welcome at this council. He said that in 1960 he had gotten some haughty letters from Archbishop Gerald O'Hara, the apostolic delegate in England, and Cardinal Godfrey of Westminster, who told him they'd "delated" *Black Popes* to the Holy Office for "the scandalous material" contained in it. Neither of them had ever bothered telling him how *Black Popes* was "scandalous." I frowned. My guess was that it wasn't just *Black Popes* that caused the trouble. After all, the book had been published more than a decade ago.

My guess was that Roberts had become an aging *enfant terrible*. He was the only bishop in the world who advised Pope Pius XII in 1950 not to define as infallible the dogma of the Assumption of Our Lady. And he had marched with Bertrand Russell in a daring, ban-the-bomb campaign at a time when Catholics didn't march with Protestants (or heathens) in any kind of cause. In a mock serious tone, I asked him how he could urge the Quakers to come to a council to look in on a debate on war and peace and The Bomb when these matters weren't even on the agenda. He wrinkled his nose and said that maybe the presence of the Quakers would help get the question on the agenda.

"Is there anything better I can do here," he said, "than to stop the world from blowing itself up?"

I had no good answer to that. I wondered to myself whether this raffish little Englishman, or even an entire council, could stop the world's leaders from starting a nuclear war if they wanted to. Only time would tell about that. So I changed the subject and asked him how an archbishop, even a Jesuit archbishop, could turn out to be so, well, different.

He said he'd tell me if I would drive him home. Bargain. He lived in a poor convent way out on the Monte del Gallo. On the drive, he told me how he'd just been minding his own business, serving as rector of a small college in Liverpool, when he got the news (from an inquiring newspaper reporter!) that Rome was making him the next archbishop of Bombay, India. He claimed that it wasn't until he had received the holy oils of episcopal consecration that some Vatican functionary discovered he'd tabbed the wrong English Jesuit. By then, of course, it was too late.

I thought to myself that this was a happy accident. Perhaps the Holy Spirit knew what she was doing. In teeming, turbulent, overcrowded, backward Bombay (where Catholics were less than one half of 1 percent of the population), T. D. Roberts became a very pastoral, very compassionate shepherd who had a surfeit of free time on his hands to do some heavy thinking about the mission of the church in the world. He thought the church had unwisely tied itself to the Latin culture in which it took such solid root, that the missionaries who then branched out from that root did so not only to Christianize Asia and Africa and South America but to Europeanize those continents as well. The missionaries were colonizers for a particular culture as much as witnesses to Christ's coming for all humankind.

Roberts soon realized he would have to abdicate his office. He could see that Gandhi's movement would eventually end with the banishment of the British. So Roberts sent Pope Pius XII a series of letters telling him that the church didn't need an Englishman in Bombay; it needed a native Indian archbishop. The pope did not agree.

Roberts knew that the pope might regret that decision. He saved the situation by a bit of cunning. In 1946, when the Atlee government in England committed itself to Indian independence, he simply got the pope to let him have an Indian auxiliary bishop. Roberts had just the chap in mind for the job, a tall, stately young priest named Valerian Gracias. Then Roberts packed a valise, walked out the door, and told Gracias over his shoulder to run the show—because he was taking a two-year trip around the world via tramp steamer. He ended up in Rome.

"You see?" Roberts told Pius XII. "Now that India has gone independent, you have an Indian in Bombay just when you need him." The pope fixed Roberts with a long, deep, unsmiling stare, then nodded and sighed in French, *Bien*. Gracias would soon become the first native Indian cardinal. As for Roberts, he had schemed himself out of a job.

The pope suggested he might return to England where he could preach at the Jesuits' famous church on Farm Street.

When we arrived at Roberts's convent, he was staring ahead through the window of my VW at the macadamed bleakness of the street, with not even a tree or a bush in sight.

"You feel isolated out here?" I asked. He nodded.

Suddenly, I suggested that he might like to come home with me to dinner—that very night. I didn't have to urge him. We drove directly back to Monteverde Vecchio, and as we did so Roberts asked me about Mrs. Kaiser. "How can she stand all these—people you bring home?"

"Mary?" I said. "She's got a thing about clerics. She loves 'em." Mary needed no prompting. She loved Archbishop Roberts. He told a lot of stories, he had a brandy or two, he bounced our little daughter Betsy on his lap, he told some more stories. Mary and I had the same idea almost simultaneously. His Grace was lonely and alone. We had a spare bedroom. Why didn't he stay with us? He pondered that invitation for a millisecond and said he'd be delighted. I moved him in the next day.

With my own council father in residence, so to speak, I had an edge on the other journalists at the council. I began learning things from Roberts that I couldn't get from the official daily briefings at the press center. For one thing, each day, he routinely handed me all the secret documents of the council. They were in Latin. But I read Latin rather well. Roberts gave me more than that. Through him, I began to see the council and its changing moods through the eyes of a council father, and from a council father who was also becoming a part of my own family. Each evening, I'd get home to find him preparing for Mass, which he celebrated conversationally, primitively, on a table at one end of our triple living room. "The biggest, most undreamed of thrill of all," Mary wrote home to her family, "is having His Grace say Mass every day in our very own living room. He says Mass facing Betsy and me, with Bob next to him, serving. What a blessing for us."

Afterward, we'd have a cocktail and some dinner, and talk about the council's proceedings, trade rumors and gossip of the day, discuss who'd said what to whom at the two bars behind the main altar at St. Peter's, the Bar Jonah and the Bar Rabbas (where they served brandy and schnapps as well as cafe espresso).

"They turned Ottaviani off today," T. D. reported one evening with a chuckle. "He had gone far beyond the ten-minute time limit. After a warning by the chair, he found he was speaking into a dead microphone."

Ottaviani boycotted the council for a number of days after that, and there was no official accounting for his absence. Then T. D. came home with a story, picked up at the Bar Jonah. "Now they say the reason why Ottaviani hasn't been coming," reported T. D. with a wrinkle of his nose, "is that his chauffeur kept him waiting so long the other morning that he called a passing taxi and told the driver, 'To the council.'" T. D. paused, then added laconically, with perfect timing, "The cabbie drove him to Trent."

The council sessions lasted until mid-day. Then T. D. would catch a municipal bus home. Sometimes, he'd nap after lunch, then receive an increasing number of visitors around tea time—allies and potential allies in his efforts to get the question of war and peace and The Bomb put on the council's agenda. His own afternoon guest list began to include a steady stream of ban-the-bombers, Czech and Polish and Hungarian bishops who wanted to go back to their governments with a pacifistic statement from the council, members of the United Nations' Food and Agricultural Organization, English civil libertarians, Indian converts in saffron-colored saris, Quakers in severe black woolen suits, ex-priests in trouble, seminarians who wanted to know how to disobey their superiors, journalists who wanted to interview him, and artists who wanted to draw him. . . .

Far from being isolated in his resistance to the antediluvian minds of the Roman curia, he found that his venturesome opinions were shared by many others, including some of the best prelates in Christendom. With him, they thought (and said out loud) that the church was overloaded with excess baggage, myth, superstition, and nonsense. With him, they voted on all the important reforms of Vatican II, most of which tended to make the church less Roman—and more Catholic.

Every morning, I'd drive Roberts to the council. He hated the regal trappings of his office, mumbled when he got tangled in his robes as we climbed into my yellow Volkswagen, and made clear his antipathy for humbug whenever he had a chance. One morning, when a pilgrim in St. Peter's Square asked him to bless her rosary, he grimaced and gave it a perfunctory wave. He wore no episcopal ring, and if anyone asked him about it (thinking they might be expected to kiss it), he said with a grin and a wrinkle of his nose that he kept it in his back pocket.

THOMAS GROOME

Who Was That Tall, Dark Stranger—
Who Introduced Me to Vatican II?

Thomas Groome was born on September 30, 1945, in County Kildare, Ireland, the youngest of ten children—nine of whom lived into adulthood. His father, Terence, was a local politician with a keen commitment to social justice—though he didn't use those terms. His mother, Margaret, was a devout Catholic with a deep spirituality—though she wouldn't have called it that either.

Groome attended St. Patrick's Seminary, Carlow, Ireland (1962-1968), received an M.A. in religious education from Fordham University (1973), and then went on for a doctorate in theology and education at the joint program of Union Theological Seminary and Columbia University's Teacher's College, graduating in 1976.

Since 1976, Groome has taught theology and religious education at Boston College, rising through the ranks to full professor in 1992. His first book was Christian Religious Education: Sharing Our Story and Vision *(Harper & Row, 1980). With it he introduced a shared Christian praxis approach to religious education; essentially this is a participative pedagogy that encourages students and teachers to bring "life to faith, and faith to life." Translated into many languages,* Christian Religious Education *continues to be used widely throughout the world. In 1998, he published* Educating for Life: A Spiritual Vision for Every Teacher and Parent, *and a few years later the best-selling* What Makes Us Catholic: Eight Gifts for Life *(Harper, 2002). His most recent book and a capstone to his scholarly writing is* Will There Be Faith? *(HarperCollins, 2011).*

Much of Groome's writing over the years has been on religion curricula. He is the primary author of the God With Us *curriculum, grades K to 8 (1984), and of* Coming to Faith, *grades K to 8 (1994). Both have been widely used, the latter in parish catechetical programs and Catholic schools all in the spirit of Vatican II. Currently he is the primary author/ editor of the new* Credo Series, *a religion curriculum for high-school-age students from Veritas, USA, following the USCCB Framework for Adolescent Catechesis. Groome currently serves as professor of theology and religious education at Boston College, and as chair of the Department of Religious Education and Pastoral Ministry within BC's School of Theology and Ministry.*

I WAS IN A FRONT-ROW seat of the crowded assembly hall of the seminary. He was a towering figure as I looked up at him, tall, trim, and handsome, with dark, bushy hair. And oh so impeccably dressed. The precise crease in his black suit meant it wasn't the tweed of my culture. His round-collar was the then-modern style, with just a sliver of white showing in front. The peeping cuff-links made for perfection in clerical attire. Ah, but more imposing still was his eloquence; he mesmerized us assembled seminarians with the "inside story" from Vatican II.

St. Patrick's, Carlow, is the oldest seminary in the English-speaking world (founded 1793) and is renowned for preparing good pastoral priests. Yet, it has always lived in the shadow of the more elite St. Patrick's, Maynooth—beside Dublin. Famous scholars visiting Ireland rarely ventured this far into the countryside. And now, here was a world-renowned theologian, and a *peritus* working on the documents that emerged from Vatican II, holding forth on the stage of our *aula maxima*.

What a night it was! Beyond his imposing stature and eloquence, the tall dark stranger's enthusiasm was infectious. Even the stiffs among the faculty seemed caught up in the moment. Everyone was clapping, hurrahing, egging him on, laughing at his jokes. By the end, there was nary a doubt among us but that the whole Catholic Church would be renewed from top to bottom—or more likely from bottom to top—and soon. And this theological maestro was setting fire in our bellies to go over the hill as front-line troops in the grand *aggiornamento*—as the beloved John XXIII called his agenda of reform and renewal that he proposed for the council.

It must have been the fall of 1965 because I was a first-year theologian at the time, and Vatican II was winding down. Our speaker clearly had first-hand knowledge about the council and could range across its many documents. Most memorable, however, were his comments about the "Decree on Ecumenism." As to the present day in Ireland, this topic can be politically loaded. But he was so persuasive. Of course Protestants are "brothers and sisters in faith," members by baptism of the same Body of Christ. Who could disagree? Beyond that, surely God's love and saving will are universal. We'd heard of "baptism of desire" already, but this theological pimpernel was saying much more, about dialogue and being open to learn from people of non-Christian faiths. What a novel and exciting notion!

Throughout the council, the Irish newspapers were fairly extensive in their coverage of Vatican II, and our seminary profs would make positive if cautious comments about what was "going on over there." But that memorable night and speaker amounted to my first existential awareness that a deep-down turning point was unfolding for the Catholic Church—and in our time. The possibilities seemed to reach beyond the horizon of our wildest dreams. How exciting!

As I recall, it was about the same time that the seminary abandoned its traditional standard textbooks. For as long as anyone could remember, we used a Nolden manual for moral theology, and texts by Ott and Tanquerey for dogma. Upon "crossing the wall" from philosophy to theology, one could pick up a set of these for a few shillings—maybe tenth hand and with invaluable cheat notes in the margins—and be well equipped for the next four years. But no more.

Pa Brophy, the dogma professor, came to epitomize the spirit of the council on our seminary faculty. He introduced an array of modern texts, including a work by Charles Davis, then making headlines. Lar Ryan, the moral professor and later bishop of Kildare and Leighlin, dropped Nolden with its emphasis on preparing priests to hear confessions and taught us moral theology as the ethics of Christian living. And the whisper of optional celibacy for priests began to waft about, a topic of more than passing interest to a seminary full of testosterone-laden Irish lads. Ah, what a heady time it was!

Let me now offer a brief retrospect on what Vatican II caused in my area of alleged expertise—religious education and catechesis. Two particular catalysts come to mind.

First, remember that Trent had overwhelmingly favored a definition of faith as *belief* in the official teachings of the church. Thereafter, and for the next four hundred years, the mode of catechesis became a question-and-answer catechism that summarized the beliefs for children to memorize. Indeed, the success of Luther's *Short Catechism* prompted Catholics to embrace this tool as well, but Trent gave the catechism its theological warrant by emphasizing faith as belief. It was precisely on this score that Vatican II put a cat among the catechetical pigeons.

In sum, and as Rahner often pointed out, the council returned the church to the ancient understanding of Christian faith that includes "right belief " (orthodoxy) but likewise "right action" (orthopraxis) and "right worship." Catholics relearned from Vatican II that their faith must engage their heads, hearts, and hands, permeating every nook and cranny of their lives. Reclaiming this wholistic Christian faith required a more wholistic approach to catechesis, one that would help people to integrate "life" and "faith" as a "living faith" in the midst of the world.

Thereafter, though the catechetical renewal encouraged by the council may have had its aberrations, in general and by God's grace it "continues to bear very welcome fruit" (*General Directory for Catechesis*, no. 24).

Second and closely related, the council revived a radical theology of baptism with major consequences for the mission of the church and its educating in faith. By radical I mean a return to the roots, reclaiming baptism as a call to transformation of life as disciples of Jesus Christ. It confers great rights and responsibilities to participate in the church's function of continuing the mission of Jesus in the world. With baptism— not just with vows or holy orders—comes "the call of the whole Church to holiness" (*Lumen gentium*, Chapter 5). In sum, Vatican II was a catalyst for Catholics to become active agents of their faith rather than passive dependents.

The spin-offs for catechesis were myriad: a huge increase of lay leadership in catechetical education, greater numbers and a higher level of training among volunteers, increased parental participation in the faith education of children because the home is where identity is formed, awareness that faith must be integrated into daily life and lived for God's reign in the world, a new emphasis on adult religious education and on Christian faith as a journey into holiness of life, requiring life-long catechesis (*General Directory for Catechesis*). The list could go on!

Now, fifty years on from Vatican II, the élan and hope of those first postcouncil years for thoroughgoing reform and renewal of the church as a sacrament of God's reign in the world, has been tempered by experiences of two steps forward and one step back (no more, we hope). Yet, the *aggiornamento* launched by the Holy Spirit on the church and world by that great council cannot be undone. Our reverence for the doctrinal authority of an ecumenical council of the church assures that its watermark will remain, and ever call our "shoulders to the wheel" with renewed commitment to realize its hopes.

And who was that tall dark stranger? It was the young Gregory Baum. Little did I imagine as a first-year theology student in Carlow seminary that some fifteen years later he would write me a cherished note of appreciation after I published my first book. Like the council, Gregory has matured since I looked up at him on stage at St. Patrick's, Carlow. But I will always cling to the hopes that he and the council engendered in our young hearts back then, that the church can ever renew itself as an effective symbol—a sacrament—of God's reign and saving work in the world. And whenever I hear people debating about the true spirit of the council, I still cling to my first vivid memory of it, personified in the great Gregory Baum.

EPILOGUE

Vatican II in Retrospect:
A Lifetime and Esteemed Companion

FERNANDO F. SEGOVIA

Fernando F. Segovia was born in La Habana, Cuba, on April 25, 1948. He immigrated as a political refugee to the United States on July 10, 1961, during what was perhaps the hottest period of the Cold War, between the Bay of Pigs invasion in Cuba, in April, and the erection of the Berlin Wall in Germany, in August. He settled in New York City, becoming an early member of the Latino/a community.

Segovia studied for the priesthood for several years at the Pontifical College Josephinum, and left seminary to pursue doctoral work in early Christian studies at the University of Notre Dame. Upon graduation, he taught first at Marquette University (1977-1984) and then at the Divinity School of Vanderbilt University (1984-), where he currently holds the Oberlin Graduate Chair of New Testament and Early Christianity.

With regard to Vatican II, the story of the council and the story of his life have gone hand in hand: the announcement of the council and the triumph of the Cuban Revolution take place within days of each other; his years of secondary education in New York coincide with the years of the council; his studies in seminary and graduate school parallel the initial implementation of the council; his professional life grows out of the spirit of the council and develops as the fate of the council undergoes reversal.

Professor Segovia has been active in biblical studies and theological studies. His interests in the former include method and theory; ideological criticism; cultural criticism. Segovia is the past president of the Academy of Catholic Hispanic Theologians in the United States. His interests in the latter encompass: liberation and political theology; non-Western theologies; minority theologies. He is the author of many

263

works, most recently editing, with R. S. Sugirtharajah, Postcolonial Commentary on the New Testament Writings *(2009), and the leader of many projects in such fields.*

THE STORY OF THE SECOND Vatican Council, I have found upon retrospection, intersects with the story of my life at several key points and marks it in quite profound ways. It does so toward the beginning, as an adolescent moving toward critical consciousness in the midst of troubled times. The announcement of the council in 1959 coincides with a major event in global affairs, the Cuban Revolution, which touched me directly and which would ultimately touch not only all of Latin America but also the world as a whole. It does so through the entire middle phase of my life, as a maturing adult with ever-developing critical acumen in a world of momentous events and changes. To begin with, the duration of the council, spanning four sessions from 1962 through 1965, matches my years of secondary education. Further, the aftermath of the council follows me in two movements: first, through its initial implementation in the late 1960s and early 1970s, precisely as I undertake studies for the priesthood; then, through its changing fortune beginning with the late 1970s, as I pursue a professional life that flows directly out of such an educational experience. It does so now toward the wane, as a senior adult in full critical consciousness in the face of momentous and troubled times. The fiftieth anniversary of the council, which this volume celebrates with reference to its inaugural session (1962-2012), forms part of a series of commemorations that prove for me highly pregnant and highly ambiguous.

In these reflections I should like to capture this twofold sense of sustained interweaving and lasting imprint that I have come to associate with Vatican II. The council was a signal event that I not only had the privilege to live through but also the blessing to have lived with—an event that I look back on as a guiding light, that I now view as in retreat, and that I still regard as a source of hope for the future. These reflections are my way of rendering honor and giving thanks to Vatican II.

Toward the Beginning: Political and Ecclesial Awakenings

I was born on April 25, 1948, in the city of La Habana, Cuba, close to fifty years to the day after the country gained its independence from the United States (May 20, 1902).[1] Such independence, I should note, was more formal than material, since the country remained very much within the imperial-colonial orbit of the United States. My parents made their way into the urban professional class and were not only practicing but also engaged Catholics. As active members of the Catholic Action movement, they stood for social justice and worked with the disadvantaged in various ways. As conscientious citizens of the country, they believed in liberal democracy and supported human as well as social rights. As imperial-colonial subjects, they respected the United States but believed firmly in self-determination for the country. I attended the same school as my father, the Colegio De La Salle (Vedado), one of the many institutions run by the Christian Brothers throughout the country. Here I received a typical Catholic education of the times, excellent in every respect, designed to make me a Catholic active in society and culture, and conversant with the English language and the United States in general. We were, therefore, very much members of the church and citizens of Cuba, and we did know our place within the historical and political American sphere of influence.

This was the preconciliar church: hierarchical and authoritarian, to be sure, but also with an underlying sense of threat and fragility. This was a church for which the specter of Communism and militant atheism loomed large on the horizon: the Soviet Union had engulfed a great part of Europe at the end of the Second World War, had recently quashed the Hungarian Revolt of 1956, and made no secret of its designs on world domination and its espousal of world struggle. This was also a trying time for the country: a coup d'état had ruptured the democratic process in 1952, leading to a dictatorial regime; a revolutionary process had begun in 1953, consisting of multiple opposition fronts, including the July 26 Movement of Fidel Castro Ruz; and a civil conflict had engulfed the nation, deteriorating year by year. The U.S. stance was typical: support for a friendly despot, until such support proved untenable. For us, both as members of the church and as citizens of Cuba, two events took place at the end of the 1950s that would change our lives forever, and radically so. Both took place in January of 1959, within days of each other.

First, in the early morning hours of January 1, the news began to spread through the city, and reached our home, that the government of President Fulgencio Batista y Zaldívar (1952-1959) had come to an end. The dictator had fled the country, and thus the revolutionary struggle that had marked my childhood and youth and that had gathered steam to the point of near-total support had triumphed. In this struggle many in the Catholic Church had taken part, either by way of guerrilla warfare or, as in the case of my parents, in the urban underground movement.[2] The months that followed were a time of great social and cultural euphoria—a time of great expectations and marvelous dreams for the future. Then, on January 25 the news reached this church that the recently elected successor to Pius XII, John XXIII, had called for a new ecumenical council, which was to address the signs of the times—to bring the church into dialogue with the modern world and to update itself for the new times accordingly. This announcement caused surprise as well as wonder, further raising expectations and dreams about the future as well. Looking back, it was as if the future of our country and the future of our church lay wide open before us.

Such a sense of possibility, alas, did not last long. On July 10 of 1961, I arrived in the United States as a political refugee, the result of my family's decision to leave the island. In the two and a half years that had elapsed since the triumph of the revolutionary struggle, elections had not been called as promised, attacks on differing political stances had sharpened alarmingly, and the government had become increasingly authoritarian and exclusivist—the broad front of the revolution had become the tight front of the *Revolution*, under the grip of Fidel Castro. Further, a large-scale policy of nationalization had begun against foreign property, leading to a rupture in relations with the United States, with recriminations of communist leanings and rumors of military intervention. Relations with the church also deteriorated badly. Many Catholics, like my parents, who had labored for the restoration of democracy and for greater social justice under the banner of the revolution, saw the emerging vision, rhetoric, and program of the revolution as a threat to their dreams and expectations for the future as Cubans as well as to their values and commitments as Catholics. When this conflict came to a head in April of 1961, in the Bay of Pigs invasion, and as President Castro called for a Marxist-Leninist Cuba, the decision was taken to emigrate to the United States. Their worst fears had come to happen: not only had the dictatorial yoke taken hold again, but also the specter of Communism had come upon the country. Cuba had gone, in effect, from one imperial-colonial orbit to another.

In my mind, therefore, the triumph of the Cuban revolution and the convocation of Vatican II have always gone and shall always go together. These were two events that were to change both Latin America and the world radically, in very different ways, for the remainder of the century. Both would emerge as beacons of liberation and hope; both would fade over time. By 1961 my own situation in this regard was clear. The aftermath of the Cuban revolution, that glorious moment of dreams and expectations that had transcended all political divisions, I had already felt in my own flesh and blood. Exile would now mark me for the rest of my life. The beginning of the council, that other moment of expectations and dreams, still lay a year away. Its aftermath would prove far more fulfilling, though only for a while.

Through the Middle: Political and Ecclesial Developments

In the United States my family settled in New York City, the immigrant city par excellence. At that time, Latin American immigration was practically nonexistent, and the Latino/a population consisted of two major and isolated groupings: Mexican Americans in the western part of the country and Puerto Ricans in the eastern part. Cubans would soon become the third largest such grouping. The nation was overwhelmingly of European descent, as was the Catholic Church (descendants of the Irish, the Germans, and southern and eastern Europeans). It was a minority church in a dominant Protestant country, but a strong and powerful one. We were now living in a country not our own, the epicenter of our imperial-colonial orbit, and in a church not our own, a minority within a minority. I attended a Catholic high school, Cardinal Hayes, an archdiocesan institution staffed by diocesan priests and a variety of religious orders. This too was a typical Catholic education of the times, quite good as well, designed to prepare us for life as faithful members of the church and loyal citizens of the country. These were the years of the council.

This was still the preconciliar church: still very much hierarchical and authoritarian and still very much in dread of Communism, but the first winds of change were in the air. Our classes in religious education— every day, every semester, every year—focused as always on the dynamics and mechanics of Catholicism. Yet, such fare came with a twist. Over the four years, such training was accompanied by news about developments at the council and reports about its adopted decrees. The country—under the administration of its first Catholic president, John F. Kennedy, young and charismatic—was deeply immersed in two conflicts. On the international front, the Cold War continued to rage, waged everywhere but most palpably in Germany, Vietnam, and, yes, Cuba. On the national front, the struggle for civil rights—spearheaded by African Americans, but also involving Latino/a Americans, Asian Americans, and the feminist movement—was becoming more confrontational and more violent. Our lives were impacted throughout by national and international developments: the Cuban Missile Crisis in 1962; the assassination of President Kennedy in 1963; the Civil Rights Act of 1964; and throughout the ever-escalating war in Vietnam, with its demand for young male bodies of our age.

At some point in the course of my sophomore year, the notion of studying for the priesthood first entered my mind—a combined result, no doubt, of an intense Catholic education and the excitement surrounding the council, among other things. This I did upon graduation, joining the archdiocese of Havana in exile, with the intention of going back to Cuba upon ordination. My mind thus remained fixed on my country of birth; I was still an exile. I was sent for philosophical studies to the Pontifical College Josephinum in Columbus, Ohio—a national seminary under the aegis of the Holy See, materially removed from the world and living in self-absorbed isolation. Such a course of action prevented any possibility of going to war in Vietnam, given our special Selective Service classification as ministry students.[3] It was from this point on that I began to experience the aftermath of the council over the course of my life: first, during my seminary years; then, over the course of my professional life.

On the Way Up: Implementation

While in seminary, I lived through the initial, gradual implementation of the spirit and reforms of the council. As the years passed, from 1966 to 1972, the way of life that had for so long marked studies for the priesthood changed drastically, from small hesitant steps at first to major structural and academic reforms later on. By the early 1970s this was a different world altogether. This was now the conciliar church in full transition—eagerly entering into conversation with modernity and updating itself in dizzying fashion, reading the signs of the times. Many were the changes. Most of the old rules and habits had been eliminated, one by one. Isolation from the world had yielded to engagement with the world, through pastoral work and an open-door policy. A separatist, defensive theological education had been replaced by a collaborative ecumenical program, involving the creation of a theological consortium with Trinity Lutheran Seminary and the Methodist Theological Seminary of Ohio. Indeed, the annual recitation of the oath against modernism had been replaced by a commemoration of Reformation Sunday. Above all, a traditionalist and dogmaticist theological education had given way to a wonderful influx of novel, liberalizing currents—new topics, new questions, new names. There was a very definite sense of excitement and freedom in the air. At the same time, the turbulent world of the late 1960s and early 1970s entered our domain in full force, unsettling all; one need only remember that fateful year of 1968.

This was also, to be sure, the conciliar church of the exodus: every year, more and more students left the seminary to pursue other careers, while entering classes became smaller and smaller. In 1972 I joined this exodus as well. I wanted to pursue doctoral studies in biblical criticism, but not within the framework of the priesthood. I was captivated by the new tendencies and readings, and I wanted to engage them full-time in the academy. This I was able to do at the University of Notre Dame (1972-1977), during which time the years of reform continued apace. It was one of the best decisions that I have ever taken in my life, preparing the way for what has turned out to be a long and productive academic career.

With this move, thoughts of a return to Cuba disappeared entirely from view. I was no longer an exile but an immigrant, here to stay. Through the 1960s and 1970s, the country had gone ever deeper into the imperial-colonial orbit of the Soviet Union, waging a worldwide struggle against imperialism and capitalism, from Latin America to Africa and Asia. My country of origin had become a most active player on the world scene, out of all proportion to its size, and had become a symbol, if not *the* symbol of liberation to many. During this period, one of the new tendencies that had come to the fore in the church was the theology of liberation, emerging out of my continent and rapidly spreading to Asia and Africa. Its concerns—the need for contextual analysis in theological production; the scandal of overwhelming poverty; the emphasis on liberation with the vision of a just society—I found most attractive, despite its own early idealization of socialism in Cuba, which I found most ironic.

On the Way Down: Retreat

During these decades, I experienced the subsequent shifting fate of the council reforms and spirit, as the initial path of reform gave way to a path of restraint and redrawing. From the late 1970s on, the after-effects of the exodus were in evident and ever-mounting display: deep losses in personnel, both in the ranks of the diocesan clergy and in the religious orders; widespread closings of seminaries, monasteries, and convents; sharp retrenchment in parish networks and school systems. In the face of such developments, rather than carrying through with resolve the project of transformation, the process of dialoguing with modernity and updating itself in new and creative ways, a program of restoration was gradually put into place, beginning with the election of Pope John Paul II in 1978 (1978-2005).

This was the postconciliar church in the wake of transition: an institutional church in steep decline and determined counter-action. Its aim now, in reading the signs of the times, was to apply the brakes to the perceived excesses of Vatican II, through a policy of law and order from the center, signaling a return to the hierarchical and authoritarian church of preconciliar times. The church was not alone in such a turn. These decades were characterized by fundamental changes in the United States: a strong reaction from the right to the perceived excesses of the 1960s, beginning with the election of President Richard M. Nixon in 1968 (1969-1974); the resurfacing of the evangelical movement as a strong political and religious force; the emergence of neo-liberalism as political economy in the wake of the Great Society. Profound changes were at work in the world as well: a shift from industrial to global capitalism; the exhaustion of socialism and the end of Communism; the emergence of the United States as the hyperpower, with a sense of triumphalism among the elite that history had come to an end. The change in Cuba was no less fundamental. The country experienced ever greater social and cultural decline, coming to a climax in the early 1990s with the end of imperial-colonial largesse from the Soviet Union. By the end of the century, it had become but a relic of a bygone era. All such changes were closely related to one another.

This turnabout I experienced as a lay critic and theologian within the world of the academy: first at Marquette University (1977-1984), and then at the Divinity School of Vanderbilt University (1984-), a non-denominational institution with a strong reformed history and tradition, where I was appointed to fulfill the role of token Catholic in a liberal faculty. Sheltered from the grasp of this developing climate of centralization, I witnessed the growth of control in theological circles and repression in ecclesiastical circles as well as the decline in the ecumenical commitment of the early years. Among the targets of this policy of interventionism was liberation theology, judged as too Marxist in orientation and too radical in mode and objective: seminaries were closed; individuals were investigated; writings were attacked. In the academy, meanwhile, these were exciting years. It was so in general, as postmodernist and poststructuralist currents affected disciplines and discourses. It was so in theological and critical studies in particular, as the disciplines underwent major developments as well. For me, these years of loss in the church were balanced by years of gain in the academy.

To my mind, consequently, the whole of my academic and professional life is intimately linked to the reforms in Catholic thought and practice brought about by the council. I would not have studied for the priesthood without its early influence during the years of secondary education. I would not have developed such a keen interest in matters religious and theological without the sense of freedom and excitement that it unleashed in religion and theology. I would have never viewed the church with the sense of dialogue and openness, of endless possibilities, that the council fostered. At the same time, these were years marked by a sense of loss with regard to those early dreams and expectations of the council, which I experienced during its initial period of implementation.[4] In sum, all that I became and have accomplished goes back, in one way or another, to the council.

Toward the End: Political and Ecclesial Ruminations

I find myself at this point in my life, since turning sixty years of age in 2008, in the midst of a series of highly significant yet decidedly bitter-sweet anniversaries. In January of 2009, I observed the fiftieth anniversary of both the birth of the Cuban Revolution and the convocation of Vatican II. On July 10 of 2011, I recalled the fiftieth anniversary of my departure from Cuba, my country of birth, and my arrival in the United States, my country of adoption. The year 2011 also marked the fortieth anniversary of the emergence of liberation theology.[5] From September of 2012 through December of 2015, I shall be thinking often of the fiftieth anniversary of the council. The years 2016 and 2017 will bring the fiftieth anniversary of my entrance into seminary and the fortieth anniversary of my professional life as an academic, respectively. Such times bring persistent retrospection, beyond control but by no means undesired. Such retrospection is responsible for these reflections.

I wish I could say that the dreams and expectations of 1959 have found fulfillment in both the church and Cuba, and indeed in the world at large. I am afraid, to the contrary, that the heady optimism that ruled those early days is matched by the somber pessimism that prevails in the present days of culmination. Wherever I look—be it the church, Cuba, or the world—the scenario is frightening.

A look at the church reveals implosion, sclerosis, embattlement. The steep institutional decline has continued unabated, as the crisis in numbers and facilities and finances has multiplied. At the same time, the church has been damaged to the core by a worldwide moral crisis involving countless revelations of sexual abuse by the clergy and systematic cover-ups of such crimes by the hierarchy. Such a crisis points to an even more fundamental crisis within the church regarding its teaching on human sexuality. The result has been a crippling loss of moral authority and respect. The restorationist project has not only utterly failed but has also led to mystification and repression: on the one hand, the multiplication and encouragement of new religious groups with ultra-papist agendas and the reflorescence of outward pageantry and mass spectacles; on the other hand, an atmosphere of intimidation and subservience and a return to traditionalist and dogmaticist theological education.

A look at my country of birth, Cuba, shows a nation in absolute exhaustion. The nation is kept barely afloat by an infusion of aid from the outside, this time from Venezuela, leading to amazing developments on the part of its octogenarian leaders, in power for over fifty years now: on the part of former president Fidel Castro, a public admission that the so-called Cuban system is no good even for Cuba; on the part of President Raúl Castro, a set of measures meant to reduce the role of the state in the economy. Such acknowledgment and such policies, however, are accompanied by as tight a clamp as ever on civil society and as harsh a repression as ever of the population.

A look at the world reveals crisis everywhere. First, a global economic meltdown beginning with the Great Recession of 2008—caused by insatiable greed, unrestrained deregulation, and massive individual as well as state indebtedness. Second, a relative decline of both Europe and the United States in terms of power and influence—giving way to a multipolar world with new players (China, India, Brazil, Russia). Third, a world of heightened insecurity beginning almost immediately upon the end of the Cold War, from the First Gulf War of 1991 to the attack of 9/11 in 2001 by al-Qaeda, to the Second Gulf War of 2003. Lastly, an ecological disaster in the making that will affect human life as we know it in all continents. A look at my country of adoption, the United States, in particular shows a nation in distress: ever-greater concentration of wealth in the hands of the elite and ever-expanding poverty, now reaching into the middle classes; an explosion of racism and ethnicism, now directed at the newer immigrants, especially Latinos/as, and at the Arab and Muslim world; a long-range set of burdens (massive indebtedness, failing wars, dialectical paralysis in government).

In my mind, therefore, the present disarray in the church, which I see as brought about by the betrayal of the council, goes hand in hand with the present disarray elsewhere—the betrayal of the revolution in Cuba, the consequences of unbridled capitalism in the world, the sheer arrogance of empire in the United States. I could go on. My observance of the milestone anniversaries mentioned earlier remains, perforce, a muted and silent affair. They appear now as but a faint memory and reminder of what could have been and should have been.

A Concluding Word

Despite such a bleak state of affairs and such a prevailing sense of doom, I remain too much a child of the Cuban Revolution and of the Vatican

Council. I am not ready to give up the struggle and relinquish hope, and will never do so, even if it is a struggle against all odds and a hope against all hope. The legacy of those early days will not let me, whether it be the vision of a different and better world instilled by my Cuban experience or the call to face the signs of the times resolutely and constructively inherited from the council. These two events of January 1959 still compel me—against all odds and all hope—toward a working vision of freedom and justice, dignity and well-being for all, a vision of a new liberation—toward a new revolution, a new church, and a new world order. For such a disposition, I am indeed most grateful to the council and render honor hereby.

Notes

Foreword: An Interpretive Introduction to Vatican II

1. Many of the negative responses were directed not at the documents of Vatican II but at the implementation of the council. Some who expressed these concerns, such as Charles Journet and Jacques Maritain, had been scholars credited with intellectual developments that helped to shape the council itself.

2. Dennis M. Doyle, "Journet, Congar, and the Roots of Communion Ecclesiology," *Theological Studies* 58 (September 1997): 461-79. See also *Communion Ecclesiology: Vision and Versions* (Maryknoll, NY: Orbis Books, 2000).

3. *Concilium* website, http://www.concilium.in/aboutus.htm (accessed October 2, 2011). Founding members of the *Concilium* board included Johann-Baptist Metz, Yves Congar, Hans Küng, Karl Rahner, and Edward Schillebeeckx.

4. *Communio* website: http://www.communio-icr.com/about.htm. Founding members of *Communio* included Henri de Lubac, Hans Urs von Balthasar, Joseph Ratzinger, and Karl Lehman. The English edition began to appear in 1974.

5. *Il Concilio ecumenico Vaticano II: Contrappunto per sua storia* (Vatican City: Liberia Editrice Vaticana, 2005); in English as *The Second Vatican Ecumenical Council: A Counterpoint for the History of the Council*, trans. Kenneth D. Whitehead (Chicago: Distributor for University of Scranton Press, 2008).

6. See the account given by Sandro Magister, a journalist for *L'espresso,* available at http://chiesa.espresso.repubblica.it/articolo/34283&eng=y. A good summary and analysis of this controversy can be found in Kristin Colberg, "The Hermeneutics of Vatican II: The Role of Reception and Authority in the Debate over the Council's Interpretation," *Horizons* 38 (Fall 2011).

7. "Christmas Greetings to the Members of the Roman Curia and Prelature," December 22, 2005, available at http://www.vatican.va/holy_father/benedict_xvi/speeches/2005/december/documents/hf_ben_xvi_spe_20051222_roman-curia_en.html (accessed October 2, 2011).

8. Magister gives his own account supporting Marchetto at http://chiesa.espresso.repubblica.it/articolo/43223&eng=y. See also Magister's account of responses given by Alberigo, Komonchak, and others; available at http://chiesa.espresso.repubblica.it/articolo/181668?eng=y (accessed October 2, 2011). This story, in my opinion blatantly biased, contains a valuable bibliography of Magister's own columns on this subject as well as other key resources. See also Joseph A. Komonchak, "Novelty in Continuity," *America,* February 2, 2009, 10-16.

9. Komonchak's "Vatican II as an Event," originally given as a lecture at St. Louis University in 1999, can be found in David G. Schultenover, ed., *Vatican II: Did Anything Happen?* (New York: Continuum, 2008), which also contains essays by John W. O'Malley and others. O'Malley further develops the approach to Vatican II as an event

in John W. O'Malley, *What Happened at Vatican II* (Cambridge, MA, and London: Belknap Press of Harvard University, 2008).

10. The remaining paragraphs are adapted from this author's review of the first edition of this book that appeared in the *National Catholic Reporter*, July 4, 2003.

Preface: All Is Story

1. Max DePree, *Leadership Is an Art* (New York: Dell Publishing, 1989), pp. 81-82.

Part One: The Council in Context

1. In making reference to "fathers," mention must also be made of "mothers" of the council. Women were there. A good place to start is Carmel Elizabeth McEnroy, *Guests in Their Own House: The Women of Vatican II* (New York: Crossroad, 1996).

2. For more on this, see *History of Vatican II*, ed. Giuseppe Alberigo and Joseph Komonchak (Maryknoll, NY: Orbis Books, 2000), 1:60-72. In Chapter 2, "The Antepreparatory Phase: The Slow Emergence from Inertia," Fouilloux asks the question whether or not the church was ready for a council.

3. For more on the reaction to the council both within and outside the church, see Giuseppe Alberigo, "The Announcement of the Council: From the Security of the Fortress to the Lure of the Quest," in *History of Vatican II*, 1:1-54. As the footnote on page 1 of the book shows, this title from the newspaper *La Croix* first appeared on January 30, 1959.

4. See J. Oscar Beozzo, "The External Climate," in *History of Vatican II*, 1:357-404.

5. Alberigo, "The Announcement," in *History of Vatican II*, 1:18-26. Here Alberigo examines in greater detail the episcopal responses, sharing one aside that Cardinal Spellman (New York) felt that the council was "destined for certain failure."

6. See Pope John's opening address in Walter M. Abbott, ed., *The Documents of Vatican II*, trans. Joseph Gallagher (New York: Guild Press, 1966), p. 716.

7. See Peter Hebblethwaite, *Pope John XXIII: Shepherd of the Modern World* (New York: Doubleday, 1985), p. 414.

8. See *History of Vatican II*, 1:33-44.

9. See *History of Vatican II*, 1:44-49.

10. These comments are found in Murphy's book review of *History of Vatican II, Vol. I: Announcing and Preparing Vatican Council II* in *Commonweal* (September 13, 1996), p. 34.

11. See *History of Vatican II*, 1:109-66.

12. See *The Documents of Vatican II*, pp. 712-13.

13. For more on the pope's opening address, see Andrea Riccardi, Chapter I, "The Tumultuous Opening Days of the Council," in *History of Vatican II*, 2:14-18.

14. For more background on this, see *History of Vatican II*, 2:26-32.

15. This and other stories and anecdotes can be found in John Deedy, *A Book of Catholic Anecdotes* (Allen, TX: Thomas More, 1997), p. 195.

16. The four volumes were *Letters from Vatican City* (1963), *The Second Session* (1964), *The Third Session* (1965), *The Fourth Session* (1966), all published by Farrar, Straus & Giroux of New York. These reflections were reprinted in 1999 by Orbis Books under the title *Vatican Council II*.

17. Richard Hooker as quoted in Samuel Johnson, *Dictionary of the English Language*, Preface (1755).

18. Leon-Joseph Suenens, *Memories and Hopes* (Dublin: Veritas Publications, 1991), p. 334.

19. John XXIII, "Opening Speech to the Council" (October 11, 1962), in *The Documents of Vatican II*, pp. 712-13.

20. Quoted in Xavier Rynne (pseudonym), *The Second Session*, p. 6.

Part Two: Vatican II and the Liturgy

1. Mark S. Massa, *Catholics and American Culture: Fulton Sheen, Dorothy Day, and the Notre Dame Football Team* (New York: Crossroad, 1999), p. 149.

2. For Jungmann's reflection on the "Constitution on the Sacred Liturgy," see *Commentary on the Documents of Vatican II*, 5 vols., ed. Herbert Vorgrimler (New York: Herder and Herder, 1966), 1:1-88.

3. See Daniel P. Grigassy, O.F.M., "The Liturgical Movement," in *The New Dictionary of Theology*, ed. Joseph A. Komonchak, Mary Collins, and Dermot A. Lane (Collegeville, MN: Liturgical Press, 1993), pp. 586-91; and Mark Searle, "Liturgical Movement," in *The HarperCollins Encyclopedia of Catholicism*, ed. Richard P. McBrien (New York: HarperCollins, 1995), pp. 783-85. Lengthier studies of the liturgical movement include Marcel Metzger, *History of the Liturgy: The Major Stages*, trans. Madeleine Beaumont (Collegeville, MN: Liturgical Press, 1999); and J. D. Crichton, *Light in the Darkness: Fore-Runners of the Liturgical Movement* (Collegeville, MN: Liturgical Press, 1996). An American perspective on the movement can be found in Keith F. Pecklers, *The Unread Vision: The Liturgical Movement in the United States of America: 1926-1955* (Collegeville, MN: Liturgical Press, 1998).

4. Father Diekmann's comments can be found in an interview ("Vatican II: There's Been Nothing Like It in 1,000 Years") with the editors of *U.S. Catholic* (November 1991): pp. 14-23.

5. Diekmann expands on this point in "The Constitution on the Sacred Liturgy," in *Vatican II: An Interfaith Appraisal*, ed. John H. Miller, C.S.C. (Notre Dame, IN: University of Notre Dame Press, 1966), p. 19.

6. I heard this example during a talk by Untener titled "The Reforms of Vatican II: How Have We Done? Where Are We Going?" The recording was made and sponsored by the Emmaus Center for Music, Prayer, and Ministry in St. Paul, MN. The tape is distributed by St. Anthony Messenger Press (Cincinnati, 1996).

7. "The Constitution on the Sacred Liturgy," no. 50, in *Vatican II: The Basic Sixteen Documents*, ed. Austin Flannery, O.P. (Northport, NY: Costello, 1996), pp. 135-36.

8. Diekmann, "The Constitution," in *Vatican II: An Interfaith Appraisal*, p. 23.

9. Cited by Diekmann, "The Constitution," in *Vatican II: An Interfaith Appraisal*, p. 23.

10. Arthur Jones, *New Catholics for a New Century: The U.S. Church Today and Where It's Headed* (Allen, TX: Thomas More Publishing, 2000), pp. 65-66.

11. Clarence R. J. Rivers, Jr., "Thank God We Ain't What We Was: The State of the Liturgy in the Black Catholic Community," *Proceedings of the Black Catholic Theological Symposium: October, 1978* (Pittsburgh: Capuchin Press, 1979), p. 69.

12. Joseph Howze et al., "'What We Have Seen and Heard': A Pastoral Letter on Evangelization from the Black Bishops of the United States" (Cincinnati: St. Anthony Messenger Press, 1984), p. 31.

13. Rivers, "Thank God We Ain't What We Was," p. 70.

14. Howze et al., "What We Have Seen and Heard," p. 8.

15. Thea Bowman, "Being a Black Catholic," in *Sister Thea Bowman: Shooting Star: Selected Writings and Speeches,* ed. Celestine Cepress (Winona, MN: Saint Mary's Press, 1993), p. 32.

16. This has been adapted from this author's *To Stand on the Rock: Meditations on Black Catholic Identity* (Maryknoll, NY: Orbis Books, 1998), pp. 115-19. During this congress, I served as the principal liturgist.

17. "The Constitution of the Sacred Liturgy (*Sacrosanctum concilium*)," in *The Basic Sixteen Documents: Vatican Council II: Constitutions, Decrees, Declarations,* gen. ed. Austin Flannery, O.P. (New York: Costello, 1996), p. 124.

18. Bernard Botte, *From Silence to Participation: An Insider's View of the Liturgical Renewal,* trans. John Sullivan, O.C.D. (Washington, DC: Pastoral Press, 1988), p. 170.

Part Three: What It Means to Be Church

1. See Vatican I, "Dogmatic Constitution on the Church of Christ" (1870) in Norman P. Tanner, ed., *Decrees of the Ecumenical Councils,* 2 vols. (London: Sheed & Ward; Washington, DC: Georgetown University Press, 1990), 2:811-12. Heinrich Denzinger et al., eds., *Enchiridion Symbolorum, Definitioneum et Declarationum de Rebus Fidei et Morum* (29th ed.; Freiburg: Herder & Herder, 1953), 1821.

2. See Tanner, *Decrees of the Ecumenical Councils,* 2:814-15; Denzinger, 1831.

3. See Tanner, *Decrees of the Ecumenical Councils,* 2:816; Denzinger, 1839.

4. In a schema on the Supreme Pastor, which was distributed but not discussed at Vatican I, we read: "The Church of Christ is not a society consisting of equal members, as though all the faithful who form part of it had the same rights. It is, on the contrary, an unequal (hierarchical) society in that some of the faithful are clergy and others are laity. It is above all such a society because there is in the church a power that is divinely instituted which some have received in order to sanctify, teach and govern and which others have not received." See J. D. Mansi, *Sacrorum conciliorum nova et amplissima collectio,* 53 vols. (Florence, Venice, Paris, Leipzig: H. Welter, 1759-1927), 51:543. Cited by Yves Congar, "Moving Towards a Pilgrim Church," in *Vatican II Revisited by Those Who Were There* (Minneapolis: Winston Press, 1986), p. 133. The understanding of the church as an unequal society, in which the duty of the faithful is "to allow themselves to be led, and, like a docile flock, to follow the Pastors" is repeated by Pope Pius X in his encyclical *Vehementer nos* (1906). See Claudia Carlen, ed., *The Papal Encyclicals* (New York: McGrath, 1981), 3:47-48.

5. See Xavier Rynne (pseud.), *Letters from Vatican City. Vatican Council II (First Session): Background and Debates* (New York: Farrar, Straus & Company, 1963), pp. 215-19, 222-31. Giuseppe Ruggieri, "Beyond an Ecclesiology of Polemics: The Debate on the Church," in *History of Vatican II,* ed. Giuseppe Alberigo and Joseph Komonchak (Maryknoll, NY: Orbis Books, 2000), 2:330-40. Gérard Philips, "History of the Constitution," in *Commentary on the Documents of Vatican II,* ed. Herbert Vorgrimler, 5 vols. (New York: Crossroad, 1989), 1:109.

6. See Giuseppe Alberigo's summary of the state of the question in 1963-1964: "Conclusion: The New Shape of the Council," in *History of Vatican II,* 3:491-98.

7. See Rynne (pseud.), *Letters from Vatican City,* p. 215.

8. Francis X. Murphy observed at the time that Chapter 2 of the constitution, deal-

ing with the church as the People of God, was "actually the heart of the Council's break-away from a scholastic approach to the theology of the Church. It described the mystery of the Church in biblical terms adapted to the existentialist world in which the Church now finds itself." Xavier Rynne (pseud.), *The Third Session: The Debates and Decrees of Vatican Council II, September 14 to November 21, 1964* (New York: Farrar, Straus & Giroux, 1965), p. 14.

9. As John O'Malley notes, the image of the "People of God," with its stress on the fundamental equality of all members of the church, "replaced the strong vertical line of ruler-subject" of the earliest draft of the constitution with a strong horizontal line. And the chapter on holiness "imbued *Lumen gentium* with its finality by saying explicitly, forcefully, and for the first time ever in a council that holiness is what the church is all about, what human life is about. By presenting the church as more than a guardian of orthodoxy and an enforcer of good behavior, this crucial document helped move the council beyond the earlier senate-model to a new modality." See *What Happened at Vatican II* (Cambridge, MA: Belknap Press of Harvard University Press, 2008), pp. 174-75.

10. "Though they differ essentially and not only in degree, the common priesthood of the faithful and the ministerial or hierarchical priesthood are none the less interrelated; each in its own way shares in the one priesthood of Christ" (no. 10). And, "The holy people of God shares also in Christ's prophetic office: it spreads abroad a living witness to him, especially by a life of faith and love and by offering to God a sacrifice of praise, the fruit of lips confessing his name (see Heb 13:15)" (no. 12). See Austin Flannery, ed., *Vatican Council II: The Basic Sixteen Documents* (Northport, NY: Costello, 1996), pp. 14 and 16.

11. *Lumen gentium*, no. 12, in Flannery, ed., *Vatican Council II*, pp. 16-17.

12. In the original draft, the council "teaches and solemnly professes that there is only one true Church of Jesus Christ, namely the one we celebrate in the creed as one, holy, catholic, and apostolic . . . which, after his resurrection, he entrusted to St. Peter and his successors, the Roman pontiffs, to be governed; therefore only the Catholic Roman has a right to be called the Church" (quoted by Giuseppe Ruggieri, "Beyond an Ecclesiology of Polemics: The Debate on the Church," in *History of Vatican II*, 2:286).

13. *Lumen gentium*, no. 8, in Flannery, ed., *Vatican Council II*, p. 9.

14. *Lumen gentium*, no. 15, in Flannery, ed., *Vatican Council II*, pp. 20-21.

15. *Lumen gentium*, no. 16, in Flannery, ed., *Vatican Council II*, p. 22.

16. Already during the first session of the council (beginning in October 1962), as the assembled bishops discussed their first topic, the liturgy, the question about the extent of the power of bishops to legislate liturgical requirements in their different nations became an issue. See Xavier Rynne (pseud.), *Letters from Vatican City*, pp. 97-98.

17. So even in the earliest phase of preparation for the council, known as the antepreparatory phase, the pope intervened so that the bishops around the world would have the opportunity to identify the items to be discussed at the council, rather than being presented with an agenda prepared by the Antepreparatory Commission and being asked for their reaction. At its May 26, 1959, meeting, the Antepreparatory Commission received from their president, Domenico Cardinal Tardini, a draft of a letter to the bishops and a questionnaire intended to guide their responses. In it, the defense of certain doctrinal and moral truths against modern errors and the return of "dissident brothers and sisters to the Roman Church" were identified as agenda items for the council. But at the meeting of the full commission on June 30, 1959, in the presence

of Pope John, the procedure for consulting the bishops was completely changed. There would be no questionnaire, but only a simple letter in which the bishops would be asked to communicate with "complete freedom and honesty" the critiques and suggestions that their pastoral concern directs them to offer as possible points of discussion at the future council. See É. Fouilloux, "The Antepreparatory Phase: The Slow Emergence from Inertia (January, 1959-October, 1962)" in *History of Vatican II*, 1:92-94.

18. Cited in Xavier Rynne (pseud.), *The Third Session*, p. 251. Cardinal Arcadio Larraona's letter to Pope Paul VI is printed in *Paolo VI e i problemi ecclesiologici al Concilio: Colloquio internazionale di studio* (Rome: Edizioni Studium and Istituto Paolo VI, 1989), pp. 619-21.

19. O'Malley, *What Happened at Vatican II*, p. 208.

20. See *Lumen gentium*, "The Explanatory Note," in Flannery, ed., *Vatican Council II*, pp. 92-95. Tanner, *Decrees of the Ecumenical Councils*, 2:899-900.

21. See Paul VI's Opening Address, cited in Rynne (pseud.), *The Third Session*, pp. 287-96; here p. 290. The pope declared that the council's deliberations on this subject "will certainly be what distinguishes this solemn and historic synod in the memory of future ages." He further emphasized the need to coordinate this council's declarations on the subject with the teaching of Vatican I:

> The fathers of the first Vatican Council defined and proclaimed the truly unique and supreme powers conferred by Christ on Peter and handed on to his successors. This recognition has appeared to some as having limited the authority of bishops, the successors of the apostles, and as having rendered superfluous and prevented the convocation of a subsequent Ecumenical Council, which, however, according to canon law has supreme authority over the entire church.
>
> The present ecumenical synod is certainly going to confirm the doctrine of the previous one regarding the prerogatives of the Roman Pontiff. But it will also have as its principal objective the task of describing and honoring the prerogatives of the episcopate. . . .
>
> Let us repeat as our own those well-known words which our distant and saintly predecessor of immortal memory, Gregory the Great, wrote to Eulogius, Bishop of Alexandria: "My honor is the honor of the universal church. My honor is the strength of my brothers. I am thus truly honored when the honor due to each and every one of them is not denied to them."
>
> The integrity of Catholic truth now calls for a clarification consonant with the doctrine of papacy which will place in its splendid light the role and mandate of the episcopate. (pp. 291-92)

See also O'Malley, *What Happened at Vatican II*, p. 176.

22. Cardinal Giuseppe Siri, a spokesman for the minority, was ecstatic that the Note had been added. Although most commentators agree that the Note did not change the fundamental meaning of the document, the Note's rejection of the idea that "college" implies equality between the head and the members of the college and the Note's affirmation of hierarchical communion as a condition of episcopal membership in the college "gave those who opposed collegiality a tool they could—and would—use to interpret the chapter as a reaffirmation of the status quo." (O'Malley, *What Happened at Vatican II*, p. 245). Joseph Ratzinger (the future Pope Benedict XVI), shortly after the council, observed that the ambiguity and ambivalence of the Note seemed to tip

the balance in favor of papal primacy. See Joseph Ratzinger, *Theological Highlights of Vatican II*, trans. Henry Traub et al. (New York: Paulist Press, 1966), pp. 114-16.

23. *Lumen gentium*, no. 22, in Flannery, ed., *Vatican Council II*, pp. 30-31.

24. Avery Dulles, "Introduction to the Dogmatic Constitution on the Church," in Walter M. Abbott, ed., *The Documents of Vatican II* (New York: Guild, 1966), p. 10. Cardinal Léger of Montreal regarded the document on the church as the hinge of the entire council. See Rynne (pseud.), *Letters from Vatican City*, p. 222. And Pope Paul VI believed that it would be the crowning achievement that "distinguishes this solemn and historic synod in the memory of future ages." See his Opening Address for the Third Session (September 14, 1964), in Rynne, *The Third Session*, p. 290.

25. See Robert McClory, "Detour: The Commission on Birth Control," *U.S. Catholic* (September 1995), p. 12. The *U.S. Catholic* article is an excerpt from Robert McClory, *Turning Point* (New York: Crossroad, 1995).

26. See Chapter 4 of *Lumen gentium*, especially nos. 33-35, in Flannery, ed., *Vatican Council II*, pp. 51-54.

Part Four: Revelation, Scripture, and Tradition

1. See R. A. F. MacKenzie, "Introduction to Dei Verbum," in Walter M. Abbott, ed., *The Documents of Vatican II* (New York: Guild, 1966), p. 107. Murphy, writing pseudonymously under the name Xavier Rynne, concurred: "There can be little doubt that the Constitution on Divine Revelation will be regarded as the most important document promulgated by the Council after the Constitution on the Church. Together with *Lumen gentium*, it enshrined and consecrated the new biblical approach to theology which has become one of the hallmarks of Vatican II." Rynne, *The Fourth Session: The Debates and Decrees of Vatican Council II, September 14 to December 8, 1965* (New York: Farrar, Straus and Giroux, 1966), p. 184.

2. Giuseppe Ruggieri, "The First Doctrinal Clash," in *History of Vatican II*, ed. Giuseppe Alberigo and Joseph Komonchak (Maryknoll, NY: Orbis Books, 2000), 2:233. See also Joseph Ratzinger, "Dogmatic Constitution on Divine Revelation, Origin and Background," in *Commentary on the Documents of Vatican II*, 3:155-67; Donald Senior, "Dogmatic Constitution on Divine Revelation," in *Vatican II and Its Documents: An American Reappraisal*, ed. Timothy E. O'Connell (Wilmington, DE: Glazier, 1986), pp. 122-40.

3. See Xavier Rynne (pseud.), *Letters from Vatican City* (New York: Farrar, Straus & Giroux, 1963), pp. 140-41. Ruggieri, "Doctrinal Clash," *History of Vatican II*, 2:235.

4. Congar, in *Informations Catholiques Internationales*, December 1, 1962, p. 2; cited in Rynne (pseud.), *Letters from Vatican City*, p. 141.

5. In his *Disquisitio*, Rahner outlined four principal criticisms of the schema on revelation. First, the schema was too long and attempted to settle theological issues that were still controverted. Second, the text lacked a pastoral orientation. Third, the text also lacked an ecumenical spirit. Fourth, the schema improperly placed all of its statements on the same dogmatic level. See Ruggieri, "Doctrinal Clash," *History of Vatican II*, 2:237-40, 260. O'Malley, *What Happened at Vatican II* (Cambridge, MA: Belknap Press of Harvard University Press, 2008), p. 145. It is interesting to note that Joseph Ratzinger (the future Pope Benedict XVI) joined Rahner, with the blessing of the German bishops, in writing an alternative text to the official one. Their alternative text circulated among the council fathers before the official schema was discussed on the floor of St. Peter's.

6. Ruggieri, "Doctrinal Clash," *History of Vatican II*, 2:240.

7. See Rynne, *Letters from Vatican City*, pp. 141-43; Ruggieri, "Doctrinal Clash," *History of Vatican II*, 2:250-51.

8. Liénart, as quoted in Rynne, *Letters from Vatican City*, p. 143.

9. Bishop Charue of Namur, Belgium, for example, rejected the suggestion that modernism needed to be condemned in the conciliar document: "It is not up to the Council to do the work of the Holy Office, or of theologians, but it is up to the Council not to set the stage for another Galileo incident! Our Council should imitate that of Jerusalem, and not put unbearable burdens on those outside the Church or the faith. The fact that the Church can house men of diverse opinions and attitudes gives us hope for the future." Cited by H. Fesquet, *Le Monde* (November 21, 1962); Rynne (pseud.), *Letters from Vatican City*, p. 158.

10. "It can be said that during the week of discussion of *De fontibus* the Council took possession of its purpose in the terms in which *Gaudet Mater Ecclesia* [John XXIII's Opening Address on October 11, 1962] had described it. It was the decisive phase of a process that was clearly articulated in Bea's intervention on November 14: (a) The Pope has given the Council a pastoral purpose; (b) the Council has already made this purpose its own in its opening 'Message'; and (c) the need now is consciously to ratify this purpose by rejecting a schema that runs counter to it. The clarity of Bea's vision of the real issue should not allow us to forget how passionate this debate was." Ruggieri, "Doctrinal Clash," *History of Vatican II*, 2:253. See also Rynne (pseud.), *Letters from Vatican City*, p. 149. In his diary entry for November 14, 1962, John XXIII wrote, "That disputes will arise can be foreseen. On the one hand, the draft [the preparatory schema] does not take into account the specific intentions of the Pope in his official discourses. On the other hand, a good eight cardinals, relying on these discourses, have discredited the main point of the draft. May the Lord help us and make us one." See Ruggieri, "Doctrinal Clash," p. 256.

11. The Rules of Procedure constituted an Appendix to the document *Motu Proprio Appropinquante Concilio* (August 6, 1962). The text can be found in *La Documentation Catholique* (October 7, 1962), p. 1231. Concerning whether the schema had papal approval, see Ruggieri, "Doctrinal Clash," *History of Vatican II*, 2:163, note #80.

12. O'Malley, *What Happened at Vatican II*, p. 148.

13. O'Malley explains the significance of De Smedt's speech: "De Smedt's speech raised the stakes. All at once on the floor of St. Peter's the bishops witnessed the spectacle of an officially constituted body of the council, now enjoying the status of a commission, asserting that it could not accept the work of another. When Bea had spoken on the opening day of the debate, he had spoken in his own name. Now De Smedt spoke in the name of the Secretariat. At this point it became clear that the council had reached a critical point in procedure." *What Happened at Vatican II*, p. 149.

14. See Rynne (pseud.), *Letters from Vatican City*, pp. 164-66; Ruggieri, "Doctrinal Clash," *History of Vatican II*, 2:262-63.

15. Rynne (pseudonym), *Letters from Vatican City*, p. 167.

16. According to O'Malley, the importance of the vote on November 20 and of the papal intervention on November 21 "can hardly be exaggerated." The intervention, which ruled in favor of the prevailing reformist sentiment in St. Peter's, set the direction that Vatican II would take from that moment forward. *What Happened at Vatican II*, p. 151. Robert Rouquette, commenting at the time in the French Jesuit journal, claimed that with the vote on November 20, "we can consider the era of the Counter-

Reformation ended and a new era for Christendom, with unforeseeable consequences, begun." "Bilan du concile," *Études* (January 1963), pp. 94-95.

17. Koenig as quoted in Xavier Rynne (pseud.), *The Third Session* (New York: Farrar, Straus & Giroux, 1965), p. 44.

18. Butler stated, "We do not want the childish comfort of averting our gaze from the truth, but a truly critical scholarship which will enable us to enter into dialogue with non-Catholic scholars." Quoted in Rynne (pseud.), *The Third Session*, p. 47.

19. See Rynne (pseud.), *The Fourth Session* (New York: Farrar, Straus & Giroux, 1966), pp. 187-96.

20. "Dogmatic Constitution on Divine Revelation" (*Dei verbum*, no. 9) in Austen Flannery, ed., *The Documents of Vatican II* (New York: Guild, 1966), p. 103.

21. See Abbot Christopher Butler, "The Constitution on Divine Revelation," in *Vatican II: An Interfaith Appraisal*, ed. John H. Miller, C.S.C. (Notre Dame, IN: University of Notre Dame Press, 1966), p. 49.

22. *Dei verbum*, no. 11 in Flannery, ed., *Vatican Council II*, p. 105.

23. Pope Benedict XVI, *Jesus of Nazareth: From the Baptism in the Jordan to the Transfiguration*, trans. from the German by Adrian J. Walker (New York: Doubleday, 2007), pp. xv and xvi.

24. Pope Benedict XVI, *Jesus of Nazareth: Holy Week. From the Entrance into Jerusalem to the Resurrection*, English translation provided by the Vatican Secretariat of State (San Francisco: Ignatius Press, 2011), pp. xiv-xv.

25. See the study Reid has done jointly with Leslie J. Hoppe, O.F.M., *Preaching from the Scriptures: New Directions in Preparing Preachers* (Pulaski, WI: Franciscan Printing, 1998).

26. See Heinrich Denzinger et al., eds., *Enchiridion symbolorum, definitionum et declarationum de rebus fidei et morum* (29th ed.; Freiburg: Herder & Herder, 1953), 4214.

27. Denzinger, *Enchiridion*, 3886.

28. Karl Rahner, "Scripture and Theology," in *Theological Investigations*, vol. 6 (Baltimore: Helicon Press, 1969), p. 93; idem, "Bible. B. Theology," in *Sacramentum Mundi*, 6 vols. (New York: Herder & Herder, 1968-70), 1:171-78, especially 176-77.

29. See Denzinger, *Enchiridion*, 4226.

30. See *Acta Apostolicae Sedis* 56 (1964), 712-18; Denzinger, *Enchiridion*, 4402-7.

31. See Denzinger, *Enchiridion*, 4404-6.

Part V: Ecumenism and Interreligious Dialogue

1. Pius XI as cited in Williston Walker et al., *A History of the Christian Church*, 4th ed. (New York: Charles Scribner's Sons, 1985), p. 686.

2. See Rynne (pseudonym), *Letters from Vatican City* (New York: Farrar, Straus, & Giroux, 1963), p. 44.

3. Rynne, *Letters from Vatican City*, p. 77.

4. See Rynne, *Letters from Vatican City*, pp. 190-91.

5. See Claude Soetens, "The Ecumenical Commitment of the Catholic Church," in *History of Vatican II*, ed. Giuseppe Alberigo and Joseph Komonchak (Maryknoll, NY: Orbis Books, 2000), 3:258-59, 264-66. Rynne (pseud.), *The Second Session* (New York: Farrar, Straus & Giroux, 1964), pp. 216-17.

6. The Spanish cardinal de Arriba y Castro, for example, stated that the promotion of dialogue with other Christians seemed to contradict current church law, which

forbade the publication or reading of books containing "heresy." From his perspective, "ecumenism" meant simply the right of the Catholic Church to engage in proselytiza- tion. Arriba y Castro proclaimed: "It should not be forgotten that only the Catholic Church has the right and duty to evangelize." Cited in Rynne, *The Second Session*, p. 238. See also pp. 250, 264, and 274.

7. Soetens, "The Ecumenical Commitment," *History of Vatican II*, 3:263. Cardi- nal Ritter of St. Louis, for example, declared that the schema marked the end of the Counter-Reformation and gave substantial impetus to the unity of Christians. Ritter declared that the text should clearly acknowledge the validity of the sacraments of the Oriental churches and should avoid any expressions offensive to Protestants. He added that there was no legitimate reason for denying the use of the term "church" to the religious groups that originated after the sixteenth century. See Rynne, *The Second Session*, p. 237. See also pp. 251 and 263.

8. O'Malley, *What Happened at Vatican II* (Cambridge, MA: Belknap Press of Harvard University Press, 2008), p. 200.

9. O'Malley, *What Happened at Vatican II*, p. 204.

10. "The emendations were sent to Cardinal Bea as 'suggestions,' but in view of the lateness of the hour—it is said that they were communicated the previous evening when it was no longer possible to discuss them in a full meeting of the Secretariat and the final decision as to whether to accept or reject them had to be made by the cardinal with some of his aides—there can be little doubt that the papal suggestions were the equiva- lent of an 'order.' To have refused them would have jeopardized the whole decree." Rynne (pseud.), *The Third Session* (New York: Farrar, Straus & Giroux, 1965), p. 264.

11. Between November 14 and 18, 1964, a list of "difficulties" and suggested changes was communicated to Johannes Willebrands, secretary of the Secretariat for Christian Unity, to which Willebrands and his associates made a reply to the pope. The pope had selected these "suggestions" for change from a longer list that he received from sources that to this day have not been definitively identified. See O'Malley, *What Happened at Vatican II*, p. 243. Luis Antonio G. Tagle, "The 'Black Week' of Vatican II (November 14-21, 1964)," in *History of Vatican II*, 4:412-13.

12. For examples of the changes that were made, see Tagle, "The 'Black Week' of Vatican II," in *History of Vatican II*, 4:414-16.

13. See Rynne, *The Third Session*, p. 265. Tagle, "The 'Black Week' of Vatican II," in *History of Vatican II*, 4:416-17.

14. "Decree on Ecumenism," in *The Basic Sixteen Documents: Vatican Council II: Constitutions, Decrees, Declarations*, gen. ed. Austin Flannery, O.P. (New York: Costello, 1996), pp. 502-3.

15. Cited by Walter Abbott, ed., in *The Documents of Vatican II* (New York: Guild Press, 1966), p. 338.

16. See Fourth Lateran Council, *Constitutions*, section 1 ("On the Catholic Faith"), in Norman P. Tanner, ed., *Decrees of the Ecumenical Councils*, 2 vols. (Washington, DC: Georgetown University Press, 1990), 1:230. For the Council of Florence, see Tan- ner, *Decrees*, 1:578.

17. The Catholic Church's Holy Office rejected Feeney's claim that only Catholics could be saved by distinguishing between those who "really" belong to the church by means of explicit faith and actual baptism and those who "belong" to the church "by desire," that is, those people of good will who would join the church if they knew it to be the one, true church of Christ. See "Feeney" in *The Harper Collins Encyclopedia of Catholicism*, ed. Richard P. McBrien (San Francisco: Harper, 1995), p. 522.

18. See Francis A. Sullivan, *Salvation Outside the Church? Tracing the History of the Catholic Response* (New York: Paulist Press, 1992), pp. 3-6.

19. "Introduction" to *Nostra aetate*, in Abbott, ed., *The Documents of Vatican II*, p. 656.

20. See Rynne, *The Second Session*, pp. 235, 239.

21. The Jewish scholar Jules Isaac played a very influential role in moving Pope John XXIII to insist that a positive statement concerning the Jews be made at the council. In 1947 Isaac helped to draw up the ten points of Seelisberg, which made recommendations to the Christian churches on how they might remedy their anti-Jewish teachings. In 1959 he published a book that challenged the caricature of Judaism as a legalistic religion and that rejected the "justification" of Jewish persecution as punishment for the crucifixion of Christ. At his audience with the pope, Isaac presented the pope with a dossier that included the Seelisberg points and asked him to have the council address them. See O'Malley, *What Happened at Vatican II*, p. 219.

22. Bea said, "The Secretariat to which the care of promoting Christian Unity is given undertook the question treating the Jews not on its own initiative, but by reason of the express command of the Supreme Pontiff, Pope John XXIII of happy memory. This was given verbally to the President of the Secretariat." Quoted in Rynne, *The Second Session*, p. 218. See also pp. 222-23.

23. See Rynne (pseud.), *The Second Session*, pp. 221, 222.

24. "Different reasons were alleged for this move: because the Pope [i.e., Paul VI] was anxious not to compromise the reception he might receive in Jordan and Jerusalem on his intended pilgrimage; because of sharp Arab protests against the document made directly to the Vatican Secretariat of State through diplomatic channels; because of misgivings on theological grounds by some of the Pope's advisers, perhaps shared by Pope Paul; because of pressure exercised by the minority in the Council" (Rynne, *The Third Session*, p. 33).

25. Whether or not to include reference to deicide was hotly debated. For some of the details, see O'Malley, *What Happened at Vatican II*, pp. 250-51.

26. *Nostra aetate*, no. 4, in Flannery, ed., *Vatican Council II*, p. 573.

27. *Nostra aetate*, no. 2, in Flannery, ed., *Vatican Council II*, p. 571.

28. It is important to read these statements together with the statements concerning Islam and Judaism in the "Dogmatic Constitution on the Church" (*Lumen gentium*), no. 16, where the possibility of salvation for those who have not received the gospel is affirmed.

29. For an excellent history of the development of Catholic thinking on the issue of salvation outside the church, see Francis A. Sullivan, *Salvation Outside the Church?*

30. See Sullivan, *Salvation Outside the Church?* pp. 70-73. This idea that some people might justifiably reject Christian faith because of the poor witness of Christians is picked up at Vatican II. See the "Pastoral Constitution on the Church in the Modern World" (*Gaudium et spes*), no. 19.

31. Sullivan, *Salvation Outside the Church?*, p. 98.

32. *Lumen gentium*, no. 13, in Flannery, ed., *Vatican Council II*, p. 19.

33. *Lumen gentium*, no. 16, in Flannery, ed., *Vatican Council II*, p. 22. See also *Gaudium et spes*, no. 22.

34. Gregor Maria Hoff, "A Realm of Differences: The Meaning of Jewish Monotheism for Christology and Trinitarian Theology," in Philip A. Cunningham, Joseph Sievers, Mary C. Boys, Hans Hermann Henrix, and Jesper Svartvik, eds., *Christ Jesus*

and the Jewish People Today: New Explorations of Theological Interrelationships (Grand Rapids, MI: Eerdmans, 2011), pp. 202-7, esp. 207.

35. As noted by Eugene J. Fisher, "Official Roman Catholic Teaching on Jews and Judaism: Commentary and Context," in Eugene J. Fisher and Leon Klenicki, eds., *In Our Time: The Flowering of Jewish-Catholic Dialogue* (New York/Mahwah, NJ: Paulist Press, 1990), p. 6.

36. See the addresses delivered by John Paul II on November 17, 1980; November 26, 1986; September 11, 1987; June 24, 1988; September 26, 1990; November 8, 1990; April 28, 1999; June 29, 1999; February 26, 2000; March 12, 2000; and March 26, 2000. All are available at: http://www.ccjr.us/dialogika-resources/documents-and-statements/roman-catholic/pope-john-paul-ii.

37. See further my essay "Official Ecclesial Documents to Implement Vatican II on Relations with Jews: 'Study Them, Become Immersed in Them, and Put Them into Practice,'" *Studies in Christian–Jewish Relations* (2009): pp. 1-36, esp. pp. 6-8. Available at http://ejournals.bc.edu/ojs/index.php/scjr/article/view/1521/1374.

38. John M. Oesterreicher, *The New Encounter between Christians and Jews* (New York: Philosophical Library, 1986), pp. 199-200.

39. So, e.g., Cardinal Avery Dulles, "Covenant and Mission," *America*, October 21, 2002, pp. 10-11; and Cardinal Albert Vanhoye, "The Plan of God Is a Union of Love with His People," address delivered at the Synod of Bishops, October 7, 2008. But against their construals, see Jesper Svartvik, "Reading the Letter to the Hebrews without Presupposing Supersessionism," in Cunningham et al., eds., *Christ Jesus and the Jewish People Today*, pp. 77-91.

40. E.g., Cardinal Christoph Schönborn, "Judaism's Way to Salvation," *The Tablet* (March 29, 2008), available at http://www.thetablet.co.uk/articles/11223/.

41. Seemingly implementing Cardinal Dulles's views, the Committees on Doctrine and on Ecumenical and Interreligious Affairs of the U.S. Conference of Catholic Bishops released "A Note on Ambiguities Contained in 'Reflections on Covenant and Mission'" on June 18, 2009. After critiquing the 2002 study "Reflections on Covenant and Mission" (issued by the Secretariat for Ecumenical and Interreligious Affairs and the National Council of Synagogues) for defining dialogue as "a mutually enriching sharing of gifts devoid of any intention whatsoever to invite the dialogue partner to baptism," it went on to say, "Though Christian participation in interreligious dialogue would not normally include an explicit invitation to baptism and entrance into the Church, the Christian dialogue partner is always giving witness to the following of Christ, to which all are implicitly invited [§7]." After an unprecedented unanimous letter from the Conservative, Orthodox, Reconstructionist, and Reform Jewish movements together with the American Jewish Committee, the Anti-Defamation League, and B'nai B'rith that this understanding would mean the end of Jewish dialogue with the Catholic Church, the leaders of the U.S. Bishops Conference replied on October 2, 2009, that both the critical quotation from "Reflections on Covenant and Mission" and the sentence about explicit and implicit invitations to baptism would be deleted from "A Note on Ambiguities." This unusual action thus reaffirmed that in the context of interreligious dialogue there should be no invitations, implicit or otherwise, to convert to Catholicism.

42. *Jesus of Nazareth*, Part Two, *Holy Week: From the Entrance into Jerusalem to the Resurrection* (San Francisco: Ignatius Press, 2011), p. 45. Hildegard Brem, a Cistercian contemplative nun, is abbess of the Mariastern-Gwiggen Abbey in Hoenweiler, Austria. Other ways of envisioning the eschaton are suggested by the Pontifical Biblical

Commission's 2001 study, *The Jewish People and Their Sacred Scriptures in the Christian Bible*, §21.

43. Editor's note: After acknowledging that the church was late in recognizing the principle of religious liberty, Murray continued as follows: "In any event, the document is a significant event in the history of the Church. It was, of course, the most controversial document of the whole Council, largely because it raised with sharp emphasis the issue that lay continually below the surface of all the conciliar debates—the issue of the development of doctrine. The notion of development, not the notion of religious freedom, was the real sticking point for many of those who opposed the Declaration even to the end." Cited in Abbott, ed., *Documents of Vatican II*, p. 673.

44. *Dignitatis humanae*, no. 4, in Flannery, ed., *Vatican II*, pp. 555-56; see alternative translation in Abbott, ed., *Documents of Vatican II*, p. 682.

45. *Dignitatis humanae*, no. 7, in Flannery, ed., *Vatican II*, pp. 558; see alternative translation in Abbott, ed., *Documents of Vatican II*, p. 687.

46. Gerald M. Costello, op-ed piece, "[A Vatican Council Footnote:] The Cardinal Stepped In," *Catholic New York*, October 10, 1982, p. 11.

47. Donald Pelotte, S.S.S., *John Courtney Murray: Theologian in Conflict* (New York and Ramsey, NJ: Paulist Press, 1976), p. 82.

48. Costello, "The Cardinal Stepped In."

49. Bernard Häring, *My Witness for the Church*, trans. Leonard Swidler (New York and Mahwah, NJ: Paulist Press, 1992), p. 576.

50. Pietro Pavan, "Ecumenism and Vatican II's Declaration on Religious Freedom," in *Religious Freedom: 1965 and 1975. A Symposium on a Historic Document*, ed. Walter J. Burghardt, S.J. (Woodstock Studies 1; New York and Ramsey, NJ: Paulist Press, 1976), pp. 7-38, at p. 12.

51. Pavan, "Ecumenism and Vatican II's Declaration on Religious Freedom," p. 10.

52. *Nostra aetate*, no. 2, in Flannery, ed., *Vatican II*, p. 571; alternative translation in Abbott, ed., *Documents of Vatican II*, p. 663.

Part Six: World Issues and Social Justice

1. *Gaudium et spes*, no. 1, in Austin Flannery, ed., *Vatican Council II: The Basic Sixteen Documents* (Northport, NY: Costello, 1996), p. 163.

2. Jay P. Dolan, *The American Catholic Experience: A History from Colonial Times to the Present* (Garden City, NJ: Doubleday, 1985), p. 228.

3. As quoted by Justo Gonzalez in *The Story of Christianity: The Reformation to the Present Day* (New York: Harper & Row, 1985), p. 298.

4. See Donal Dorr, *Option for the Poor: A Hundred Years of Catholic Social Teaching*, revised and expanded edition (Maryknoll, NY: Orbis Books, 1992); John A. Coleman, ed., *One Hundred Years of Catholic Social Thought: Celebration and Challenge* (Maryknoll, NY: Orbis Books, 1991); and Michael Walsh and Brian Davies, eds., *Proclaiming Justice and Peace: Papal Documents from Rerum Novarum through Centesimus Annus*, revised and expanded edition (Mystic, CT: Twenty-Third Publications, 1991).

5. See Michael J. Schultheis, Edward P. De Berri, and Peter J. Henriot, *Our Best Kept Secret: The Rich Heritage of Catholic Social Teaching* (Washington, DC: Center of Concern, 1987).

6. See Campion's Introduction to the "Pastoral Constitution on the Church in the

Modern World," in Walter M. Abbott, ed., *The Documents of Vatican II*, trans. Joseph Gallagher (New York: Guild Press, 1966), p. 183.

7. For this conversation and the remarks of Suenens concerning the plan for the council, see his article "A Plan for the Whole Council," in *Vatican II Revisited by Those Who Were There*, ed. Alberic Stacpoole (Minneapolis, MN: Winston Press, 1986), pp. 88-105.

8. Cardinal Leon-Joseph Suenens, *Memories and Hopes*, trans. Elena French (Dublin: Veritas Publications, 1992), p. 78.

9. See Suenens, "A Plan for the Whole Council," in Stacpoole, ed., *Vatican II Revisited*, p. 88.

10. Suenens, *Memories and Hopes*, p. 78.

11. Suenens, *Memories and Hopes,* pp. 97-98.

12. Quote from Pope John XXIII's September 11, 1962, radio address, cited in *History of Vatican II*, ed. Giuseppe Alberigo; English version ed. Joseph A. Komonchak (Maryknoll, NY: Orbis Books, 1995-2000), 2:437.

13. See Charles Moeller's "History of the Constitution," in Herbert Vorgrimler, ed., *Commentary on the Documents of Vatican II*, 5 vols. (New York: Herder & Herder, 1966), 5:10-11.

14. Alberigo, ed., *History of Vatican II*, 2:200-203.

15. Vorgrimler, ed., *Commentary on the Documents of Vatican II*, 5:10-11.

16. Suenens, *Memories and Hopes*, p. 86.

17. Suenens, *Memories and Hopes*, p. 87.

18. For those desiring more information than this brief introduction can provide, see volume 5 of *Commentary on the Documents of Vatican II*, ed. Vorgrimler. This whole volume is devoted to the "Pastoral Constitution on the Church." Two other sources, though much shorter in their overview, include "The Church in the Modern World," by Enda McDonagh in *Contemporary Catholic Theology: A Reader*, ed. Michael A. Hayes and Liam Gearon (New York: Continuum, 1998), and "The Constitution on the Church in the Modern World," by Bishop Mark G. McGrath, C.S.C., in *Vatican II: An Interfaith Appraisal*, ed. John H. Miller, C.S.C. (Notre Dame, IN: University of Notre Dame Press, 1966), pp. 397-412.

19. Alberigo, ed., *History of Vatican II*, 2:412.

20. Joseph Ratzinger, *The Theological Highlights of Vatican II* (New York: Paulist Press, 1966), p. 148.

21. Vorgrimler, ed., *Commentary on the Documents of Vatican II*, 5:3.

22. Miller, ed., *Vatican II: An Interfaith Appraisal*, p. 296. For more on the story of the Birth Control Commission, see Robert Blair Kaiser, *The Politics of Sex and Religion* (Kansas City: Leaven, 1985).

23. See Häring's article, "Marriage and the Family," in Miller, ed., *Vatican II: An Interfaith Appraisal*, p. 439.

24. See Charles Moeller, "Man, the Church and Society," in Miller, ed., *Vatican II: An Interfaith Appraisal*, p. 417.

25. McDonagh, "The Church in the Modern World," p. 306.

26. McGrath, "The Constitution on the Church in the Modern World, " in Miller, ed., *Vatican II: An Interfaith Appraisal*, p. 397.

27. McDonagh, "The Church in the Modern World," pp. 300-301.

28. *Gaudium et spes*, no. 29, in Flannery, ed., *Vatican Council II*, p. 194; alternative translation in Abbott, ed., *Documents of Vatican II*, p. 58.

29. *Lumen gentium*, no. 32, in Flannery, ed., *Vatican Council II*, pp. 49-50; alternative translation in Abbott, ed., *Documents of Vatican II*, p. 58.

30. *Statutes of the Federation of Asian Bishops' Conferences* (Hong Kong: FABC Central Secretariat, 1992), Article 2, A-G.

31. Peter C. Phan, ed., *The Asian Synod: Texts and Commentaries* (Maryknoll, NY: Orbis Books, 2002), p. 39.

32. "Toward a Fundamental Theological Interpretation of Vatican II," *Theological Studies* 40 (December 1979): 716-27.

33. "Toward a Fundamental Theological Interpretation of Vatican II," 716-27.

34. See Samuel Huntington, "Religion and the Third Wave," *National Interest* 24 (Summer 1991): 29-42.

Epilogue: Vatican II in Retrospect: A Lifetime and Esteemed Companion

1. Cuba had come—along with a number of other islands and archipelagos (Guam and the Philippines in the Pacific Ocean; Puerto Rico in the Caribbean Sea)—into the possession of the United States, a swiftly rising imperial power, upon acquisition from Spain, a just as swiftly expiring imperial power, as a result of the Spanish-Cuban-American War of 1898 and the Treaty of Paris.

2. Indeed, I have always regarded such involvement of Catholics in the mid- to late 1950s as a first example of the revolutionary church that would so mark Latin America in the 1960s and beyond.

3. Unlike many, I did not pursue ministerial studies to avoid the war. In fact, under the lottery system instituted subsequently, whereby a number was assigned every year based on date of birth, I drew a very high number indeed, somewhere in the 320s as I recall, and thus I would have never been drafted. I did enter the seminary with a genuine sense of vocation, although, needless to say, I was only too glad to avoid Vietnam.

4. A small but definite comfort in this regard has been the development of a laity that was ever more sophisticated and independent, duly critical and free-thinking, to which I proudly belong and which may ultimately prove to be the salvation of the church.

5. There is no pure point of origin for liberation theology, given the many voices and the span of time involved. I take the publication in Spanish of Gustavo Gutiérrez's signal volume (*Teología de la liberación: Perspectivas*) as point of reference.

Index

Commission for Religious Relations with
the Jews, 207, 209
Commission for Religious Relations with
the Muslims, 207
communicatio in sacris, 195, 196
Communio, xvi
community, and Vatican II, 37
Community of Sant'Egidio, 207
Concilium, xv, xvi, xvii
Conference of Major Superiors of
Women, 228
Confirmation, 59
Congar, Yves, 38, 95, 117, 121, 129, 138,
204, 229, 232, 251
Constitution on Sacred Liturgy. *See
Sacrosanctum concilium*
Cooke, Bernard, 60, 190
CORPUS, 27
Cosgrove, Monsignor Henry, 9
Council of Florence, 23, 171, 173
Council of Trent, 3, 30, 46, 82, 86, 129,
130, 186, 189, 257, 260
Counter-Reformation, 132, 171
Cousins, Ewart, 190
Cronin, Monsignor Daniel, 124
Cross, Frank M., 146
Crossan, John Dominic, 148-51, 213,
214
Crowley, Patty, 100
Cuban Missile Crisis, 267
Cuban Revolution, 264, 265, 266, 271,
272
Cullmann, Oscar, 173, 196
Cunningham, Lawrence S., 119-22
Cunningham, Philip A., 183-87
curia, Roman, 3, 4, 5, 7, 8, 16, 17, 18, 41,
42, 88, 97, 104, 105, 110, 112, 132,
137, 138, 206, 228, 257
Curran, Charles, 102-5
Cushing, Cardinal Richard, 123, 124,
173, 175, 199

Daniélou, Jean, 12, 121, 251
Danneels, Cardinal Godfried, 42
Darwin, Charles, 86
Davis, Charles, 260
Davis, Cyprian, O.S.B., 75-80
Day, Dorothy, 190
De ecclesia, 88

De fontibus revelationis, 128, 129, 130,
131
De historica evangeliorum veritate,
165
De Smedt, Emile Joseph, 88, 131, 204
Declaration on the Jews, 137
Declaration on the Relationship of
the Church to Non-Christian
Religions, 171, 173-78. *See also
Nostra aetate*
Declaration on Religious Freedom, 37,
38, 99, 137, 171, 198-200. *See also
Dignitatis humanae*
Decree for the Jacobites, 173
Decree on Ecumenism, 137, 138, 170,
171, 172, 174, 196, 259. *See also
Unitatis redintegratio*
Decree on Missionary Activity of the
Church, 206. *See also Ad gentes*
Decree on the Appropriate Renewal of
the Religious Life, 250. *See also
Perfectae caritatis*
Dei verbum (Dogmatic Constitution on
Divine Revelation), 115, 128, 138,
141, 143, 145, 147, 152, 153, 158,
164, 165, 166
Delhaye, Philippe, 157
Descamps, Albert, 157
devotions
Catholic, 64, 65, 127
Marian, 64, 65, 120, 127
Diekmann, Godfrey, O.S.B., 17, 45, 46,
48, 49, 72, 197, 228, 229
Dignitatis humanae, 198, 203, 204
Divine Office, 47, 78, 83
Divino afflante spiritu, 133, 141, 142,
158, 162
Dolan, Jay P., 218, 219
Dominus Jesus, 24
Döpfner, Cardinal Julius, 88, 232
Dozier, Carroll T., 191
Drinan, Robert F., S.J., 198-200
and civil liberties/human rights, 199
Dulles, Cardinal Avery, S.J., xvi, 136-38,
190, 215

Eastern Orthodox, reunion with, 170
Ecclesiam suam, 16, 171, 172
ecclesiologies, conflicting, 110, 111, 112